DATE DUE

The Christian Right and Congress

THE CHRISTIAN RIGHT AND CONGRESS

Matthew C. Moen

The University of Alabama Press

Tuscaloosa and London

Library of Congress Cataloging-in-Publication Data

Moen, Matthew C., 1958–
The Christian right and Congress / Matthew C. Moen.
p. cm.
Bibliography: p.
Includes index.
ISBN 0-8173-0445-2
1. Evangelicalism—United States—History—20th Century.
2. Fundamentalism—History—20th Century. 3. Christianity and
politics—History—20th century. 4. United States. Congress.
5. United States—Politics and government—1981– 6. Conservatism—
United States—History—20th century. 7. United States—Church
history—20th century. I. Title.
BR1642.U5M64
328.73'078—dc19   88-34010
CIP

British Library Cataloguing-in-Publication Data available

To Kenneth and Verona Moen
from a loving son

Contents

    10. Reputation Problems   151

    11. The Transition Period   160

    12. Off the Hill   169

              Notes   176

         Bibliography   209

              Index   226

Preface

The manner in which the Christian Right influenced the agenda of the U.S. Congress during the Reagan years is the central focus of this book. The answers that are provided about this subject have been derived from some objective indices, such as the number of bills introduced and hearings held on their issues, and more importantly, from personal interviews with about three dozen individuals who were involved in various ways in the Christian Right's struggles on Capitol Hill.

Ever since it arose in the late 1970s, the Christian Right has attracted the interest of scholars. Those from different academic disciplines began early to examine such facets of the movement as its historical roots, its electoral influence, and its theological underpinnings. When I embarked upon this project, researchers had almost entirely ignored the impact of the Christian Right on Capitol Hill. It was an understandable omission, given the problems they faced in ascertaining interest-group influence on legislative struggles in the nation's capital; it was also an unfortunate omission because the Christian Right was resolute in taking its grievances to Congress for a good deal of the Reagan presidency. As conservative activist Paul Weyrich explained it so succinctly in 1980, when queried by a reporter about the need to focus attention on Capitol Hill: "If you want to change America, you have to change the Congress."

The subject of this book was approached with few preconceptions. After completing about a dozen interviews, it seemed to me that any influence of the Christian Right on Congress that existed was minimal. After completing more interviews and weighing some of the empirical indices, however, I came to a rather different conclusion. Of course, the view that the movement was influential, particularly in the first Reagan term, will not surprise one early interviewee, who mischievously pointed out that the mere fact that I was poking around Capitol Hill asking questions about the impact of the movement was testimony to its effectiveness.

This book has been written for several different audiences. It is hoped that scholars will appreciate my attempt to tackle the subject; students of social movements, interest groups, and Congress will benefit from the tale that is told; historians will find useful the "snapshot" of Christian Right activity during the first decade of its existence; and interviewees will be interested in the detailed treatments of struggles in which they were personally involved. Because the book is grounded in interviews and is therefore non-technical, it should serve a wide readership.

The debts incurred during the course of this project are numerous. The American Political Science Association's Congressional Fellowship Program and the Carl Albert Congressional Research and Studies Center, at the University of Oklahoma, provided me the opportunity to conduct personal interviews in Washington. The interviewees graciously donated time from their busy schedules to converse with an academic who had little to offer them in return. Ronald M. Peters, Jr., Director and Curator of the Carl Albert Center, and Gary W. Copeland, its Associate Director, provided sagacious counsel during that period and subsequently on drafts of a number of the chapters.

The office of Congressman Phil Sharp, where I spent my fellowship year on the Hill, provided a hospitable environment for my interview forays. My warmest thanks go to Phil Sharp, Mike Kraft, Tom Wanley, Donna Imus, Lita Levine Kleger, Don Kaufman, John DeLap, and Frank Meinhold for their interest and constant encouragement. It was clear what an honorable group they were when in absentia I won the office lottery for the one available ticket to President Reagan's 1984 State of the Union speech.

A number of scholars offered valuable suggestions at various points, including Larry B. Hill, Donald J. Maletz, and Rob Griswold. Frederic D. Ogden, formerly of Eastern Kentucky University, and Anson Shupe, Chairman of the Department of Sociology and Anthropology at Indiana University-Purdue University at Fort Wayne, graciously provided detailed suggestions from which I profited immensely. I thank them for their efforts. Of course, none of the people mentioned should be held responsible for the book's interpretations or shortcomings.

My departmental colleagues at the University of Maine have provided a pleasant milieu in which to work. Chairman Ed Collins supported the project in every possible way, managing to find both time and resources whenever I needed them. Bahman Bakhtiari and Kenneth Palmer provided written suggestions about the manuscript. During the latter stages of the project, Carol MacMannus supplied valuable research and typing assistance. Finally, the Faculty Research Fund Committee and Greg Brown, Vice-President for Research and Public Service, graciously offered monies in support of the project.

The University of Alabama Press has been extraordinarily helpful throughout the publication process, for which I am very grateful. Malcolm MacDonald, Director of the Press, kindly took interest in the project, steered it through the review process, and kept me abreast of its status. Judith Knight assisted in a variety of ways thereafter, and Robert Ferris did a superb job of editing. It has been both an educational and enjoyable experience working with them.

Finally, thanks of a different sort must be accorded Donna Lynn Shalley, whose willingness to tackle some of the pedestrian aspects of life during the time I was busy with this study was a godsend. Her acceptance of a marriage proposal along Maine's rocky coast on a foggy summer evening, while I was in the midst of writing this book, was a glorious day in the life of this political scientist.

The Christian Right and Congress

Introduction

The central objective of this book is to explain the agenda activities and influence of the Christian Right. The fundamental question this study seeks to answer is this: In what manner and degree has the movement shaped the political agenda?

In their seminal work on agenda-building, Cobb and Elder posited two different types of political agendas. The first one they called the "systematic agenda," defined as the "general set of political controversies that will be viewed at any point in time as falling within the range of legitimate concerns meriting the attention of the polity."[1] The second type they called the "institutional agenda," defined as a "set of concrete, specific items scheduled for active and serious consideration by a particular institutional decision-making body."[2] As the definitions imply, the systematic agenda always will be more abstract, general, and broad in scope than any particular institutional agenda, such as that of a legislature or a court.[3]

This volume deals with both the systematic and the institutional agendas, as well as with the relationship between them. The purpose is to explain not only the manner in which the Christian Right placed its concerns on the systematic agenda, but also how it placed them on the specific institutional agenda of the Congress. Beyond that, both the process by and the degree to which the movement has affected the Congress will be examined. In fact, the activities and impact of the Christian Right vis-à-vis the Congress are the main focus of the book.

The thesis undergirding this study is that the movement has been quite successful in influencing the agenda. It has taken numerous issues that were lying virtually dormant on the agenda, redefined and enlarged their appeal, and then placed them on both the systematic and the congressional agendas. Moreover, it has obtained action on many of those issues, which is no small accomplishment. Cobb and Elder have shown that it is tremendously difficult even to place items on an agenda because so many are carried over from year to year.[4] In a more recent study of agenda-building, Kingdon made a similar point.[5] As the agenda activities of the Christian Right are explored in this volume, the theme of influence will recur.

This book proposes to answer a variety of intriguing questions: What caused the Christian Right to arise so suddenly in the late 1970s? How did it initially focus public and congressional attention on its issues? What groups and individuals are responsible for pushing its political agenda? What does that agenda tell us about its nature? From what quarters did it receive support on Capitol Hill? To what extent are its agenda and its actions symbolic rather than substantive? In what ways has it influenced Congress? What considerations explain its relative success rate?

In the attempt to answer those questions, this volume draws upon Christian Right documents, such as the mass mailings of the various organizations; congressional documents, such as bills, hearings, and the record of floor debates; and personal interviews with key individuals who were involved in the Christian Right's struggle to gain access and inroads to the systematic and the congressional agendas. Among the individuals interviewed were the legislative directors of the major Christian Right organizations, members of Congress and their staffs, the White House liaison to the conservative religious community, and the lobbyists of major religious denominations as well as secular organizations that were opposed to the Christian Right and its goals.

The interviews were conducted near the end of the 98th Congress (1983–84). The timing was fortuitous because the rise of the Christian Right was still fresh in the minds of the interviewees, and the high-water mark of the movement on Capitol Hill was the 98th Congress. A total of thirty-three personal interviews were conducted. (For a complete listing of them and a description of the interview process, see the "Special Interviews" section at the end of the Bibliography.)

Rationale for Study

As late as 1977, the conservative Christian community that later coalesced to form the Christian Right was considered a "sleeping giant" in American politics.[6] Charles Cade, the first operations director of the Moral Majority, once suggested that the political hibernation of the conservative Christian community was grounded in an inability to relate to the problems of secular society: "Abortion, pornography, homosexuality—those are hard for average Christians to relate to. They don't read *Playboy*, their daughters aren't pregnant, and they don't know any queers."[7] By 1979, though, the "sleeping giant" had awakened from its political slumber in a bearish mood. Its leaders quickly became household names, and its support was solicited by politicians of both major political parties.

The fact the Christian Right arose and grew into a significant political force so rapidly is one reason why it is worth examining. The sheer swiftness of its rise not only strongly suggests that its supporters were deeply troubled about the existing state of affairs in the late 1970s, but it also indicates that the leaders were adept at tapping that widespread discontent. A better understanding of the contemporary appeal of social conservatism as well as the process by which elites can build significant political movements in the 1980s requires an examination of the Christian Right.

Second, the movement is worth studying because it has been involved in such a wide range of contemporary political affairs. Among other things, it has recruited conservative Christians to run for public office and to work in government bureaucracies; solicited support for the election and the reelection of Ronald Reagan; registered thousands of voters; assumed control of the Republican party apparatus in select locales; and lobbied the Congress on a variety of legislative issues, including abortion, school prayer, and tuition tax credits. Given that sheer range of activities, the movement warrants greater examination. That is especially true of its congressional activities, which heretofore have virtually been ignored.[8]

Third, the Christian Right is worth analyzing because it is such a unique political hybrid. For instance, it is composed of citizens who generally lack the socioeconomic attributes (for example, education and wealth) conducive to high levels of political participation and to pressure-group membership. Shupe and Stacey found that the movement consists mainly of less-educated, lower-status citizens.[9] Nevertheless, they are heavily involved in politics.[10]

Then, too, the Christian Right is composed of citizens who are appreciably more conservative than the rest of the public on a wide range of political issues. Shupe and Stacey found that they are strong conservatives, especially on matters involving religion, education, and the family.[11] More recently, Wilcox demonstrated that, on a variety of domestic policy, foreign policy, and civil-liberties issues, they are "quite extreme in their conservatism."[12]

The Christian Right also consists of individuals who have historically eschewed politics, preferring to concentrate their energies on their own spiritual lives and salvation.[13] The reason for their apolitical behavior may be traced to a belief in "dispensational" theology, which teaches that the Second Coming of Christ is imminent and that in the interim it is futile to attempt to redeem human institutions. As Christian Right leaders tried to recruit conservative Christians into politics, they had to strive mightily to overcome the dispensational view embraced by many of their supporters, which was orthodoxy for them.

Finally, the Christian Right is made up of individuals hailing from the conservative wing of Protestantism. Menendez has argued that the movement consists of evangelical, fundamentalist, pentecostal, and charismatic Christians.[14] As these terms are commonly understood, evangelicals are conservatives who stress traditional morality, mission work, and individual commitment to Christ; fundamentalists share those views, as well as a belief in a literal interpretation of the Bible; pentecostals embrace evangelical and/or fundamentalist views, and place emphasis upon gifts from the Holy Spirit, such as speaking in tongues; and charismatics are pentecostals from traditionally non-pentecostal denominations (for example, United Methodist). The conservative wing of Protestantism, as well as the Christian Right, is represented by such denominations as the Southern Baptist Convention, the Assemblies of God, the Church of the Nazarene, the Church of God, and the Independent Baptist churches. In lesser numbers, of course, other Protestant denominations are represented as well.

In short, the Christian Right is a unique political movement. Its supporters lack the socioeconomic attributes of political participation and historically have steered clear of politics, but today are involved heavily in it. Moreover, they are unusually conservative politically and theologically. That uniqueness, combined with the rapid rise of the movement and its range of political actions, justifies an extended inquiry into its agenda activities and influence.

Before proceeding further, one brief point must be interjected. The fact that evangelical, fundamentalist, pentecostal, and charismatic Christians participate in the movement has led to considerable confusion over terminology. Different writers have described the supporters of the Christian Right by these various labels at different times. Recent research has suggested, however, that the fundamentalist wing may be the most prevalent and the most powerful.[15] For that reason, as well as a matter of literary convenience, the term "fundamentalist" will consistently be employed throughout this book to describe the supporters of the Christian Right, keeping in mind that this particular variant of conservative Protestantism is not the only one represented in the movement. It is simply too awkward to draw distinctions each and every time.

Outline of Book

This volume is divided into four major parts. Part I examines why the Christian Right arose and how it placed its concerns on the systematic and the congressional agendas. The process of politicizing the conservative Christian community, the reasons why that community suddenly entered politics en masse in the late 1970s, and the manner in which it mobilized backing for its concerns and gained the attention of policymakers will all be discussed. In addition, the use of political symbols and other techniques of mass mobilization will be treated.

Part II examines the players of the Christian Right as well as the politicians who have promoted its agenda, including President Reagan, New Right senators, and the House Conservative Opportunity Society. Also analyzed are the roles of the conservative television preachers, the New Right secular conservatives, and congressional staff members in struggles over the political agenda. Finally, Part II discusses in considerable detail the formation of the major Christian Right groups and their Washington, D.C., operations.

Part III focuses on the activities and influence of the Christian Right on Capitol Hill. It begins with a look at the political agenda that the movement advocated there, with an eye toward what that agenda reveals about the nature of the movement. The narrative then provides an indepth discussion of the legislative struggles of the Christian Right in both the 97th and 98th Congresses (1981–84). In this part of the book, the ways in which it failed and succeeded will be examined, as well as what explains its success rate.

Part IV opens with an evaluation of the problems faced by the Christian Right as the second Reagan term began. A brief discussion follows of the 99th and 100th Congresses (1985–88), noting how the movement altered its strategy on the Hill during that time. The book closes with a chapter on the emergence of new opportunities for the Christian Right off Capitol Hill: in the bureaucracy, the courts, and the state/local arenas.

Part I

Gaining Access

1. Politicizing the Faithful

It took the Reverend Jerry Falwell about fourteen years to change his mind completely about the propriety of fundamentalist Christians participating in politics. In 1965, in a sermon entitled "Ministers and Marches," he preached against involvement in the civil rights and anti-war struggles of the time, based upon the understanding that Jesus was essentially apolitical while He was on earth.[1] In 1979 Falwell was encouraging fundamentalists to participate in politics via the conservative interest group he assented to lead: the Moral Majority. The evolution of his thought on this subject stemmed from a conviction that the secular state had gradually become intrusive of fundamentalist institutions and oppressive of its values. The general thrust of this chapter confirms that view.

Falwell's antipathy for the secular state was shared widely within fundamentalist circles in the late 1970s. Bob Billings, for instance, who later became the first executive director of the Moral Majority, launched a 1977 campaign to stem attempted government intrusiveness into the affairs of fundamentalist, private schools.[2] Although he did not form his own group at the time, the Reverend Pat Robertson was similarly displeased with the secular state, reflected in this 1980 comment: "We used to think that if we stayed home and prayed it would be enough. Well, we are fed up. We think it is time to put God back in government."[3]

Concerns of the Fundamentalists

What persuaded these men to shed their apolitical leanings and to exhort their followers to do likewise? The simple answer is that, having witnessed the politics and culture of the 1960s and 1970s, fundamentalists believed figuratively (and perhaps literally) that the nation was "going to hell." The Reverend James Robison made just such a point in 1980, when he said that America was in such a state that it was time to "either sound the charge or blow taps."[4] The Reverend Del Fehsenfeld, a youth evangelist from Chicago, also remarked: "If America does not go to her knees [and repent], she will go to her grave."[5] The Reverend Adrian Rogers, president of the Southern Baptist Convention, put the matter even more bluntly: "Most Americans are egomaniacs strutting their way to hell."[6] Clearly, fundamentalist leaders were deeply disturbed by the nature of American society as it existed circa 1980.

Of course, many non-fundamentalist citizens subscribed to the view that the country had "gone to hell" throughout the 1960s and 1970s. During that period, citizens became far less trustful of politicians, less confident of political institutions, less enamored with political parties, and less sanguine that the future would bring better times.[7] This study, however, does not seek to explain that trend, which has already been performed by others.[8] Instead, the purpose here is to identify the concerns that alienated fundamentalists and caused them to rethink their abstinence from politics. Those concerns may be separated into four broad categories: domestic policy, foreign policy, culture, and religion. Most of this chapter focuses on developments within those categories.

Cash, Courts, and Corruption

In domestic policy, three trends were particularly galling to fundamentalists. First, the federal government increased markedly in scope, both raising and spending money at unprecendented levels. In 1960, for instance, it raised $92 billion and spent about the same; in 1979, the year the three major Christian Right groups were formed, it raised $465 billion and spent $493 billion—more than a 400 percent increase in revenues and expenditures.[9] Granted, this trend appalled many secular conservatives as well as religious fundamentalists who believed that they did not receive benefits commensurate with their tax burden, that the government had expanded its scope beyond reasonable bounds, that a large government posed a threat to individual citizen liberties, and/or that the government was purposefully undertaking a redistribution of wealth. What disturbed fundamentalists in a unique way, however, was the manner in which the trend toward "big government" resulted in the assumption of tasks historically performed by the family.

It is easy to identify ways in which "big government" impinged upon the fundamentalist way of life. Assumption of the retirement burden via the Social Security program, for example, had the twin effects of placing elderly grandparents outside the home as well as alleviating their sons and daughters of the direct responsibility of caring for them. Congressman Phil Crane (R.-Ill.), speaking of the Medicare portion of Social Security, put the matter this way: "The liberals sold Medicare to the public on the basis that it would allow people to shirk responsibility for their parents when they got old."[10] A second example is welfare benefits. The governmental assistance of indigents led to such consequences as allowing unwed pregnant adolescents to keep their babies, to live outside their homes, and not to marry upon becoming pregnant. A third example is programs that provided contraceptives to adolescents; despite the protestations of Planned Parenthood, a deducible corollary was increased sexual promiscuity by at least some of this group. A final example is the government's assumption of a greater burden for child day care, which provided some women another incentive to live outside their homes.

In recognition of those developments, James McKenna remarked that the tax structure was a major reason behind the politicized state of the fundamentalists.[11] Attacking particularly the Internal Revenue Service (IRS), he stated, "The IRS uses its power to trod upon many things people consider moral issues. The IRS retribution [upon the traditional family structure], as best as I can figure it, stems from a simple lust for money."[12] The motivation of the IRS aside, McKenna makes an important point. Increased government spending in the 1960s and 1970s led to the usurpation of functions historically associated with the family. To fundamentalists, that was an Orwellian nightmare. There was no way to reconcile biblical teachings about the virtues of the family structure with policies that often worked to dismember it.

The attack upon the fundamentalist subculture by the secular state was probably unwitting, despite the views of conspiratorial-minded fundamentalists, who regarded it as deliberate. (Those individuals who thought in conspiratorial terms responded with an attack upon "secular humanism," which will be addressed in the next chapter.) Even by 1984, after several years of Christian Right rhetoric about the usurpation of family functions by the state, liberals seemed remarkably oblivious of the whole issue. Not a single interviewee for this research who would be considered a "liberal" in the contemporary lexicon so much as broached the issue when queried about the reasons behind the fundamentalist entrance into politics.[13] It is a small, but perhaps revealing, piece of evidence about liberal sensitivities to the concerns of the fundamentalist community.

The second trend in domestic policy that exasperated fundamentalists was the judicial activism of the Supreme Court. That activism, especially as it was embodied in the Warren Court, was highly offensive on both philosophical and policy grounds.

On a philosophical plane, fundamentalists were suspicious of the institution of the Supreme Court. Their misgivings stemmed from some key differences: the justices tended to be wealthy, well educated, and consumed with the affairs of state; the fundamentalists, less wealthy, less educated, and preoccupied with religious rather than secular affairs; the Supreme Court was elitist, consisting of nine unelected members serving virtually life terms; and Christian fundamentalism was mass-based and participatory. American Civil Liberties Union Legislative Counsel Barry Lynn aptly summed up the anti-elitist sentiments of fundamentalists: "As a practical matter, the Christian Right dislikes the idea of only nine [Supreme Court] people deciding whether abortions should be outlawed or whether their kids should get to pray in school. It really bothers them."[14]

On the policy level, the content of numerous Supreme Court rulings was objectionable. The litany of cases that offended the fundamentalist community is well known and involves several of the most controversial decisions of the post-World War II period: *McCollum* v. *Board of Education* (1948), where the Court ruled that religious instruction in the public schools was unconstitutional; *Engel* v. *Vitale* (1962) and *Abington School District* v. *Schempp* (1963), in which the Court held that voluntary recitation of a non-denominational prayer and devotional Bible reading in the public schools, respectively, were unconstitutional; *Epperson* v. *Arkansas* (1968), where the Court contended that an Arkansas statute forbidding the teaching of the theory of evolution in the schools was unconstitutional; *Swann* v. *Charlotte-Mecklenburg Board of Education* (1971), in which the practice of school busing to facilitate desegregation was upheld; and *Roe* v. *Wade* (1973), where the Court defended the right of women to obtain abortions.[15]

Especially irksome were the *Engel* school-prayer and *Roe* abortion decisions. They were consistently mentioned by interviewees. Roy Jones, legislative director of the Moral Majority, said his group "was originally set up to move on school prayer and abortion legislation."[16] Gary Jarmin, legislative director of Christian Voice, remarked that school prayer was his organization's top priority.[17] Congressmen Phil Crane (R.-Ill.) and Henry Hyde (R.-Ill.) as well as Forest Montgomery, of the National Association of Evangelicals, all mentioned those two issues in the context of discussions on the entrance of fundamentalists into politics.[18]

The reason that those particular issues were singled out among the others by interviewees is not entirely clear. It could be that Christian Right supporters viewed them as the most important (particularly abortion, which in their eyes involved murder). It could also be a process of elimination: the *McCollum* decision forbidding religious instruction in the public schools was more than thirty years' old and no longer a matter of controversy; the *Epperson* decision allowing the teaching of evolution was not all that objectionable to most fundamentalists, despite the clamor of some;[19] the *Swann* decision allowing school busing was narrowed, if not repudiated. The objectionable school-prayer and abortion decisions, in contrast, are generally more recent and strongly opposed by fundamentalists. In one study, 95 percent of Moral Majority supporters disagreed with the gist of the school-prayer decision and 66 percent with the one on abortion.[20] One related explanation for the saliency of these issues is that they are an effective means of raising money for the Christian Right organizations. A sampling of Moral Majority fund-raising letters provides evidence to that effect.[21]

It would be erroneous to suggest that the school-prayer and abortion decisions directly spawned the Christian Right. The timing is way off to assert such a causal relationship. The school-prayer ruling was handed down seventeen years and the one on abortion six years before the major Christian Right groups formed in 1979. Because of that lag time, it is erroneous to argue that those decisions gave rise to the movement.[22] What they did was help politicize fundamentalists.

Christian Right antipathy for the Supreme Court is evidenced both in interviewee comments already cited and in backing "court-stripping" schemes restricting the jurisdiction of the Court.[23] It is also evident in a 1977 Gallup Poll, which found that citizens who fit the general profile of Christian Right supporters had less confidence in the Supreme Court than other citizens. By 55 to 34 percent, college-educated versus grade-school-educated persons registered a favorable opinion of the Court; by 50 to 30 percent, high-income versus low-income citizens also did so.[24]

A third trend in domestic policy particularly objectionable to fundamentalists was the widespread corruption among high government officials during the 1960s and 1970s. The litany of scandals is incredible: the use of the Senate majority leader's office by Bobby Baker to accumulate a fortune; the improper use of campaign contributions and travel money by Senator Thomas Dodd; the misuse of Education Committee funds by Adam Clayton Powell; the illegal use of government agencies, violations of civil liberties, and disregard for election laws lumped under the rubric of Watergate; the "no contest" plea of Vice-President Spiro Agnew to charges of misconduct; the money donated by Tongsun Park to members of Congress in what became known as "Koreagate"; the indictment of Congressmen Joshua Eilberg and Daniel Flood for taking bribes; the conviction of Congressman Charles Diggs for padding his office payroll and accepting employee "kickbacks"; the resignation of Congressman Wayne Hays after it was revealed that he kept staff member

Elizabeth Ray on the office payroll in return for sexual favors; the arrest of inebriated Congressman Wilbur Mills after his companion, stripper Fanne Fox, jumped out of his car and leaped into the Washington, D.C., Tidal Basin; and the illegal campaign contributions by Gulf Oil Corporation to various members of Congress.[25] It was no coincidence that Congress paid great attention to ethics by the late 1970s, reflected in the adoption of codes of conduct for members and their staffs.[26]

One effect of those scandals was probably to drive away a segment of the populace from political participation, including some fundamentalists. Others, however, were convinced that it was time to become involved in politics, that what the nation needed was a strong infusion of morally concerned citizens. Politics was too "dirty" to ignore any longer in a country that was theirs too.

Political pundit Kevin Phillips has argued that Watergate in particular helped politicize fundamentalists. In his view, it directly helped elect President Jimmy Carter in 1976—the "born-again" Baptist who promised in the post-Watergate period never to knowingly "tell a lie" while in office.[27] His presidency, in turn, convinced fundamentalists that it was not sufficient to have a president who looked and sounded like them, but often did not think like them. (The manner in which Carter proved offensive to many fundamentalists will be discussed later in this chapter.) Similarly, Woods has argued that the Christian Right arose from the political malaise of the Vietnam and Watergate period.[28]

Wuthnow has provided a fairly similar, albeit more theoretical, analysis. He believes that Watergate helped activate a sense among fundamentalists that the private morality of individual citizens had consequences for the public good by revealing a clear connection between personal moral codes and collective outcomes.[29] The injection of a deep sense of morality might head off further national calamities like Watergate. Who better to make such an injection than fundamentalists grounded in bedrock biblical values? Wuthnow's contention is evidenced by archival materials.[30]

His analysis is compelling, though it cannot stand alone as the sole cause that politicized fundamentalists. At most, it is a piece of the puzzle because it does not account for foreign policy trends that were equally disturbing to the conservative Christian community.

Foreign Policy

Two trends during the decade of the 1970s that helped politicize fundamentalists may be extracted from the milieu of American foreign policy.

The trends, which may be set apart because they disturbed fundamentalists on theological as well as policy grounds, were an increased emphasis on détente with the Soviet Union and a decreased acceptance of the Israeli cause vis-à-vis the Arabs in the Middle East.[31]

The American emphasis on détente began in earnest during the Nixon presidency, when Henry Kissinger was secretary of state. The reality underpinning the new policy of cooperation with the Soviets was that their military strength was equivalent to that of the United States. The hope behind détente was to create a vested Soviet interest in "peaceful coexistence" through increased trade, technological transfers, and citizen-exchange programs.

On policy grounds, fundamentalists opposed this policy because they (along with many secular conservatives) believed the Soviets would use the period of peaceful cooperation to steal technology, engage in subversion, export revolution, and violate arms-control agreements.

On theological grounds, fundamentalists simply abhorred the thought of cooperation with a Marxist regime. A common (and fundamentalist) understanding of Marxism is that it is atheistic (with religion serving as an "opiate" of the people), that it is humanistic (with a "heaven on earth" obtainable in the perfect communist society), and that it is founded on communal rather than individual rights. Fundamentalist Christianity flatly rejects those teachings. It views religion as life's guiding philosophy rather than as an opiate assuaging the masses; it denies that mankind, in the absence of God, can progress to a more perfect condition; it champions personal rather than communal rights, based upon the intrinsic worth of the individual in the eyes of God. Many fundamentalists may not have been able to articulate those differences, but they sensed them. One interviewee who could articulate them was Congressman Phil Crane:

> [Some] . . . champion the view that man is progressing to a higher level, approaching that of angels. I find that train of thought dangerous, and emanating from the Marxist view that we can obtain a "heaven on earth." In order to have an angelic world, men would have to be angels. In justifying the dictatorship of the proletariat, Marx argues that some have become angels before others. Again, that strikes me as a dangerous idea, because it is a means by which to justify a concentration of power and any sort of crime against humanity.[32]

For fundamentalists, the détente policy was not only bad politics, but also bad form. It was morally bankrupt.

The anti-communist strain in fundamentalist thought has a rich history.

In the 1950s, for example, the Reverend Billy James Hargis formed the "Christian Anti-Communist Crusade," and the Reverend Carl McIntire organized the American Council of Churches (an alternative to the National Council of Churches, which he believed was too internationalist and sympathetic to Marxism) to combat "godless" international communism.[33] The driving force behind their organizational entrepreneurship was their view that communism had a Satanic nature.[34]

Although it is tempting to write those trends off as excesses of the cold war period, it would be erroneous to do so. Contemporary fundamentalists have strongly espoused the anti-communist message, Reverend Falwell once identifying communism as the chief adversary of "God's plan" for America.[35] Likewise, the Reverend Tim LaHaye once referred to Soviet and Chinese leaders as "international gangsters and murderers" whose regimes were oppressive and dangerous.[36] Nearly two decades ago, fundamentalist Hal Lindsey wrote *The Late Great Planet Earth*, which interpreted biblical prophecy so as to place the Soviet Union on the side of "evil" in the final world conflagration depicted in the New Testament book of Revelation.[37] Given that outlook, it is easy to see how the emphasis on détente aroused fundamentalists.

The second trend that disturbed and helped politicize them was the decreased acceptance by the United States of the Israeli cause in the Middle East. This trend started after the 1973 Arab oil embargo. At the time, the embargo created bitterness among Americans, but over the long term it served to raise the saliency of the Arab case vis-à-vis Israel. Throughout the 1970s, Americans became more aware of the plight of the Palestinians, the intransigence of Israel with regard to occupied lands, and the power of its lobby in Washington.[38] This awareness did not automatically translate into greater backing for the Arab cause, but it did lead to an erosion of support for Israel. The *Congressional Quarterly* summed it up this way:

> Recent public opinion polls have generally shown that the Arabs still have a long way to go before they would substantially shift traditional American support from Israel to the Arab cause. However, according to a 1975 Gallup Poll, there has been a notable erosion of strong pro-Israeli support to an "even-handed" position . . . But in shifting away from one-sided support for Israel, Americans have moved into neutral, not pro-Arab positions.[39]

On theological grounds, fundamentalists found any shift away from Israel, however slight, wholly unacceptable. As articulated by Lindsey in his popular book on biblical prophecy, many fundamentalists believe on eschatological grounds that America must stand firmly behind Israel. Their view is that the Middle East will be the focal point of Armageddon, the "final battle" to be waged on earth between the forces of good and evil.[40] The forces of "good," as might be expected, are identified specifically as Israel and her allies and the forces of evil as the Soviet Union and her allies.[41] The world is spared from this final conflagration only by the Second Coming of Christ.[42] It is essential to fundamentalists that America be on God's side (Israel) in the coming conflagration. Backing for Israel is especially crucial in contemporary times because of the view that Armageddon and the Second Coming are imminent.[43]

Liberal theologians are keenly aware that eschatological understandings lie behind the fundamentalist espousal of Israel's cause. The Reverend John Kater, Jr., for instance, argues that it is on eschatological grounds rather than an assessment of political strategy that fundamentalists strongly support Israel.[44] Similarly, specifically referring to Falwell, the Reverend Stan Hastey said, "Israel is so important to Falwell because it must be in place for the eschatological events to occur. Anyone who opposes Israel opposes God, when that view is taken to its logical conclusion."[45] Scholar A. James Reichley has noted in the same vein: "The fundamentalist's expectation, based on biblical prediction, that Jews will return to Israel just before the millenium provides a linkage."[46]

The fundamentalists' support for Israel is fraught with irony. They do so because of her role in the predicted eschatological events, but their traditional dogma teaches that salvation is denied to those individuals who are not "born-again" Christians. Then too, fundamentalists espouse foreign policy initiatives that bolster Israel, but are often at odds with American Jews over domestic civil liberties issues like school prayer and abortion. Finally, despite their strong stance behind Israel, many fundamentalists seem to be anti-Semitic. The Reverend Bailey Smith once remarked that God did not hear the prayers of Jews—a position presidential candidate Ronald Reagan quickly distanced himself from when it was enunciated at an event he attended.[47] The Reverend Jerry Falwell once quipped that most people disliked Jews because they could make more money accidentally than most people can on purpose.[48]

Despite the irony and the tensions, fundamentalists have grown close to the Jewish community over time. The opposite is the case with liberal Protestants and Catholics, who have parted company with Jews over defense policy and the Palestinian issue. Reichley sums up the shifting alliances: "As liberal Protestant and Catholic groups drifted away from support for Israel . . . Jews have found a new and unexpected, and for some alarming, ally in some fundamentalist Christian groups, notably Jerry Falwell's Moral Majority."[49] The rift between liberal Protestants and Catholics with Jews should not be overstated, for they still work in tandem on a variety of social welfare and civil-liberties issues. However, the erosion of that relationship is facilitating an increasingly cozy, albeit irony-laden, relationship between fundamentalists and Jews.

The Counterculture

As if the domestic and foreign policy trends were not enough, American culture changed in the 1960s and 1970s in ways that shocked fundamentalist sensibilities. The drift of culture during that time was embodied and described by the omnibus phrase "counterculture." It remains difficult to define that phenomenon, but it is easy to reel off some of the specific trends and events that made it objectionable to fundamentalists: the anti-war protests in the streets; the takeover of campus buildings; the burning of ROTC buildings and draft cards; the sexual revolution; the miniskirt craze; the New York Easter "love-in" of 1967; the burning of brassieres; the rise of "rock and roll" music; the Woodstock concert; the rock musical *Hair*; the rise of the drug culture centered on "pot" and LSD; the disdain for such symbols of authority as police, politicians, and parents; the "flower children"; the two-fingered "peace" sign; the display of small American flags on the seats of blue jeans; and the appearance of the "Hippies" and "Yippies," including the Yippie nomination of a hog named "Pigasus" for the presidency of the United States. On the heels of those events was the gay rights movement, which also involved protest marches and claims against established traditions.

To at least some degree, liberals welcomed these trends as progress against militarism, sexism, and authoritarianism. In contrast, fundamentalists abhorred them, viewing the life-styles embedded within the counterculture as immoral and irreligious; they disdained the fact that such matters could even find their way onto the nation's systematic agenda. They were evidence of a morally bankrupt society.

The acute concern of the fundamentalists with the problem of moral decline is easily demonstrated. The policy positions of the contemporary Christian Right, for instance, are predicated on arresting a perceived decline in traditional morality. The movement seeks to restrict abortion, contraceptives for minors, and pornography, while simultaneously promoting chastity and school prayer.

A number of Christian Right leaders have also focused repeatedly on the theme of moral decline, reflecting the seriousness of the matter from their perspective. The Reverend Jerry Falwell serves as a prime example.

First, he assented to head an organization called the *Moral* Majority—a name that was not happenstance. Second, he said at the time he became politically active that the "moral fiber" of the nation was eroding visibly over time.[50] Third, after becoming politically active, he continued to solicit money from supporters based on moral themes. One fund-raising letter, for instance, declared that "*moral* cancers [are] destroying America and the *Moral* Majority has been fighting to return American to *moral* sanity."[51] Falwell is not alone among fundamentalists in focusing on this theme. The Reverend Tim LaHaye and the Reverend James Robison both wrote books lamenting the moral decline of America.[52]

Public opinion polls also show fundamentalist alarm about moral decline. One survey, for instance, found that 65 percent of Moral Majority supporters compared to 19 percent of non-supporters agreed with the statement "We need more laws on morality."[53] The same survey also revealed that 55 percent of Moral Majority supporters compared to 25 percent of non-supporters agreed with the statement "If the American government does not support religion, the government cannot uphold morality."[54] Although the second measure of morality is less direct than the first, it addresses the theme of moral decline with similar results.

The view that the Christian Right arose in response to the decline of traditional morality, or put another way, the rise of "alternative life-styles," is shared by some sociologists. They argue, via the "status politics" framework, that citizens whose social status and/or cherished life-styles have been devalued form right-wing protest movements as a means of reassertion. In such a framework, the Christian Right is understood to be a right-wing protest movement intent upon restraining or prohibiting non-traditional or "alternative" life-styles. Lorentzen has argued for just such an interpretation, asserting that the Christian Right emerged to "legitimate and protect the conservative evangelical life-style."[55] Similarly, Shupe and Stacey contend that "the defense of a cherished lifestyle from the perceived ill effects of secularization . . . present a plausible framework for understanding the goals of the New Christian Right."[56]

The problem with such an interpretation is that it is monocausal. The Christian Right was disturbed about a number of issues outside the realm of life-styles. The behavior of the liberal clergy in America constitutes a case in point.

Liberals and Liberation

As fundamentalist leaders surveyed the political landscape in the 1960s and 1970s, they surely noticed the political activism of their liberal religious brethren. The activism itself was not so disturbing because clergy had long been active in secular policy matters such as abolition and prohibition. The intensity and outspokenness of the liberal clergy during the 1960s and 1970s, however, was another matter. They helped politicize the fundamentalists.

The liberal clergy who were active at that time are well known: the Reverend William Sloane Coffin, the Reverend Richard John Neuhaus, the Reverend Jesse Jackson, Father Daniel Berrigan, Father John Cronin, and Father Theodore Hesburgh. Many others could be named. The two major issues attracting these clergymen were civil rights and the Vietnam War. Their activities on these issues included the delivery of sermons, "op-ed" pieces for newspapers, testimony before Congress, lobbying, street marches, civil disobedience, and even some minor violence such as raids on draft boards. Reichley again provides a nice summary: "The civil rights struggle and the Vietnam War, the two most visible public issues of the period, caused intense controversy and soul-searching within most denominations . . . [a] general response among the churches was to become more deeply involved, in one way or another, in secular politics."[57] The liberal-clergy activism in secular affairs helped politicize fundamentalist leaders, who believed the task of injecting religious values into secular politics was in poor hands.

Proof that the fundamentalist clergy and its supporters were politicized in part by liberal-clergy activism is easy to locate. The Reverend Jerry Falwell said as much in a fund-raising letter:

> Liberal clergyman like Jesse Jackson have long been involved in the political process. But the other side does not want you or Jerry Falwell in the act. If you and I buy their argument that "religion and politics don't mix"— they will win. If you and I accept the "double-standard" that liberal clergymen can mix politics and religion—but you and I cannot—they will win. So I am angry and fearful at the same time.[58]

Likewise, Congressman Henry Hyde (R.-Ill.) suggested:

> For too long the religious right has left politics to the religious left and to all sorts of trendy clergy . . . [Then] the conservative preachers looked around in the 1970s, and they saw the influence that the liberal preachers were exerting in politics, be it macro issues like civil rights or more micro issues like the lettuce boycott. The realized that this was their country too, and that they had to get active if they wanted to turn things around . . . I

welcome them on the scene, because I disliked the one-sided activities of the liberal clergy.[59]

Finally, New Right direct-mail whiz Richard Viguerie wrote:

> During the 25 years that I've been active in politics, most of the major religious leaders in America have been liberals who were in the forefront of almost every liberal political cause—civil rights battles, Vietnam war rallies, reduction in military spending, and expansion of welfare . . . [now] conservative preachers are beginning to lead and speak out on politics just as liberals like Protestants Rev. Andrew Young, Rev. Jesse Jackson, Rev. William Sloane Coffin, Rev. Martin Luther King, Jr., and Catholics Rev. Theodore Hesburgh, and Father Robert Drinan have done . . . [Yet] liberals are now complaining about conservative ministers who are doing just what liberal ministers have been doing for decades.[60]

These statements reflect both disgust with liberal-clergy activism and recognition of the reality that clerical advocacy in secular affairs had been left to the liberals. The latter point is widely agreed upon. The Reverend Charles Bergstrom, of the Lutheran Council, explained it nicely: "There is truth in the view that the conservative clergy is simply doing what the liberal clergy has been doing for some time."[61]

Related to, and to some extent underlying, the disdain for liberal-clergy activism was fundamentalist contempt for Catholic "liberation" theology. The essence of that theology, stated clearly after a meeting of Latin American bishops in Colombia in 1968, is that the social structure of certain nations should be remade to achieve a greater degree of equity.[62] Although the bishops did not embrace Marxism, the call to restructure society along the lines of assisting the less fortunate (proletariat) clearly sounded like Marxism. In view of the serious reservations of fundamentalists about that doctrine, discussed earlier, it is not surprising that they found "liberation" theology unpalatable. Catholic advocacy of it helped politicize them.

The Growing Numbers

The response of the fundamentalist community to the confluence of the trends in domestic and foreign policy, culture, and religion took two opposite forms: some fundamentalists withdrew further from secular society, and others began to become politicized. For those in the latter group, a political agenda was already taking shape. Because "big government" was intrusive of fundamentalist institutions and hostile to its values, a somewhat libertarian, anti-statist agenda was in the works, stressing budget cuts, less government regulation, and less judicial activism. Because of the rapprochement with the Soviets, a militaristic agenda was also taking shape, emphasizing "peace through strength." Due to concerns over existing moral standards, an intense moral agenda was also being defined by fundamentalists. It emphasized issues like school prayer, abortion, pornography, and homosexuality. Those general agenda objectives had to be tailored considerably before fundamentalists could hope to place them on any institutional agenda, like that of the Congress. It was a big step to move from a general anti-statist agenda to specific budget plans or from a moral agenda to specific wording for a school-prayer constitutional amendment. For now, only the broad outline of an agenda that reflected unhappy experiences with the secular state was taking shape. The other steps came later.

The timing could not have been much better for those fundamentalists who were contemplating political involvement. Even as they were doing so, their numbers were growing as more and more citizens were brought into the more conservative, often fundamentalist, churches. The conservative churches enjoyed the following gains in membership over the course of the 1970s: Church of Jesus Christ of Latter-Day Saints (Mormons), from 2,180,064 to 2,592,000 (16%), Seventh-Day Adventists, from 396,097 to 535,705 (26%), Jehovah's Witnesses, from 333,672 to 519,281 (36%), Southern Baptist Convention, from 11,330,481 to 13,191,394 (14%), Church of God (Pentecostal), from 252,349 to 373,501 (32%), Assemblies of God, from 1,066,128 to 1,293,394 (18%), and Church of the Nazarene, from 850,655 to 896,989 (5%).[63]

In contrast, the "main-line" Protestant churches suffered the following declines in membership during the 1970s: Disciples of Christ, from 1,592,609 to 1,231,817 (23%), Episcopal Church, from 3,373,890 to 2,815,359 (17%), Presbyterian Church in the U.S. (Southern), from 961,767 to 862,416 (10%), Lutheran Church in America, from 3,279,517 to 2,942,002 (10%), United Church of Christ, from 2,032,648 to 1,769,104 (13%), United Methodist Church, from 10,990,720 to 9,731,779 (11%), and United Presbyterian Church in the U.S.A., from 3,222,663 to 2,520,367 (22%).[64]

What explains the growth of the conservative churches and the decline of the main-line churches? Kelley argues that more and more people simply left the latter for the former churches out of the conviction that the latter were offering a diluted form of Christianity.[65] As he sees it, "The mainline denominations will continue to exist on a diminishing scale for decades, perhaps for centuries, and will continue to supply some people with a dilute and undemanding form of meaning, which may be all they want. These dwindling denominations may spawn new movements which, if they pursue the hard road of strictness, may have vital effects on human life, such as the declining churches had in their youth but can no longer achieve."[66]

A different and probably more telling explanation has been offered by Roof and McKinney, who argue that demographics play a key role. They cite polls which show that the main-line churches have aging constituencies, noting that fully 42 percent of all Disciples of Christ, 41 percent of Methodists, and 43 percent of United Church of Christ followers are 55 years of age or older.[67] In contrast, none of the conservative churches reach a 40 percent threshold. Along the same lines, Johnson demonstrated that the conservative churches have higher birth rates and better retention of their youthful members than their main-line counterparts.[68] Taken together, the evidence suggests that the conservative churches grew of their own accord, not at the expense of the main-line churches. In any case, the significant point is that, while fundamentalist leaders were being politicized, their potential base of support was expanding.

Enough Is Enough

Still lacking for the fundamentalist leaders in their attempts to build a constituency were any specific events that could crystallize their community. An amorphous discontent existed within that community, but it was one brought about very gradually by long-term trends. Some "triggers" were needed that would make the politicized masses take the further step of actual political involvement. Those triggers came in the late 1970s, courtesy of the Federal Communications Commission, the Internal Revenue Service, and the Carter administration.

Federal Communications Commission

In March 1979 WFAA television, in Dallas, decided to suspend the regular broadcast of the Reverend James Robison, a fundamentalist preacher headquartered in Fort Worth. The decision to preempt the broadcast, which was a strong attack upon the gay rights movement and homosexual life-styles, was based on a concern that the "Fairness Doctrine" (or at least its subset, the "equal time" provision) might be violated by showing only the anti-gay point of view.[69] Executives of the station reasoned that it might be compelled to televise a "pro-gay" show of some sort to comply with the Fairness Doctrine, a prospect they found alarming, even if remote. Rather than risk such an outcome, they canceled the broadcast. Moreover, in order to avoid similar incidents in the future, they dropped Reverend Robison from the regular programming schedule.[70]

He was outraged. The preemption of the anti-gay program smacked of secular intrusion into religious affairs as well as violation of the First Amendment guarantee of free speech. Moreover, the decision to drop Robison from the programming schedule signaled to him and his followers the real power of the gay rights constituency they so disdained. Quickly counterattacking, he organized and led a "Dallas Freedom Rally" in June to protest the WFAA decisions to preempt his broadcast and to remove him from the schedule. The rally was attended by an estimated 12,000 citizens, and it raised more than $100,000 in legal expenses for him to bring suit against WFAA.[71] Faced with that local reaction, the station offered a compromise that he accepted: the anti-gay program was not aired, but he was reinstated in the programming schedule. Within three months after the rally, he accepted a position as vice-president of the newly formed Christian Right organization known as the Religious Roundtable. He took the step into politics.

The significance of this incident for Reverend Robison personally and for his supporters must be understood against the backdrop of another issue involving the Federal Communications Commission (FCC) and the television preachers. Only then will the intense reaction of the fundamentalists be fully appreciated.

The issue began in December 1974, when California professors Jeremy Lansman and Lorenzo Milam petitioned the FCC to investigate the practices of non-commercial educational and broadcasting systems, including religious television and radio stations. Additionally, they requested a "freeze" on all license applications by "religious Bible, Christian, and other sectarian schools, colleges, and institutes" until such time as the investigation was completed.[72] The simple fact that such a petition was under FCC consideration, let alone its possible acceptance, understandably alarmed religious broadcasters. If the FCC accepted the petition, their growth and outreach might well be curtailed. Besides, the matter once again smacked of secular interference with religious affairs: a branch of the federal government was investigating religious ministries. For those various reasons, religious broadcasters implored their audiences to contact the FCC and encourage its commissioners to dismiss the petition brought by the two professors. The bulk of the audiences were fundamentalists.

The pleas of the religious broadcasters worked. Early in the following year, letters and telegrams began arriving at the FCC requesting the rejection of "Petition 2493," the number that was routinely assigned to the petition by the agency. By the time the FCC ruled on the petition in August, an estimated 700,000 letters had arrived requesting its rejection.[73] The FCC denied the petition on the grounds that it was too extreme and that it potentially violated the First Amendment.[74] The language of the opinion was so strong that there was little doubt what the commissioners thought about the petition. They said that the professors brought forth an "impermissible proposition" due to their "personal distaste" for religious programming.[75]

The denial of Petition 2493 in August 1975, however, is only a part of the story. As time elapsed, rumors about the origin and nature of "2493" grew and spread, quite possibly at the hand of religious broadcasters who wished to make certain the issue was buried conclusively. Whatever the source of the rumors, many citizens came to understand that "2493" had been filed by famed atheist Madalyn Murray O'Hair and that it was designed to "ban the broadcast of all religious programs including church services," rather than simply freeze license applications.[76] Moreover, thousands of citizens apparently refused to believe that the FCC denied the petition because letters have continued to roll into the FCC ever since 1975 at the rate of 130,000 per month.[77] A phone conversation with an FCC official in May 1984 confirmed that finding; the official revealed that more than 500,000 letters were received in the first few months of that year requesting rejection of "2493" and making reference to O'Hair and a total ban on religious broadcasting.[78]

In response, the FCC for years has been sending form-letter replies back to citizens who have contacted the agency on this matter, informing them that the petition had not been brought by O'Hair, had not been drafted to ban all religious broadcasting, and in any case, had been denied in 1975. Despite its efforts, the FCC has failed to stem the flow of letters, which could be the result of poor dissemination of information within the fundamentalist community. More likely, the citizens contacting the agency are purposefully keeping pressure on it to keep its distance from religious programming.

That backdrop provides a better understanding of why the WFAA preemption caused such an uproar among fundamentalists. The FCC was already a suspect entity.

In a narrow sense, the cancellation of Reverend Robison's broadcast spurred him into politics and helped institutionalize the Religious Roundtable. In a broader sense, it signaled to other television preachers that the almost total freedom they enjoyed over program content could swiftly be taken away, as well as emphasized to fundamentalist followers like those attending the "Dallas Freedom Rally" that political involvement might be necessary in the America of the late 1970s—perhaps even involvement that was continuous and intense.

The Tax Collectors

The FCC was by no means the only government agency to incur the wrath of many fundamentalists. Two years after it entertained and denied Petition 2493, the Internal Revenue Service (IRS) began to enforce provisions revoking the tax-exempt status of racially discriminatory private schools. Regulations prohibiting a grant of tax-exempt status to such schools had been on the books since 1970, when they were added as an extension of the civil rights movement.[79] For seven years though, they were not enforced. Only in 1977 did the tax-exempt issue really surface, when the IRS began its crackdown.

The reason the tax-exempt issue lay dormant for seven years before it was enforced is difficult to explain. Simple bureaucratic inertia is a possible explanation, but not a likely one. A seven-year lag between policy decision and program action stretches credibility. A more likely explanation is that the IRS decided to enforce the civil rights measures once a Democratic president came to office (Carter in 1977). Another reason may be that the IRS simply responded to the proliferation of private, fundamentalist (and possible discriminatory) schools over the decade of the 1970s. Unfortunately, no firm figures are available on the number (or rate of growth) of private Christian schools, in large part because most states do not require that they be licensed.[80] The general consensus, however, is that the number skyrocketed in the 1970s in response to the secularization of the public schools caused by the evolution, school-prayer, and school-busing court decisions, as well as the professionalization of the National Education Association and its concomitant hostility to forms of religious expression in the public schools.[81] Those trends caused the creation of a fundamentalist school infrastructure; that caught the attention of IRS officials by 1977.

The IRS crackdown enraged the conservative religious community. Prominent ministers like Jerry Falwell, Oral Roberts, Jim Bakker, and Pat Robertson either had or wished to build private colleges, and they felt threatened by the move. Beyond those elites, church leaders, parents, professors, and college administrators connected with fundamentalist schools felt threatened and harassed by the IRS.[82] As they viewed the matter, the crackdown was rather arbitrary (coming seven years after the regulations were promulgated); was a violation of the First Amendment principle of church-state separation and First Amendment religious guarantees; was a symbol of the intrusiveness of the secular state; and was notoriously unfair because it was enforced in some cases not on the basis that fundamentalist schools practiced discriminatory admission policies, but on the basis that they prohibited interracial dating and marriage. Fundamentalists argued that such a policy was not discriminatory because it applied both to black and white students and, in any case, was made known to students before they voluntarily entered the private school in question.[83]

It is necessary to recall that fundamentalists felt betrayed by the secularization of the schools wrought by the Supreme Court. In response, they formed their own private schools. The IRS crackdown seemed like an attempt to track them down just to "get" them.

Proof that this issue helped trigger fundamentalist political activism may be found in the words of Christian Right elites. Reverend Falwell put the matter bluntly in 1980: "It was the IRS trying to take away our tax exemptions that made us realize that we had to fight for our lives."[84] Bob Billings, who formed the Christian School Action in 1977 in direct response to the IRS move, similarly remarked, "The IRS ignited the dynamite [within the fundamentalist community] that had been lying around for years."[85] One anonymous minister was quoted in the *Los Angeles Times* as saying, "Why we are so angry at [IRS Commissioner Jerome] Kurtz, we would like to kill him and tell God it was an accident."[86] As these quotes indicate, this was probably the single issue among all others that directly spurred many fundamentalists into politics.

The intensity of their feeling about this issue is further demonstrated by the fact that the Reagan administration initially sought to change IRS policy as a reward to fundamentalists for their role in the 1980 victory over Carter. The Reagan administration entered into the test case on this issue, *Bob Jones University* v. *United States*.[87] Before the Supreme Court in 1982, a "friend of the court" brief was filed on behalf of Bob Jones University, a fundamentalist school whose tax-exempt status was threatened.[88] The position of the administration was unusual: it argued on behalf of a private school against its own IRS.

This position, which was part and parcel of a conscious Justice Department effort led by Brad Reynolds to relax civil rights legislation,[89] created an outcry among civil rights organizations and liberals in Congress. In response, the administration backed away from its position—sort of. Rather than switch sides, it retreated, arguing that the IRS lacked the power to deny tax-exempt status by promulgating regulations, and that only the Congress by statute could render such judgments.[90] The administration did not change sides, but did alter its justification for its stance to ameliorate criticism. The change of position allowed it to oppose the IRS decision on purely procedural grounds.

Subsequently, the Supreme Court flatly rejected the fundamentalist (and administration) arguments in the *Bob Jones* case. In an 8–1 decision handed down in 1983, the Court rebuked administration efforts: "It would be wholly inconsistent with the concepts underlying tax exemption to grant the benefit of tax-exempt status to racially discriminatory educational entities."[91] The question of whether the IRS could promulgate regulations to that effect was never really an issue for the Court; not even the administration, which championed that idea to extricate itself from a difficult position, seriously believed the IRS lacked such regulatory power.

A Baptist Gone Amiss

Even as the fundamentalists were embroiled in controversy with two government agencies, the Carter administration took a number of steps that further impelled the group into politics. The Carter presidency was of great symbolic importance to the fundamentalist community. After all, he was an unabashed "born-again" Christian who publicly proclaimed that he had experienced a religious conversion at one point in his life.[92] Moreover, he professed a fondness for lay missionary work, attending church and teaching Sunday school.[93] Because ostensibly he was "one of them," fundamentalists (especially in the South) had high expectations of his presidency. Against that aura of high expectations, it proved to be a major disappointment.

To some extent, this was true even before Carter assumed office in 1977. His "eleventh-hour" interview with *Playboy* magazine, published just prior to the 1976 election, alienated fundamentalists because of the content, the language he used, and the forum in which it was published.[94] Among other things, Carter remarked that he had looked upon "a lot of women with lust," committed "adultery in my heart many times," and recognized that "Christ says don't consider yourself better than someone else because one guy screws a whole bunch of women."[95] The interview was intended to allay the fears of moderate-to-liberal Democrats that Carter was "holier than thou." It probably achieved that goal, but certainly did not sit well with the fundamentalist community.

Besides, the interview had consequences beyond the general public reaction to it because Reverend Falwell taped a program in which he lambasted Carter for granting an interview to such a magazine and questioned his judgement and "fitness" to serve as president.[96] A pro-Carter "mole" spirited out a transcript of the program, which was scheduled to air on Falwell's "Old Time Gospel Hour." In the few days prior to the broadcast of the show, the Carter campaign contacted a host of local television stations that were to carry the program and advised them that, in airing it, they might be in violation of the "equal time" provision regulating air time during political campaigns (another FCC-grounded controversy). Concerned local stations took heed and refused to broadcast the program, which had already cost Falwell an estimated $75,000 to produce. In a panic, he offered Carter time on the broadcast to make a statement that would be edited into the final program. The Carter camp politely refused the offer publicly, but one aide was quoted as saying privately: "We rejected that idea with the contempt it deserved."[97] Reverend Falwell was out $75,000.

This incident was not the only "personal" issue between the two men. Heading into the 1980 campaign, Carter tried to woo fundamentalists to his side by inviting leading ministers to meet with him. Following one of those meetings, Falwell told supporters that the two men had discussed Carter's role in harboring homosexuals on his senior staff.[98] Moreover, Falwell said he "lectured" Carter about such a practice. The White House subsequently produced a transcript of the meeting which showed not only that the "lecture" had never occurred, but also that the question of homosexuals on the White House staff had never been broached; the only remarks even related to the topic involved whether the president disapproved of homosexual marriages, to which he assented.[99] The incident made Falwell appear as a liar.

Apart from personal disputes, a variety of happenings in the Carter administration disillusioned fundamentalists with the president. For one, in accordance with the historic position of the Baptist church, he affirmed his support for the principle of church/state separation.[100] That affirmation did not win him the hearts of fundamentalists, who at that very time felt that certain agencies of the government were intruding into their religious programs and schools. Second, in accordance with traditional Democratic policy stances, Carter declared his opposition to anti-abortion legislation, school prayer, public aid to religious schools, and restriction of sex education programs in schools.[101] As shall be seen later in this book, those items were the central agenda objectives of the major Christian Right organizations lobbying on Capitol Hill. Third, Carter's presiding over the FCC and IRS controversies deeply disturbed the fundamentalist community. Here was a president who was thought to be "one of them" who refused to "call off" the FCC and IRS. Fourth, he was involved with the Iranian hostage crisis—a focal point for dissatisfaction within the staunchly pro-American conservative Christian community.

Collectively, those matters created strong fundamentalist displeasure with the Carter administration, evidenced in several ways. First, leading conservative preachers like Jerry Falwell, Pat Robertson, James Robison, Richard Zone, Bailey Smith, Robert Grant, and Tim LaHaye opposed Carter when he sought reelection. They stood solidly in the Reagan camp by 1980, frequently expressing their utter contempt for Carter.

Second, evidence shows that Carter's fundamentalist support slipped from 1976 to 1980. The measures are not precise, but a 1976 Gallup Poll found that, by 31 to 3 percent, Baptist voters agreed that his religious orientation made them more likely to support him; in contrast, a study of the 1980 presidential vote found that citizens with fundamentalist beliefs voted overwhelmingly for Reagan.[102] Carter personally believed such a slippage occurred, lamenting after the 1980 election that his fundamentalist/evangelical support had deserted him.[103]

Third, attempts to organize and mobilize a fundamentalist political constituency failed until the waning months of the Carter presidency. As early as 1974, Bill Bright (Campus Crusade for Christ), Ed McAteer, and Congressman John Conlan (R.-Ariz.) tried to mobilize fundamentalists via such groups as the Christian Freedom Foundation, Intercessors for America, Christian Embassy, and Third Century Publishers.[104] Those efforts met with little success until the Carter presidency was nearly over, and then took root in the form of such groups as the Moral Majority and the Christian Voice.

Summary

Placed on top of all the trends that helped politicize fundamentalists, the specific "triggers" were too much for them to accept. By the late 1970s, they were convinced that the secular state was deliberately savaging their institutions and values. That view, to which this study lends credence, refutes suggestions that the Christian Right is primarily a technological creation and artifact built from the "top down" via television evangelism.[105] The television evangelists did not create a social movement where the conditions for one did not exist. To assert they did, is to be insensitive to the grievances of the fundamentalist community vis-à-vis the secular state.

The "triggers" also set into place a somewhat more specific political agenda. Already the fundamentalists had formulated the broad outline of an anti-statist, militaristic, and moral agenda as a result of their experiences with the secular state. As a result of the "triggers," that agenda became more focused. The fights with the FCC and IRS focused attention on the specific problem of government agencies intruding into religious broadcasts and fundamentalist schools. The conflict over the broadcast of an anti-gay rights program stressed the clout of the cultural opposition. As before, it was still a big step from that level of specificity to the level required for an institutional agenda like that of the Congress. The process, however, began as a result of clashes with the secular state.

2. Rallies and Tallies

By 1979, fundamentalist leaders were eager to accept the challenge brought by the secular state. What they needed to do was expand their budding movement within a nationwide fundamentalist constituency and then gain the attention of the nation's policymakers. How could the fledgling political movement be expanded? How was the attention of the policymakers to be won? Those were the questions the leaders of the Christian Right faced.

Symbolic Politics

From the very beginning, Christian Right elites proved adept at creating political symbols that had mass appeal. The very process of naming the various organizations constituting the movement served as a case in point. Over time, groups like the "Moral Majority," the "Christian Voice," and the "Religious Roundtable" acquired negative connotations; initially, however, they were extremely clever names that served to expand the movement by connoting much that was central historically to the American experience: religiosity, morality, majoritarianism, Christianity. The Reverend Charles Bergstrom aptly noted: "The Christian Right here in Washington consists of a set of well-funded political lobbying offices. . . . These offices have nothing to do with the church, but they convey such an affiliation through clever use of rhetoric and words. They speak . . . in such a way as to connote a religious affiliation."[1] The adept naming of organizations continued with the formation of the "American Coalition for Traditional Values" (ACTV—pronounced "active") in 1984, the "Freedom Council" in 1985, and the "Liberty Federation" in 1986.

The promulgation of clever organizational names is far from automatic.

A frequent Christian Right rival is "Americans United for the Separation of Church and State," a non-denominational group devoted to church/state separation. Even its leaders concede that its name had an unfortunate, if unintended, anti-Catholic bent to it.[2] The Christian Right clearly avoided names with negative connotations; in fact, it devised those that had highly positive ones. Of course, it must be emphasized that it was not merely clever names that accounted for the successful rise of the Christian Right. The war with the secular state was the central factor, to which the names simply contributed.

The intelligent use of rhetorical symbols by the Christian Right went beyond the simple naming of organizations in the late 1970s. The movement also began to frame public policy issues in ways that had intuitive mass appeal. Thus, the issue of voluntary prayer in the public schools was characterized as an issue of whether "God should be put back in the schools"; the issue of voluntary religious groups meeting on school facilities was framed as one of "equal access"; the issue of teenagers receiving contraceptives from government agencies without the consent of their parents was touted as the "sneak rule"; and the issue of the right of women to an abortion was described as one of "ensuring the rights of the unborn." In the cases of "equal access" and the "sneak rule," the Christian Right helped frame what were essentially new issues; with respect to school prayer and abortion, issues that clearly preceded the movement by a number of years, the Christian Right helped popularize the existing phraseology used by conservatives. Thus, if the movement did not invent all that rhetoric itself, it at least exhibited the good sense to employ it.

There is nothing sinister about framing issues in ways that prove beneficial to one's cause. Indeed, Edelman has shown that characterizing an issue for public discourse is part and parcel of the art of politics.[3] It is no accident that secular conservatives consistently refer to the space-based missile system as the "Strategic Defense Initiative," the Nicaraguan rebels as the "freedom fighters," and the MX missile as the "peace keeper." Likewise, liberals deliberately refer to the space-based missile system as "Star Wars" and to advantaging minorities as "affirmative action." Then too, who can forget the liberals' characterization of Nixon's "Committee to Reelect the President" as "CREEP" or the 1986 Reagan administration's massive continuing appropriations bill as the "Bloated Omnibus Money Bill" or BOMB? When the Christian Right began to frame issues, it was following a time-honored tradition in politics.

The use of rhetorical symbols went beyond the naming of organizations and the framing of issues, however, into the creation of an omnipresent symbolic enemy. Such a creation is also a time-honored tradition in American politics, particularly from the right wing. Lipset and Rabb have shown how historically the right wing has created "enemies" in America. At various times, they have been "immigrants and Catholics" (1840s), the "Masons" (pre-Civil War), the "godless communists" (1950s), and the "intellectuals and 'pointy-headed' bureaucrats" (1960s).[4] In the 1980s, the omnipresent enemy created by the Christian Right is "secular humanism."

As developed by the Reverend Tim LaHaye, John Whitehead, and Gary North—all of whom have written books exposing the "danger"—"secular humanism" may be understood broadly as "man's attempts to solve his problems independently of God."[5] Yet, the term also has a much narrower, conspiratorial usage. Secular humanism is identified as an elite cadre of avowed humanists who are hostile to Christian values and traditional morality. Those humanists, argues Reverend LaHaye in deeply conspiratorial fashion, practice "mind control" on the adult population and *intentionally* create a climate of "crime and violence in our streets, promiscuity, divorce, shattered dreams, and broken hearts."[6] The conspiratorial elite is both sinister and omnipresent.

The Christian Right's attack upon the secular humanist enemy has been apparent from the outset. (Whether it has been sincere is a question that will be discussed shortly.) Countless Moral Majority fund-raising letters, for example, identified secular humanism as a very real force with which to contend, that sometimes was even responsible for unfavorable policy outcomes in the Congress.[7] Likewise, Reverend LaHaye's *Battle for the Mind* was written to "wake up Christians" before the humanists "accomplish their goal of complete world takeover by the year 2,000."[8] In recognition of their concern, Stan Hastey remarked that some individuals in the Christian Right "truly believe it [secular humanism] is a demonic force, conspiratorially created, that can rain moral disaster upon our country."[9] Also noting that fact, but mocking it, famed psychologist B. F. Skinner entitled a document warning of the dangers of fundamentalist Christianity the "Secular Humanist Declaration."[10]

Whether Christian Right leaders actually believe such an enemy exists, or whether they simply employ it as a symbolic technique of mass mobilization, is unclear. It is difficult to imagine that they actually believe it in a conspiratorial sense, where it is so preposterous. It might be the case that they believe it in a more reasonable sense, along the lines expressed by Forest Montgomery, of the National Association of Evangelicals: "While there is no secular humanist conspiracy, we do have a society that is to a large degree a humanist society."[11] Senator Orrin

Hatch (R.-Utah) expressed a similar sentiment on a Phil Donahue show that focused on the "Hatch Amendment" to a math/science bill forbidding the teaching of secular humanism in the public schools: " . . . if you are going to keep absolute religious values [out of the schools] and the values of parents throughout the country, then you ought to keep out the values of the secular humanist which basically evolve around the individual and a belief that God does not exist and that He has no values."[12] Taking note of all of the controversy surrounding secular humanism, Congressman Bob Edgar (D.-Pa.) wryly observed: "I suppose in the absence of communists, 'secular humanism' is the next best umbrella term to describe what they consider to be societal ills."[13]

Underlying this remark, which was intended to be humorous, was a more sober tone, for the creation of a symbolic enemy was a serious matter. Unlike the naming of organizations and the framing of issues, which were tactics designed to win the hearts of some of the less sophisticated members of society, the creation of a symbolic enemy was a ploy intended to exploit the fears and anxieties of those people. The Introduction to this volume noted that many Christian Right supporters are lower-class, less-educated citizens; the creation of a symbolic enemy to play upon their fears certainly did not serve their need for heightened political awareness nor the polity's need for sober, rational discourse.

It is clear that Christian Right elites promoted a secular humanist enemy to assist in the process of expanding the movement. Was it a successful ploy? Unfortunately, that is a question which is virtually impossible to answer. Father Robert Drinan suggested that the device was not an especially effective technique for enlarging the movement: "The agitation about 'secular humanism' always strikes me as an approach of the radical right which somehow does not seem to attract a wide constituency."[14] There is no evidence to question that assertion. Of course, it could still be the case that the use of such a symbolic enemy intensified the efforts of the already committed. The sheer staying power of the secular humanist rhetoric leads one to believe that it either has been of some benefit to Christian Right leaders or that they actually believe in its existence. If the latter is true, it suggests the intellectual foundations of the Christian Right are very weak and that the movement will be unable to sustain itself over time.

Finally, in the realm of political symbolism, it is worth noting that the Christian Right produced a number of symbolic artifacts for supporters. Included in this list were such items as armbands (protesting abortion), "Vote" lapel pins in the shape of the cross, eagles (symbolizing patriotism), and all varieties of certificates denoting a "morally concerned citizen." Again, those artifacts by themselves were not the sole reason for the success of Christian Right elites in expanding their movement. At best, they were a contributory factor, bringing people into the movement psychologically and financially, because the artifacts were commonly doled out for modest contributions.

The value of political symbolism for building the Christian Right is hard to overstate. Above all else, symbols are designed to simplify complex phenomena. The lower-class, less-educated fundamentalists were a prime constituency for such simplification. Christian Right leaders happily distilled and simplified complex matters for their followers, informing them that the problem was "secular humanists" who had "kicked God out of the schools" and "denied the rights of the unborn"—the answer to which was a "Moral Majority" and a "Christian Voice" in political affairs. The successful rise of the movement was testimony to the manner in which those symbols resonated in the ears of politicized fundamentalists.

The Mass Rallies

Although engaging in symbolic politics was fine for expanding the movement within a nationwide fundamentalist constituency, it was by no means a way to garner the attention of policymakers. They were not susceptible to ploys like the clever naming of organizations and the framing of issues. Members of Congress, for instance, dealt almost daily with misnamed interest groups and mischaracterized issues. Because most policymakers were also educated elites involved in a pluralistic political process, they would write off beliefs in conspiratorial enemies as absurd. If the Christian Right was to gain the attention of politicians, it had to demonstrate it was a significant political player with some electoral clout. That was the type of thing that would win the attention, perhaps even the affection, of policymakers.

Toward that end, the Christian Right organized two major rallies in 1980. Both of them were staged events, designed to capture the attention of the mass media and, ipso facto, that of the policymakers. It was a clever move. What could be a more fascinating story than a mass rally led by previously apolitical fundamentalist ministers that was attended by thousands of erstwhile apolitical Christians who were hostile to the secular state? That story had all of the necessary ingredients: large numbers of people, protest, clergy activism, unhappiness with the status quo, church/

state separation questions, slogans, and electoral implications. The Christian Right was clever enough to let the mass media carry its message to policymakers.

"Washington For Jesus"

The first rally, called "Washington for Jesus," was a two-day affair held April 28–29, 1980, on the Mall in Washington, D.C. The idea for the rally came from the Reverend John Giminez, of Virginia Beach (Va.), who claimed that the idea came from a 1978 "vision" from God.[15] The rally was organized officially under the auspices of "One Nation Under God," an umbrella group composed of such early Christian Right luminaries as Rex Humbard, Pat Robertson, Jim Bakker, Bill Bright, Paul Crouch, James Robison, and Robert Schuller.[16] A number of those ministers would later distance themselves from the Christian Right, but for now they were intent on staging a spectacle. Conspicuously absent from the list was the Reverend Falwell, who, believing the planned mass rally would fail, decided to stage his own series of "I Love America" rallies at state capitols in order to build a constituency for the fledgling Moral Majority.[17] The "Washington for Jesus" rally was vintage Christian Right, carefully intertwining a conservative political and a spiritual message.

The political component of the rally was evident in several different ways. First, a document entitled "A Christian Declaration" was distributed as a statement of purpose for the rally. Drafted several months earlier, it enunciated conservative policy positions on a host of economic, defense, and social issues; it was withdrawn after the National Council of Churches condemned the document and the IRS suggested it might investigate the tax-exempt status of "One Nation Under God."[18] (Once again, conflict with a government agency was in the offing.)

Second, the first day of the rally (April 28) was set aside for visitation of lawmakers by rally participants, for the express purpose of communicating the "increasing concern of Christians throughout America for morality in government and righteousness in our nation."[19] In addition to the Washington, D.C., visits, a group called "Intercessors for Congress" simultaneously turned out hundreds of conservative Christians to visit the state and district offices of members of Congress.[20]

Third, the second day of the rally (April 29) was marked by partisan speeches to the estimated 200,000 in attendance.[21] According to one observer of the event, struck by its partisan tone: "In all of the more

than one hundred sermons I heard during the two days of 'Washington
For Jesus' meetings, only one mentioned the sins of war, poverty, injustice, and bigotry."[22]

The spiritual component was also present. Rally participant Tom Bovard, of the Separation of Powers Subcommittee of the Senate Judiciary
Committee, emphasized that fact: "Some individuals likened the rally to
a 'repentance' rally analogous to those of Old Testament days. For instance, it was likened to the rally which occurred in Josiah's time, when
he read the book of law to the masses, and thousands of them repented.
The 'Washington for Jesus' rally was not a condemnation of non-Christian people, but a spiritual renewal for those who attended."[23]

The theological underpinning for the rally was the Bible verse found
in Chronicles II, 7:14, which reads: "If my people who are called by my
name humble themselves, and pray and seek my face, and turn from their
wicked ways, then I will hear from heaven, and will forgive their sin,
and heal their land."[24] Use of this verse was evident in a statement of
principles of the rally, which said it was designed as a "national day of
humiliation, fasting, and prayer" so that "God's mind" might be heard.[25]
The importance of that Bible verse to the Christian Right transcends
"Washington for Jesus." It has really been the movement's statement of
purpose: to turn an immoral United States toward God so that He might
forgive her and rebuild her glory. Recognizing the significance of that
passage, Stan Hastey labeled it "the controlling text of the religious
right."[26]

Interpretation of that verse also served as a source of controversy between the liberal and fundamentalist clergy. The fundamentalists, as one
might expect, accept the verse literally, believing that any modern state
that humbles itself before God may be healed. The liberal clergy, on the
other hand, accept the verse contextually, believing that it applied to
Israel in a specific historical situation, but subsequently was supplanted
by the New Testament understanding that the "church" rather than any
nation is "God's chosen people."[27] The liberal clergy view with bemusement the fundamentalist's use of this text as a justification for their
political activities—the product of an ill-informed, literalist understanding of the Old Testament.

The combination of political and spiritual components raised the aura
of excitement surrounding the rally. The perspective of Bovard is again
instructive:

> The atmosphere at the rally was one of great excitement. People had come
> to the rally from all around the country via their own cars and in buses

and in other means of transportation, but all at their own expense . . . It was a symbolic affair and it had great symbolic importance. More than that though, it also was of great spiritual importance to the Christian people who attended. In fact, it may be fair to say that it was of symbolic importance to non-religious people but of spiritual importance to religious people.[28]

Whomever the rally served, it certainly worked to alert policymakers to the budding Christian Right. Hundreds of activists visited lawmakers in their district and Washington offices, while thousands of activists fasted, prayed, and sang on the Mall in a rally estimated to be the second largest ever held there.[29]

Interestingly, from all accounts, the rally did not alert the mass public to the Christian Right as it did policymakers. After studying media coverage of the event, Hadden and Swann suggested: "The most amazing thing about the April gathering was that it received so little attention . . . the attention it got from both print and broadcast media was far less than has often been devoted to gatherings only a fraction of that size."[30] That neglect was surprising given the newsworthy nature of the rally. Explanations for the lack of coverage centered around the liberal bias of the press and/or the failure of the media to understand the significance of this event and to differentiate it from other Washington, D.C., rallies.[31] The latter point was amplified by Bovard, who contended: "Perhaps in ten years, they [the media] will realize its importance, but to date they have failed to comprehend the strength of religious commitment and the changes such commitment is capable of bringing about."[32]

If the media were psychologically incapable of dealing with "Washington For Jesus" in April, however, they certainly were ready by the fall of that year, when the second major Christian Right rally was held. To make certain that the rally was fully covered, prominent politicians were invited to speak at it, including the man who shortly thereafter ascended to the presidency of the United States.

"National Affairs Briefing"

The second rally was covered by as many as 350 reporters representing virtually all the major news outlets in the United States.[33] Known as the "National Affairs Briefing," it took place in August 1980 and was attended by an estimated 15,000 people (about half of whom were clergy) on the basis of 160,000 invitations sent nationwide.[34] Participants received instruction in the arts of grass-roots politicking and listened to more than sixty speakers, including such Christian Right "heavyweights" as Reverends Jerry Falwell, James Robison, Pat Robertson, and Bailey Smith and such politicians as Congressman Phil Crane, Senator Jesse Helms, and Republican presidential nominee Ronald Reagan.[35]

Although small in comparison to "Washington For Jesus," the "National Affairs Briefing" received considerably more publicity, and not only because the media were psychologically and logistically better equipped to deal with it.[36] The element serving to maximize the amount of coverage, to borrow a *Reader's Digest* phrase, was the number of "quotable quotes" provided by rally speakers. The enticing snippets were plentiful. The Reverend James Robison lamented: "I am sick and tired of hearing about all of the radicals and the perverts and the liberals and the leftists and the communists coming out of the closet. It is time for God's people to come out of the closet and the churches and change America."[37] Candidate Reagan publicly suggested that creationism should be taught alongside evolution in the public schools.[38] Finally, in a widely publicized and highly controversial remark, the Reverend Bailey Smith (President of the Southern Baptist Convention) said: "It is interesting at great political rallies how you have a Protestant to pray, and a Catholic to pray, and then you have a Jew to pray. With all due respect to these dear people, my friends, God Almighty does not hear the prayer of a Jew."[39]

That statement created a clamor not only because of its content, but also because of its context. Set against rally emphases on patriotism, Christian fundamentalism, and political activism, the comment struck many people as highly anti-Semitic. Rally leaders moved quickly to repair the damage as best they could. Reverends Robison and Falwell both tried to recast the remark, stating that God heard the prayers of "redeemed Gentiles and Jews."[40] Those comments did not still the controversy, however, because they left in God's good graces only "redeemed" (or Christianized) Jews. In the face of continued public outcry, Falwell later issued a statement that applauded religious pluralism: "God hears the cry of any sincere person who calls on Him."[41]

Other rally participants distanced themselves more directly from Smith's intemperate remark. Pat Robertson quit the Roundtable organization, claiming it was too controversial.[42] He did not stay in fundamentalist coalition politics thereafter, preferring to go his own way through the "700 Club" and the Freedom Council until he began his quest for the 1988 Republican party presidential nomination.[43] Candidate Reagan likewise distanced himself, saying at a press conference: "Since both the Christian and Judaic religions are based on the same

God . . . I'm quite sure that these prayers [of Jews] are heard."[44] President Carter, who had failed in his effort to woo fundamentalist leaders, tried to capitalize on the remark by pointing out that Christian-Jewish tensions would be heightened in a Reagan administration.[45]

Ironically, the unguarded remark of Reverend Smith probably served the Christian Right well by raising its visibility. It is impossible to say with certainty. However, it is known that after the remark the media remained focused on the Christian Right for the rest of the 1980 campaign and well beyond.

Coupled with smart symbolic politics, those two rallies gained widespread attention for the movement and capped its attempts to win the attention of policymakers and of a nationwide fundamentalist constituency. The Christian Right was established as a legitimate political force. The fundamentalist constituency was well aware of its existence; the broader mass public knew about the likes of the Reverend Jerry Falwell and the Moral Majority; the politicians on the Hill were aware of the Christian Right, its leaders, and its objectives. All those things were even more true after the triumphant 1980 election.

The Liberal Surprise

The liberals were caught almost completely by surprise by the rapid fundamentalist mobilization in the late 1970s. Forest Montgomery, legal counsel for the National Association of Evangelicals, nicely summed up their surprise in an interview: "There is no way the liberals could have headed it off [the rise of the Christian Right] because they did not see it coming. One cannot provide a solution when one has yet to recognize a problem, which was the case with the liberals and the evangelicals."[46]

To some extent, the liberals should not have been caught so flat-footed, for, as was noted in the preceding chapter, the seeds of fundamentalist political involvement had been sown long before they were harvested by the Republican party in the 1980 election. On the other hand, the astonishment of the liberals over the fundamentalist mobilization was quite understandable. For one thing, political involvement by those people constituted a significant departure from past practices. Fundamentalists had long eschewed politics out of the twin convictions that it would tarnish their personal lives (politics being a nasty business) and detract from the time and attention they could devote to their spiritual lives. Summing up such sentiments in his 1965 "Ministers and Marches" sermon, Falwell remarked: "I believe that if we spent enough effort trying to clean up our churches, rather than trying to clean up state and national government, we would do well."[47] Given a history of such rhetoric and a long track record of non-involvement in politics, it was no wonder that liberals were caught by surprise by the mobilization.

Second, the liberals had every reason to believe that any "fundamentalist issue" had been laid to rest with the 1976 election of Jimmy Carter, the "born-again" Baptist Sunday school teacher. At issue in 1976, particularly among Catholic and Jewish voters, was whether an openly evangelical Christian should be elected as president. When Carter was elected, the issue was quickly laid to rest, not unlike the way the "Catholic issue" was buried after the election of John Kennedy. Hence, there was little reason to believe that a "fundamentalist issue" would arise again circa 1980, let alone that it would work against the "born-again" Baptist president. Such a scenario was inconceivable.

Third, the liberals had no particular reason to believe that a fundamentalist mobilization would occur based on the unfolding 1980 campaign. At the presidential level, the issues commonly thought to agitate fundamentalists—abortion, school prayer, pornography, and gay rights—were relegated to the back burner during the bulk of the campaign season. The major issues of the campaign were traditional foreign policy (SALT II, hostages in Iran) and domestic policy (inflation) issues. There did not appear to be any major issues that would cause fundamentalists to mobilize.

As was pointed out earlier, many different issues were of concern to fundamentalists of which the liberals were simply oblivious. The reason for their apparent unawareness is unclear. It may have been that they simply were so out of touch with the fundamentalist subculture that they failed to recognize its grievances, that they recognized the grievances but considered them illegitimate, or that they recognized the grievances but were skeptical that the fundamentalists would act on them. Eventually, the liberals recognized the growing power of fundamentalists and tried to win them over. For instance, President Carter invited some of the leaders to the White House for a bit of personal lobbying and dispatched the Reverend Robert Maddox, himself a Southern Baptist, to repair relations with fundamentalists in the South.[48] Those efforts, however, were too little, too late, and too clearly motivated by electoral considerations.

Liberal activists were not alone in their surprise at the fundamentalist mobilization. The mass media were also caught flat-footed. The titles accorded various articles in the nation's leading newspapers and popular periodicals reflected the surprise wrought by mobilization. Writing in 1980, the *Chicago Tribune* claimed that the nation's "evangelists seek political clout," the *New York Times* that "militant television preachers [sought] to weld fundamentalist Christian's political power," the *Los Angeles Times* that "evangelicals [were] seeking to establish political force," and the *Boston Globe* that there was "growing political clout of America's Christian Right."[49] Similarly, leading periodicals like *U.S. News and World Report* remarked that "old time religion [was] on the offensive," *Time* suggested that the "Protestant Right [was] born-again at the ballot box," and *Newsweek* argued the United States was experiencing "a tide of born-again."[50] Even the usually staid, non-partisan *Congressional Quarterly* reported that conservative Christians were moving "from pews to polls."[51]

Archival evidence verifies the advances of the Christian Right. During 1979, the year in which the Moral Majority, the Christian Voice, and the Religious Roundtable all formed, the *Reader's Guide to Periodical Literature* had only two articles under its "Religion and Politics" subtitle from March 1979 through February 1980, compared to sixty-eight the following year.[52] Similarly, the *Social Sciences Index* had no references under its "Christianity and Politics" subtitle from April 1979 through March 1980, compared to four articles in each of the next three years.[53] Finally, the *New York Times Index* had no references under its "Religion and Churches" subtitle for all of 1979, compared to eighteen the following year.[54] The lack of media attention to the fundamentalist subculture, even as it was arising, was ample evidence of the surprise wrought by the mobilization. Except for some secular right-wing political activists who sought to capitalize on it, virtually no one saw it coming.[55]

The Liberal Response

Perhaps because they were so surprised, liberals reacted to the fundamentalist mobilization with a vengeance. This intensity may also have been a calculated attempt to discredit the burgeoning Christian Right, even if that meant engaging in a fair amount of distortion. Edelman has shown how political hyperbole is used to label and destroy political opponents.[56] Perhaps the reaction was by design.

In any case, one tack taken by the liberals was to organize a set of countervailing groups.[57] Their purpose was to combat the Christian Right in the battle for popular support. One such group, created by television producer Norman Lear, was People For the American Way. Designed to be a non-profit, non-partisan educational organization, it quickly assumed a relatively high profile, at least in interested circles.[58]

It attracted considerable attention at the time it came into being because its founding members included former Senator Harold Hughes (D.-Iowa), Father Theodore Hesburgh (president of Notre Dame University), Rabbi Marc Tannenbaum (American Jewish Committee), and Dr. William Howard and Dr. William Thompson, both one-time presidents of the National Council of Churches. Moreover, the group soon was headed by the Reverend John Buchanan, a Republican congressman from Alabama who had been ousted by Christian Right-backed candidate Albert Lee Smith in a bitter 1980 primary contest.[59] The succession of a moderate, Southern Baptist Republican preacher to head an anti-Christian Right group understandably claimed considerable attention.

Today, People for the American Way continues to thrive, regularly disseminating news releases on the perceived threat posed by fundamentalists. A news release preceding the 1986 congressional elections typifies the group's product: "The report [we compiled] found that the religious right continues to practice a new form of intolerance which says there is only one way for godly people to vote, declares Biblical principles require adherence to a narrow set of political opinions, and claims divine endorsement for political candidates."[60]

A second group organized to combat the Christian Right was Americans for Common Sense. It was the brainchild of long-serving liberal Senator George McGovern (D.-S. Dak.). Convinced that he was the victim of a "miserable, yet effective negative politics" practiced by the right wing during his 1980 electoral defeat, he announced the formation of Americans for Common Sense in his concession speech.[61] For several years, the organization was headquartered in Washington, D.C., modestly funded, and run by McGovern and his longtime Senate administrative assistant, George Cunningham. The thrust of the group's activity was never clear. It dissolved completely in 1984, when both of its leaders aspired to elective office: McGovern to the presidency and Cunningham to the U.S. Senate seat from South Dakota held by Republican Larry Pressler. Neither candidate was successful in his quest.

A third countervailing organization was Moral Alternatives in Politics. Begun by Marquette University theologian Daniel Maguire, it sought to stimulate liberal clergy to speak out against the Christian Right. Composed of a handful of Catholic, Protestant, and Jewish religious leaders, Moral Alternatives encouraged clergy to submit "op-ed" pieces to newspapers, to deliver "sample" sermons composed by Moral Alternatives to their congregations, and to hold news conferences and release press statements.[62] As furor over the Christian Right gradually subsided in the 1980s, the organization fell into oblivion.

A fourth group was the Interchange Resource Center. Formed by the National Education Association (NEA), it was ostensibly created to serve as an "information clearinghouse" on right-wing activities; in reality, the organization, which was located at NEA headquarters in Washington, D.C., was a highly politicized operation whose archival holdings consisted mainly of critical articles and "exposés" of the Christian Right.[63] The reason the NEA formed such a group was that fundamentalists were attacking the schools on such issues as the content of textbooks, the teaching of evolution, the lack of school prayer, the perceived "liberal values" of teachers, and the instruction of students in "situation ethics." The organization achieved visibility within NEA, but never achieved any substantive outside publicity.

A second tack taken by the liberals was to launch a (sometimes vitriolic) public relations campaign focused on the Christian Right. Liberal intellectuals, led by famed psychologist B. F. Skinner and science writer Isaac Asimov, for instance, issued their sardonic "Secular Humanist Declaration," mentioned earlier, which warned against "fundamentalist, literalist, and doctrinaire Christianity."[64] Similarly, one scholar wrote an article suggesting that close parallels existed between the American Christian Right of the 1980s and European fascism of the 1940s.[65] Likewise, liberal theologians from thirteen Protestant denominations signed a statement criticizing the Moral Majority and the Christian Voice which in part read: "There is no place in the Christian manner of political life for arrogance, manipulation, subterfuge, or holding others in contempt."[66] The famed anti-war activist, Reverend William Sloane Coffin, gave a more earthy evaluation of matters: "I would agree [with Christian Right leaders] that the Bible contains all the answers, at least all the significant ones. But the Bible is something like a mirror; if an ass peers in, you cannot expect an apostle to peer out."[67]

Government officials also became involved in the public relations assault. Federal Communications Commission Director Tyrone Brown suggested that "Moral Majority" was simply an idiom for white racism.[68] Senator Carl Levin drafted a ten-point program to meet "the threat to civil liberties posed by the radical religious right."[69] Carter administration Health and Human Services Secretary Patricia Harris delivered the coup de grace, presumably at the behest of the administration, when she compared the Christian Right leaders to Iranian mullahs and the Reverend Jerry Falwell to the Ayatollah Khomeini.[70] As Harris stated it, in a contextual reference to Falwell: "I am beginning to fear that we could have an Ayatollah Khomeini in this country, but that he will not have a beard, but he will have a television program."[71]

The rhetorical excesses testified to the rapid and significant mobilization of the fundamentalists. Unfortunately, they were also evidence of some hypocrisy because the liberals had decried comments like those of Reverend Robison about the "radicals, perverts, and liberals" and those of Reverend Smith about God hearing the prayers of Jews. Yet, here the liberals were comparing the Christian Right to the Nazis and the Reverend Jerry Falwell to the Ayatollah Khomeini—comparisons that were grossly simplistic and little more than the rhetorical excesses of which they accused the Christian Right.

Promoting the Agenda

Having gained the attention of policymakers, Christian Right elites now had to win them over. That formidable task required the aggressive promotion of the movement's agenda by a variety of actors. As has been seen thus far in this volume, the agenda itself was multifaceted. It was partly anti-statist, disdaining a large and intrusive federal government; it was also militaristic, emphasizing as it did firmness vis-à-vis the Soviets and its displeasure with the Carter administration for "soft-peddling" the Iranian incarceration of American hostages. Then too, the agenda was partly moral, bent as it was toward traditional morality and such issues as abortion, school prayer, pornography, and gay rights.

As the Christian Right looked toward Capitol Hill and influencing the nation's lawmakers, it began to focus primarily upon the moral element of its agenda. That element was its niche within the budding conservative movement of the period. Like the Christian Right, the secular conservatives were deeply committed to an anti-statist and militaristic agenda; they were not as deeply committed to the moral agenda, either in principle (in the case of the moderates) or in practice, because they believed it was desirable to focus attention on budgetary and rearmament goals before proceeding to the divisive moral agenda. Thus, in part out of a deep commitment to the moral agenda and in part due to strategic placement within the conservative movement, the Christian Right began to emphasize the moral element of its agenda as it looked toward the Hill. The next part of this book examines the individuals and organizations which promoted that moral agenda and how they did so.

Part II

THE PLAYERS

3. The Visible Actors

On an evening in November 1980, the electoral efforts of the secular and religious conservatives within the Republican party were rewarded. Before election night was over, the nation witnessed the elevation of Ronald Reagan to the presidency, the takeover of the Senate by Republicans for the first time in twenty-five years after a gain of twelve seats, and the increase of thirty-three Republican seats in the House of Representatives. These victories in the Congress were especially gratifying because many nationally prominent liberal Democrats were defeated, including Senators Frank Church (Idaho), John Culver (Iowa), George McGovern (S. Dak.), and Birch Bayh (Ind.). Results like those created nothing but euphoria in Republican ranks.

For their part, the leaders of the Christian Right reveled in the victory that they helped engineer by registering and turning out thousands, perhaps millions, of fundamentalist voters. The precise number was the focus of much subsequent debate among pundits, pollsters, and scholars;[1] to the leaders of the Christian Right, however, such debates were truly academic. They believed that they delivered on their promise to produce fundamentalist votes for the Republican party, as did the secular conservatives within the party. The view that the fundamentalists contributed to the winning electoral coalition, perhaps substantially, made them an integral part of the new governing coalition.

Yet, the Christian Right leaders knew that they could not bask in the glory of their hard-fought victory. They were well aware that within the "Beltway," that euphemism used to describe the Washington, D.C., area, the struggle was just beginning. The attention of the policymakers had been gained via the mass rallies and was reinforced by the 1980 election results, but no policy battles were yet won. If that were to occur, the political agenda of the Christian Right had to be promoted aggressively by its organizations and secular allies. Furthermore, the promotion had to occur in the first Reagan term (1981–84) because there was no guarantee that the Republicans would retain control of the White House in four years, nor for that matter, the Senate in two years after the midterm elections. People had to speak on behalf of the agenda and soon. Who did so is the focus of this part of the book.

In a recent study of agenda-setting in the policy areas of health and transportation, Kingdon posited the existence of a rough division of labor between those policymakers who "set the agenda" and those who "specify alternatives."[2] The former group is viewed as a "visible cluster" of individuals who determine which issues are ripe for discussion and treatment—such as the president, the White House staff, and members of Congress.[3] Lacking the political incentives to "see issues through" to their conclusion, however, those visible policymakers do not become heavily involved in details; rather, they move on to develop and frame new issues, a tactic that pays richer political dividends.

The group of policymakers who "specify alternatives" are a "hidden cluster" of career bureaucrats, congressional staff members, and academics.[4] (Interest groups are seen as moving between agenda-setting and alternative specification.)[5] Those people lack the requisite position and visibility necessary to set the agenda, but they are able to specify particular courses of action once issues are established and framed. Their influence is just as real, though not as vital.

This chapter will focus specifically upon the "visible cluster" of actors responsible for placing and promoting the concerns of the Christian Right on the agenda, including President Reagan, the New Right senators, the House "Young Turks," and the television preachers. (The next chapter will examine the "hidden cluster" of actors, including the Christian Right groups.)[6] Each of those actors has assisted the Christian Right in placing its concerns on the nation's political agenda, be it the broader public agenda or the narrower institutional agenda of the Congress.[7] The manner in which they did so during the first Reagan term is described below.

President Reagan

The triumph of Ronald Reagan in the 1980 presidential race meant considerably more to the Christian Right than the election of a like-minded conservative. Throughout his first term, he assisted the Christian Right in a variety of ways apart from his pursuit of an anti-statist, militaristic political agenda. It is rather ironic that such was the case, given that he never expressed much of an interest in organized religion nor attended church with any regularity after becoming president.[8]

As early as the 1980 presidential campaign, Reagan began to perform a crucial task for the Christian Right. It required virtually no effort on his part, but entailed some political risk and was of central importance to the burgeoning Christian Right. What he did was "mainstream" fundamentalists into politics, giving them the political credentials they sorely needed. After all, for years many of them had been apolitical, if not even on the "fringes" of society.[9] They needed to be welcomed into politics and gain credibility as legitimate political participants. Who could better provide such credentials than a presidential party nominee? From his simple willingness to share a platform with them, Reagan provided the fundamentalists with some legitimacy and political credentials.

The platform-sharing occurred both in Washington, D.C., at the president's request and in various locales around the nation at the behest of the fundamentalist preachers. To cite a specific example of the former, the administration invited a number of the "chapter chairmen" of the American Coalition for Traditional Values (ACTV) to Washington, D.C., on July 9–10, 1984. Those individuals, according to ACTV Deputy Field Director Doug Shaddix, were "big name" conservative preachers from major cities.[10] The purpose of ACTV was to register and turn out conservative Christian, pro-Reagan voters in twenty-two targeted states in the 1984 election. The purpose of the two-day meeting was to agitate those in attendance about the election. Toward that end, President Reagan formally addressed and informally met with the group, as did such administration figures as Vice-President Bush, Ed Meese, James Watt, and Surgeon General C. Everett Koop (who spoke about abortion).[11] That major instance aside, on a more routine basis, Christian Right leaders were regularly invited to the White House. That point was confirmed by the Reverend Charles Bergstrom, of the Lutheran Council: "Unlike preceding administrations, this one has been inaccessible to the mainline [Protestant] churches. The mainline churches simply lack access to the White House, while fundamentalists go in and out of there like a revolving door."[12]

The president also journeyed to meet with the conservative preachers on their "turf." The first and most visible instance was his journey to Dallas in August 1980 to speak before 15,000 conservative Christians in attendance at the "National Affairs Briefing."[13] Later that year, he also spoke before the National Religious Broadcasters Association (NRB) in Lynchburg, Virginia—the location of Reverend Falwell's home, church, and college.[14] In 1983 he repeated an appearance before the

NRB in Washington, D.C., and then later that year appeared at Orlando before the annual meeting of the National Association of Evangelicals (NAE).[15] It was in the latter speech that he called the Soviet Union an "evil empire," reflecting his view that the Soviets were not only aggressive and totalitarian, but also morally corrupt—the precise view of the Christian Right. Finally, he appeared before the NAE again the ensuing year in Columbus at their annual gathering.[16] Quite clearly, during his first term he both reached out to and received the conservative religious community, many of whom were fundamentalists. In so doing, he helped establish them as legitimate political actors.

Several points must be interjected before discussing yet other ways that Reagan assisted the Christian Right. First, his appearances before the fundamentalist preachers fell disproportionately in presidential election years, four of the six appearances mentioned occurring in the election years of 1980 and 1984. From that observation, one might reasonably conclude that to some extent he "used" the Christian Right for his own political purposes. One member of Congress who requested anonymity provided just such an interpretation, arguing that the president "used the religious right for his own purposes, including whipping them up when he needs to divert attention from the main issues."[17] Although that observation has some merit, it must be remembered that Reagan granted fundamentalist leaders access to his administration on an informal basis, so that his formal election appearances were not the only time he reached out to them. Moreover, the correlation between appearances and election years is understandable in a representative system. As an integral part of it, politicians appear before their natural reelection constituencies in election years.

A second point that must be interjected is that Reagan did not make the fundamentalist preachers involved with the Christian Right any more popular with the public. His first-term personal popularity never "rubbed off" on those individuals, who still retained high negative ratings among the citizenry. One poll, for instance, found that, even among those citizens who voted for Reagan, a clear plurality had an "unfavorable" opinion of Reverend Falwell.[18] A similar point was made in a lighthearted sense during the 1984 campaign season when Reagan campaign aides joked that Falwell had higher "negatives" in the polls than anyone except the Ayatollah Khomeini. What the president could do he did: mainstream the fundamentalist leaders into politics. He was unable to make them be loved by the public, as he was throughout most of his first term.

Third, the fundamentalist preachers certainly did not "own" the administration. Even though the president demonstrated a willingness to reach out and receive them among all religious leaders, he was predominantly occupied during his first term with defense and economic matters, which, by comparison, dwarfed the amount of attention he devoted to the preachers and their moral agenda. It would be erroneous to assume that he was immersed in their concerns. He granted them access to his administration, but not ascendancy.

Another way that Reagan assisted the Christian Right, in addition to his providing them with political credentials, was through rhetoric. In a specific sense, he continually voiced backing for the moral agenda of the Christian Right in major speeches. Not surprisingly, the enunciated support often came in the appearances before the NRB and the NAE, mentioned earlier. Likewise, the president expressed support in his State of the Union messages. In 1983, for instance, he said he favored "passage of tuition tax credits for parents who want to send their children to private or religiously affiliated schools," as well as "a constitutional amendment to permit voluntary school prayer . . . [since] God should never have been expelled from America's classrooms in the first place."[19] Similarly, in his 1984 speech, the president reiterated his support for those objectives and added his desire "to restore protection of the law to unborn children," thereby mentioning several top legislative objectives of the Christian Right in a single speech.[20] Kingdon has argued persuasively that mere mention in a State of the Union message brings issues prominence on the agenda, which is why various interests compete so hard to have their issues mentioned in that one speech.[21] The president's mention of those issues was no small service, and was proof of his willingness to place and promote the concerns of the Christian Right on the agenda.

Yet, Reagan's aid was even more far-reaching. In addition to references to specific items on the moral agenda, he also made carte blanche statements of support. Before one group of secular conservatives, he stated: "We do not have a separate social agenda, a separate economic agenda, and a separate foreign policy agenda. We have one agenda. Just as surely as we seek to put our financial house in order and rebuild our nation's defenses, so too we seek to protect the unborn, to end manipulation of school children by utopian planners and permit the acknowledgement of a Supreme Being in our classrooms."[22] He made a similar sort of statement about the political agenda of the Christian Right at a White House press conference: "I think I've made over the months and even years my position clear on most of those social issues, and I shall be happy to see them come to my desk for signature [into law]."[23] Admittedly, this was a rather passive endorsement, but a sweeping one nonetheless.

The point may be advanced one step further. Apart from issue references, both narrow and broad, the president also promoted the broader concerns of the Christian Right: family, marriage, religion, and work. The 1984 State of the Union message is again illustrative. Perhaps intentionally drawing upon the pro-Reagan American Coalition for Traditional Values, formed in that year, Reagan devoted an entire section of his speech to the theme of "traditional values," asserting that the strengthening "of our community of shared values revolving around faith, work, family, neighborhood, freedom and peace" was one of four "great goals" our nation must achieve.[24] When Reagan's list is compared with the primary concerns of the Christian Right as they were once articulated by Cal Thomas, a one-time vice-president of the Moral Majority—pro-life, pro-morality, pro-traditional family, and pro-American—it is clear how the president reflected its concerns.[25]

One final point about Reagan's backing of the Christian Right is distinct from the previous ones. During his first term, the president came to embody fundamentalist Christianity in a real, personal sense. Evidence to that effect was everywhere: he claimed a conversion experience something akin to being "born-again" in the 1980 election; said that the Bible provided him great guidance for daily living; invoked God in many speeches and statements; publicly supported the designation of 1983 as the "Year of the Bible"; and, after the intense fundamentalist uproar when he uttered the word "damn" once, was careful not to swear.[26] Taking stock of these facts, the Reverend John Buchanan was prompted to remark in an interview: "While prior to his presidency Reagan never demonstrated much of an interest in organized religion, he is now a part of the religious right, and acts and sounds like a fundamentalist Christian. I believe he is sincere about it too."[27] Whether the president was really as sincere as Buchanan believed or simply trying to shore up fundamentalist aid for his 1984 reelection bid is to some extent irrelevant, though not uninteresting. Perhaps the commitment was genuine—Reagan would not be the first person to find religion late in life. What mattered, however, was that at a minimum he assumed the trappings of a fundamentalist Christian. Even if that was all he did, he probably helped Christian Right leaders with their constituencies by appearing to be one of them.

In short, the president accomplished much for the movement in his first term. He met formally and informally with its leaders many times, helped mainstream them into politics, provided them a visibility in fundamentalist circles that probably helped fill their organizational coffers, voiced support for their moral agenda objectives, backed their values, and even came to embody fundamentalist Christianity personally.

For all those reasons, the Christian Right was very happy with him, particularly early in his administration. In 1982, for instance, Reverend

Falwell was quoted as saying that, thus far, he could not take real issue with anything Reagan had done as president.[28] Similarly, Cal Thomas, of the Moral Majority, stated his satisfaction with White House efforts to enact the Christian Right agenda.[29] Bill Billings, of the National Christian Action Coalition, contended that the administration had done all that it could within the climate created for it by the Christian Right.[30]

The president's strong support should not be misconstrued to mean that the Christian Right was universally pleased with him, though that would not be too far off the mark. At various times, the movement sought more access to him, more personal lobbying on Capitol Hill, and greater effort on the campaign trail. Yet, those complaints were familiar ones, voiced year in and year out by even the strongest backers of any president. Reagan was in a position to assist the Christian Right and it understandably sought that assistance. The larger wave in the ripple of protest, however, was support of the president because, in the "old-fashioned way, he earned it."

Other observers were more cynical of the president and offered different explanations than that "he earned it" for the strong backing he received from the Christian Right in his first term. One such explanation was that, being relatively new to politics, the Christian Right was oblivious to the manner in which it was used. Stan Hastey said as much: "The lack of complaint on the part of the religious right reflects their political naivete."[31] That assessment was shared by one individual on the Hill, who requested anonymity: "The Christian Right has been unable to recognize sincere from half-hearted Administration efforts." Some of the more experienced activists of the Christian Right indirectly confirmed that point. Gary Jarmin, of the Christian Voice, for instance, wryly observed: "In general, the level of political sophistication among the Christian Right is low . . . there is no question in time the level of sophistication will increase, but in the meantime, let me say there is still room for improvement."[32] Given the low level of sophistication, it is reasonable to assume the heavy support accorded Reagan was partly a function of political naiveté. Of course, any naiveté that existed did not necessarily hold uniformly across the Christian Right, but instead affected mostly its mass followers and less politically experienced leaders.

A second explanation for the solid backing of the Christian Right for the president is that it made itself a victim of its own initial loyalty to the administration. The Reverend Falwell, for example, once called President Reagan and Vice-President Bush "God's instruments in rebuilding America," and suggested they were the central figures in this "Decade of Destiny."[33] According to this argument, having so closely allied himself with the administration, Falwell left no opportunity for himself to back away. After all, how could a Christian minister possibly retreat from "God's instruments?" Former Congressman Bob Edgar presented this explanation for support, finding humor in the ineptness of Falwell and other fundamentalists to extricate themselves from their position of wholehearted support for the president: "They did it [supported Reagan] with a sense of mission, reflecting the simplicity which is their way of life. Once at the political altar they were captured, and people cashed in on their efforts."[34]

A third explanation for the Christian Right's stance behind the president is that he provided them the political symbolism they desired. Edelman has demonstrated the powerful symbolic component in politics,[35] and it is plausible that the Christian Right was content with the type of symbolic affirmation of its values that the president provided in his rhetoric. Particularly for the fundamentalist masses that was perhaps the case, for they were probably unaware that his substantive actions with respect to the moral agenda did not always measure up to his rhetoric. Of course, they may also have been aware of the incongruity, but were undisturbed by it because they truly valued the symbolism.

The various explanations are by no means mutually exclusive. The Christian Right probably did ally itself too closely with the administration out of political naiveté, from which it could extricate itself only by losing face. At the same time, it benefited from and was pleased with the symbolism. Before one becomes too cynical, however, it must be recalled that the president treated the Christian Right well during his first term. He met with its leaders regularly, expressed sympathy for its legislative objectives in major addresses, and even began to behave and sound like a fundamentalist. Solely on the basis of what Reagan did for the Christian Right, it had ample reason to back him in good conscience and with enthusiasm. Perhaps that was the reason it did.

New Right Senators

In addition to electing Ronald Reagan in 1980, voters also saw fit to remove a number of long-serving Senate liberals. Elected in their place were a coterie of extremely conservative New Right senators, such as Republicans John East (N.C.), Steve Symms (Idaho), Jeremiah Denton (Ala.), Paula Hawkins (Fla.), and Don Nickles (Okla.). Along with the dean of the New Right, Republican Senator Jesse Helms (N.C.), those senators were the driving force behind Senate action on the Christian Right agenda. They were able to play an active role because of the erosion of the norm of "apprenticeship," which in an earlier era would have forbade their active participation at such an early stage in their careers.[36]

There was nothing particularly complicated about how the New Right senators assisted the Christian Right. They did so by scheduling legislative action when they were able (for example, Senator John East's antiabortion hearings in his Judiciary subcommittee in 1981); or, more commonly, by pressuring the Republican party and its Senate leadership during Reagan's first term to entertain Christian Right issues. They were quite successful in the latter regard in particular. For example, in the 97th Congress (1981–82), Senate committees held a total of five hearings on three major issues of the movement: abortion, school prayer, and tuition tax credits.[37] Similarly, in the 98th Congress (1983–84), four sets of hearings were held on those same issues.[38] Likewise, the full Senate voted on bills on all three issues in the 98th Congress.

Those actions may not seem like much, but it must be recalled that the enactment of any agenda often takes considerable time while citizens gradually are sensitized to it.[39] In helping place its concerns on the agenda, the New Right senators performed an immensely valuable function for the Christian Right. They initiated the difficult process of putting items on a crowded congressional agenda and then mobilizing support for them. Although not the kind of activity that customarily gains much attention, it was absolutely essential if there was to be any hope for the enactment of agenda objectives.

It was clear that the push for action in the Senate on the moral agenda came primarily from the New Right senators. From the outset, they were a vocal group, determined to reconstitute what they perceived to be the nation's fixation with a welfare-statist, secularist political agenda. They made some inroads in both respects, pressuring the Senate to consider reductions in entitlements and to take up issues like school prayer and abortion, which had not been considered seriously in the chamber for well over a decade. That significant point and the individual activities of the New Right senators will later be discussed in far more detail in the chapters dealing with the struggles in Congress. For now, the point is simply that the New Right senators achieved measurable success in promoting the moral agenda of the Christian Right in committees and on the Senate floor.

House "Young Turks"

During the first Reagan term, a small cadre of extremely conservative, junior House Republicans began to form. Led by such members as Vin

Weber (Minn.), Bob Walker (Pa.), Newt Gingrich (Ga.), and Bill Danne-meyer (Calif.), those "Young Turks" formed an organization formally known as the Conservative Opportunity Society (COS). It had really begun in 1983 out of informal discussions of fifty House Republicans at a retreat in Baltimore. Later, the COS institutionalized itself, holding regular strategy meetings in the offices of its members.[40]

The impetus for the formation of the COS was provided by the ma-jority-party Democrats. They continually thwarted Republican efforts in the House, refusing to schedule hearings on their issues, stacking com-mittees and subcommittees out of proportion to party ratios in the full House, similarly skewing staff support, and outvoting Republicans in committees through use of proxies even though they had a majority of members in attendance.[41] More galling than the use of House rules and procedures by the majority party to its advantage, which was simply astute politics, was the proclivity of the Democratic leadership to wield its power on the House floor for blatantly partisan purposes. In fact, it was just such an exercise of power which crystallized the convictions of the junior House Republicans that they should form the COS.

The specific incident that infuriated the Republicans was a 1983 vote on the Equal Rights Amendment (ERA). In order to put the Republicans on record against the ERA heading into the 1984 campaign season, the House leadership brought the ERA to the floor under "suspension of the rules." That procedure, usually reserved for non-controversial matters or those that required expeditious treatment, allowed only forty minutes of debate before a vote. Bringing up the ERA in this manner meant that the Democratic leadership was permitting only forty minutes of formal debate on a proposed constitutional amendment. The leadership sought to justify its misuse of the "suspension" procedure, stating that the ERA was a familiar issue that had already been extensively debated.[42] That explanation did not sit well with the Republicans, who knew full well that the leadership was using the ERA for crass partisan purposes. The ERA stood no chance of moving beyond the House when a Republican Senate and president were opposed to it. In defense of the Democratic leadership, at that time the Republicans were continually engaged in the very same process of trying to embarrass the opposition party by raising issues like school prayer and abortion on every possible occasion. The Democratic leadership was just getting even.

The Republicans were able to turn back the ERA with the help of moderate party members who had supported it previously, but this time voted against it because of the procedure under which it was raised. Winning the vote, however, was less significant than the subsequent decision of junior House Republicans to strike back at the Democratic leadership.

The counterattack came mainly in the form of inventive use of C-SPAN (the cable network responsible for televising House proceedings) and the "special orders" procedure allowing members to broach any topic at the end of the legislative day. The "Young Turks" began to use that technique daily to lambast the Democratic leadership before a nationwide cable television audience for refusing to schedule action on such issues as school prayer, abortion, and a balanced budget. The speeches they delivered were passionate, and seemingly directed to the full House because the rules did not allow the C-SPAN cameras to pan the chamber to show that no one was listening to the speeches. All the other House members, less the junior Republicans, had gone home. Over time, that situation proved unpalatable to the Democratic leadership: on a daily basis it was the object of scathing attacks by junior Republicans to a nationwide cable television audience who was unaware that the full House was not listening to the speeches. The attacks were evidently making an impact, too, at least if a story told by presidential aspirant Congressman Jack Kemp (N.Y.) is true. He said that while passing through an airport he was stopped by a woman who was not interested in him, but instead wanted to learn if he knew COS ringleader Bob Walker.[43]

In response to the situation, as was his prerogative, Speaker "Tip" O'Neill promulgated new rules with regard to the C-SPAN cameras. Specifically, he ordered them to pan the House chamber periodically during proceedings, which showed that the impassioned speeches were being delivered to an empty chamber. Moreover, he ordered the display of a caption on the television screen, which stated that the House had finished its legislative work for the day. When were the new rules put into effect? Precisely at a time when COS member Bob Walker (Pa.) was delivering one of his "special orders" speeches attacking the Democrats. Having "neglected" in advance to inform the COS members of the new rules regarding camera usage, the Speaker was the focal point of heated criticism from junior Republicans. Inside the "Beltway," the turning of the cameras even achieved official scandal status, becoming known as "CamScam."[44]

Following the ERA vote and the "CamScam" incident, the posture of the COS members toward the Democratic leadership was openly confrontational. COS members began acting on the premise that it was futile to play the legislative game within the rules of the House because the majority party was so arbitrary and dictatorial with those rules.

The connection of all that activity with the Christian Right was simple:

the issues that the COS members regularly complained about being "bot-
tled up" by the Democratic leadership during the "special orders" procedure were such issues of the movement as abortion and school prayer.
The bottom line was that the COS members placed and promoted the
concerns of the Christian Right on the House agenda, particularly in the
98th Congress.[45] The helpfulness of the COS members to the Christian
Right was no accident either, for subsequent collusive actions took place,
such as an all-night vigil at the Capitol in 1984 to attract support for a
school-prayer amendment being considered in the Senate.[46] Because the
task of agenda promotion was being performed for them in the House,
Christian Right activists were free to focus their efforts upon the Senate.

That COS members acted as proxies for the Christian Right in the
House was mentioned in many separate interviews. Gary Jarmin, of
Christian Voice, acknowledged as much: "The 'Young Turks' headed by
Gingrich are doing the work for us in the House by bringing up the social
agenda themselves. In the absence of their work, and the work being
done at the grassroots level, it is folly for me to knock on doors [to lobby
members] in the House. It is like knocking my head against a wall."[47]

A similar sentiment was expressed by Morton Blackwell, the White
House liaison to the conservative religious community,

> The rise of Vin Weber, Bob Walker, Newt Gingrich, and Bill Dannemeyer
> and the Conservative Opportunity Society is a good development, because
> those people see the need to bring issues to votes in the Congress. They
> are willing to risk a small defeat rather than make a small retreat from
> principles. They are willing to launch legislative struggles they ultimately
> lose legislatively, but win politically. The COS people electrify the public,
> in part because citizens like to see Tip [O'Neill] blow up on television.[48]

Finally, Congressman Phil Crane summed up a variety of matters related to the COS and Democratic control of the House agenda:

> Gingrich and the others [in the COS] have recognized that O'Neill, with
> his 100 member working majority, needs to be circumvented because the
> majority party controls the agenda. We [Republicans] are given no op-
> portunity to present an alternative agenda to the one O'Neill sets. More-
> over, when we then learn how to exploit his rules to combat him and his
> agenda, he and the Democratic caucus change the rules . . . Hence, I think
> Gingrich and the others are . . . [combating O'Neill] in a persuasive way,
> using things like the one-minute speeches to ask why we cannot have de-
> bates and votes on issues like abortion, school prayer, and a balanced

budget. I believe the more of these guys we have the better. We need a few more bomb throwers to pitch issue grenades on the floor of the House.[49]

Together with the president and the New Right senators, the COS members clearly moved the moral agenda from the "general set of political controversies that will be viewed at any point in time as falling within the range of legitimate concerns meriting the attention of the polity" (that is, the systematic agenda) to the institutional agenda of the Congress. The general process by which this occurred demonstrates the view of Cobb and Elder of how agenda-setting commonly works; that "visible actors" actually forced the movement undergirds the position of Kingdon that distinctions must be made between agenda-setters and alternative-specifiers. Rather than finding those two perspectives on agenda-setting at odds, as Kingdon seems to,[50] this study suggests a synthesis of the two might be appropriate. A set of "visible actors" was responsible for moving items from the systematic agenda to the institutional agenda of the Congress. That finding indicates the work of Cobb and Elder as well as that of Kingdon requires synthesis, though the essential premises of both perspectives remain intact. Other studies in different policy areas would help confirm or refute the view that items move from broad to narrow agendas with the help of "visible actors."

Television Preachers

The final group of actors who assisted the Christian Right during Reagan's first term was the television preachers, also called the "electronic preachers" and the "televangelists." Considerable attention has been devoted to those men because of their personal and political activities.

The list of those who were active during the period was impressive: James Robison, Paul Crouch, Jimmy Swaggart, Tim LaHaye, Jim Bakker, Oral Roberts, Rex Humbard, Jerry Falwell, Kenneth Copeland, Ernest Angley, and Pat Robertson. Together, they reached millions of citizens. Early estimates placed the total audience as high as a hundred million; more systematic Arbitron and Nielson ratings estimated the total audience watching the top sixty-six religious programs (some of which were not fundamentalist) at about twenty-two million, not counting the many possible repeaters.[51] Of those approximately twenty-two million viewers, fully 60 percent (13.2 million) were thought to watch the top six religious programs, four of which were led by conservative Protestants Oral Roberts, Rex Humbard, Jerry Falwell, and Jimmy Swaggart.[52] Together, they probably had an audience of eight to ten million, but perhaps less given the likelihood of repeaters. Although those numbers were far less than the wildly inflated one-hundred million figure for all of the television ministries, they were still quite impressive. Viewership was in the millions; the only riddle was how many millions.

Why did the conservative preachers so dominate the religious airwaves at that time? The answer was that they demonstrated a willingness to pay for air time previously donated outright by the networks or given for a token price to main-line Protestant and Catholic ministries. The conservative television preachers literally "bumped" their main-line brethren off the air. That trend created considerable dissension and consternation within the religious community, a point made by Hadden and Swann: "To be unaware of this [trend] or to forget it, is to miss one of the important sources of tension between mainliners and evangelicals."[53]

Not only did the conservative Protestant preachers control the airwaves, but they also exercised considerable discretion over the nature of their programming, which helped them promote the Christian Right's moral agenda. Under existing law, on their programs they were able to endorse political candidates personally (even from the pulpit if it was made clear that the endorsement was in fact a personal one), give their name and position for endorsement purposes, engage in ostensibly "nonpartisan" voter registration drives, and allow politicans and political activists to appear.[54] Apart from their actual telecasts, they were also allowed to give church mailing lists to politicans on the same basis as they were given to other organizations.[55]

Not surprisingly, the television preachers used their programs to preach a blatantly conservative political message that embraced elements of the anti-statist, militaristic, and moral agendas.[56] By itself, that was an enormous contribution to the Christian Right. Yet, the preachers performed two other major functions as well during Reagan's first term of office.

First, at certain times they undertook grass-roots agitation on behalf of Christian Right lobbying efforts on Capitol Hill. A case in point was the Senate vote on a school-prayer constitutional amendment in 1984. As anti-prayer amendment lobbyist Frances Zwenig noted after the struggle: "The issue was way different this time, because for the first time the television evangelists were really heavily involved. They organized an amazing outpouring of communications and put pressure on the Hill . . . the timing of the pressure was orchestrated."[57] Likewise, Stan Hastey, of the Baptist Joint Committee, remarked with specific reference to the Reverend Pat Robertson and his "700 Club" shortly after the prayer issue was settled: "The volume of calls he stimulated during the school prayer debate was extraordinary."[58] That specific struggle will be discussed in considerable detail in a later chapter.

Second, and more importantly, the television preachers assisted the process of selling politics to fundamentalists who historically had eschewed it and preferred to concentrate upon personal salvation. Congressman Crane explained the matter this way:

> I believe that people like Falwell and Pat Robertson deserve much of the credit for getting people involved, by legitimating politics to them over the airwaves. When I was in a Baptist church in New Hampshire during my [1980] presidential campaign, I actually witnessed a pastor, prior to the service, asking people not registered [to vote] to raise their hands, after which he gave them a lecture on civic responsibility. The system depends on good people being involved, and Falwell and Robertson and others have helped get that point across ... I would credit the various personalities, the creative use of television, and the times themselves—that is, the awareness that democracy is not a spectator sport—for attracting and coalescing people who historically have eschewed politics.[59]

In a similar vein, Roy Jones, of Moral Majority, remarked, "Falwell broke the mold [among fundamentalist preachers] by demonstrating his willingness to address political issues."[60] Tom Bovard provided a more theologically grounded explanation of the same point:

> Basically, following the Civil War, the [more conservative] churches turned inward, and concentrated on saving the individual soul. It is the result of that turning inward that had people like Dwight Moody going around preaching only salvation, and not taking the time to dabble in other things ... This dispensational view was orthodoxy for people like Falwell and Robertson. What is amazing about them is that they have turned this entire idea around, and gotten people involved in politics.[61]

Perhaps the best proof that the television preachers were successful in legitimizing politics to many fundamentalists was that the leaders who were still members of the dispensational school were extremely critical of preachers like Reverend Falwell.[62] Had the legitimization attempts failed, there would not have been such a clamor on the part of the dispensationalists.

During the time that the television preachers and the other "visible actors" were promoting the Christian Right agenda, a cadre of equally significant actors were quietly supplementing those efforts. Who were those people? How did they do so? Answers to those questions are the focus of the next chapter.

4. The Hidden Contingent

In contrast to the relatively finite number of "visible actors" involved in agenda-setting, the number of "hidden actors" who were specifying alternatives is large. Among those who fit in that category are congressional staff members, academics, bureaucrats, and interest-group activists. This discussion will focus on congressional staff members and interest-group activists, especially the latter. The decision to concentrate on those two sets of individuals is a practical one, reflecting both the need to restrict the discussion and, more importantly, the simple reality that almost no one mentioned the role of any academics or bureaucrats in the interviews conducted for this book.[1] This indicates that their roles were limited with regard to the moral agenda of the Christian Right, a view confirmed by secondary research.[2]

Congressional Staff Members

Kingdon has argued that congressional staff members are prominent in specifying alternatives. As he views it, "Staff impact on the [agenda] alternatives and on the specific provisions of legislative proposals is very great. They have considerable latitude in shaping legislative language and in inserting some proposals and not others."[3] The research for this volume confirms the veracity of that proposition. In the few instances where the names of Capitol Hill staffers were mentioned during the interviews, it was in the context of alternative specification.

Tom Bovard, counsel for the Separation of Powers Subcommittee of the Senate Judiciary Committee, provided two helpful examples in two separate interviews. In the first interview, he noted that the Senate battle over S. 158 (an anti-abortion bill) was the brainchild of former Separation of Powers Subcommittee staff member James McClellan, who provided the idea to "strip" the Supreme Court of jurisdiction as a way of restricting abortion.[4] Clearly, he was involved in specifying an alternative (court-stripping). He did not place the issue of abortion on the national political agenda—a task most people would credit to the Supreme Court.

In the second interview, Bovard provided an example of his own work in specifying alternatives, this time in the context of working with the Christian Right:

> Let me give you an example of how we here at the Subcommittee work with the Christian Right groups. We are presently working on the wording of a federal rape bill which has provisions relating to spouse rape. The Christian Right groups basically are wary of any provisions regulating marital sexual relations, and are concerned that any wording on this matter be very carefully done. We have spoken with these groups on the issue.[5]

Once again, the congressional staff member did not place an issue on the agenda; the issue of rape was around long before any bill that included provisions relating to instances of spouse rape. Rather, what Bovard did was work to specify alternatives and language with regard to marital rape, trying to accommodate concerns that the federal government might become unduly involved in the private sex lives of married couples.

A third example of congressional staff action with respect to alternative specification was provided by Gary Jarmin, of Christian Voice. When strategy meetings were first held to drum up backing for a school-prayer constitutional amendment in 1983, they were attended by a small cadre of pro-prayer activists. At the second of those meetings, staff director Stephen Markman, of the Senate Judiciary Committee, floated the idea of a silent-prayer proposal coupled with provisions allowing student religious groups access to school facilities.[6] The idea was rejected ultimately in the Senate, but it did come to a test vote. Once again, the congressional staff member did not place the issue on the agenda per se—an accomplishment that again most people would credit to the Supreme Court. What he did was specify an alternative on the prayer issue that ultimately was considered by senators during the school-prayer fight.

Interest-Group Activists: The New Right

The role of the New Right politicos in creating and nurturing the Christian Right has been well documented.[7] The consensus of individuals who have investigated that connection is that top New Right figures like Paul Weyrich (Committee for the Survival of a Free Congress), Howard Phillips (Conservative Caucus), Phyllis Schlafly (Eagle Forum), Connie Marshner (Library Court), and Richard Viguerie (RAVCO—the Richard A. Viguerie Co.) all set out deliberately to recruit fundamentalist leaders into politics. Their hope and expectation, subsequently borne out, was that those leaders could bring hundreds of thousands of previously uninvolved conservative Christians into the Republican party. The New Right leaders began their drive to recruit fundamentalist leaders in 1979, in what Viguerie's *Conservative Digest* called the "Preachers Into Politics Movement," in order to have them mobilized in time for the 1980 election.[8] The leaders traveled to meet with fundamentalist preachers and encouraged them to become involved in politics, speak out on issues, and form interest groups. Subsequent events served as testimony to the success enjoyed by the New Right operatives.

Following the initial period of cooperation, the New Right secular conservatives and the Christian Right fundamentalists continued to retain close ties. The most visible link between them was the regular meetings at forums like Library Court (so named because the meetings were held in a building near the Library of Congress) and the Kingston group (origin of the name unknown). The former meetings were described by one regular participant who requested anonymity as a "coffee and doughnuts" affair; the latter meetings were more substantive gatherings that were concerned with policy and current happenings.[9] A less visible link, but one that existed according to one interviewee who sought anonymity, was regular meetings to plan strategy and tactics. They were attended by the "heavy-hitters" of the New Right and the Christian Right. As the interviewee explained it, "Those meetings (Library Court and Kingston) are part of the coalition meetings, but there are others at a higher level that are smaller in scope." The existence of that ongoing relationship prompted some observers to think in terms of a secret right-wing conspiracy.[10] That paranoia was especially ludicrous coming from the left wing, which historically accused the right wing of being too conspiratorially minded.

Despite the early cooperation, over time the nature of the relationship between the New Right and the Christian Right changed. Initially, the New Right secular conservatives were clearly the leaders. The reason they were was logical enough: they were seasoned politicos giving guidance and direction to fundamentalists just entering politics. As New Right leader Paul Weyrich pointed out in 1984: "Five years ago, the leadership was clear, and people were in a definite hierarchy . . . in 1980 the reli-

gious right's leadership was to some extent subservient; they were so new
to politics, they deferred to people like Howard Phillips or myself."[11]
The dominance of the secular conservatives prompted some liberals to
assert that the fundamentalists unwittingly were being used.[12] At the
time, it was a natural conclusion to draw, given that a handful of experienced secular conservatives persuaded apolitical fundamentalists to
become bedrock Republicans. The conclusion was all the more natural
because the New Right recruiters were not themselves fundamentalists:
Viguerie and Weyrich were Catholics and Phillips a Jew.

As time passed, however, the view that the New Right conservatives
were "using" the fundamentalists pretty much abated. Congressman Bob
Edgar (D.-Pa.), for instance, remarked in a 1984 interview that the leading
Christian Right figures were "big boys" who certainly were not being
manipulated then and probably never were at the outset either.[13] Conservative Jim McKenna, aide to former Congressman George Hansen
(R.-Idaho), voiced a similar thought with specific reference to the Reverend Falwell: "I do not think Falwell is being duped [by the secular
conservatives]. What you have to realize about Falwell is that he was a
highly successful minister long before he ever got involved in the Christian
Right stuff. He and the secular conservatives are using each other, and
there is nothing evil about that type of symbiosis."[14] Congressman Crane
echoed a similar theme, again with references to specific individuals: "I
would point out that Falwell has his own [mailing] list, his own constituency, quite apart from that of Viguerie. It is safe to say that Falwell's
list of his own constituency is much better than that of Viguerie . . . The
point is that it seems dubious, given those circumstances, that Viguerie
is in any way 'using' Falwell."[15]

Common to all those quotes is the theme that the secular conservatives
lacked any strategic position from which to manipulate the Christian
Right. It was a view that was well founded. Although during the formation and early months of the Christian Right its leaders may have been
subject to manipulation by seasoned political activists (though there is
no evidence they were), any subservience that existed was short-lived.
Over time, any preeminence by the secular conservatives over their fundamentalist brethren abated; in fact, in time the very alliance between
the two forces abated somewhat. Why was that the case?

First, the fundamentalists gained political experience after they entered
politics. Throughout the first Reagan term, they often fell short of being
accomplished political actors—a point that will be made forcefully in a
later chapter of this book. Yet, the simple fact that they gained political
experience depreciated their need for the advice and guidance of the New
Right political veterans. Perhaps hubris on the part of highly successful

ministers also came into play. They could not and would not forever remain the students of their secular political mentors.

Second, the fundamentalists and the secular conservatives parted company somewhat over the Reagan administration. As shown earlier, the fundamentalists were extremely enthusiastic about it; the secular conservatives, on the other hand, were highly critical at times. Their displeasure dated back as far as the 1980 campaign and encompassed the following events: (1) unhappiness with the selection of the moderate, "silk-stocking" George Bush for the vice-presidency rather than "hard-liner" Congressman Jack Kemp; (2) discontent over the initial appointment of moderates in the White House like David Gergen, James Baker, and Michael Deaver; (3) disgruntlement over the lack of progress on the "social issues" in the Congress; and (4) irritation with the eastern, financial bent of the Republican party under Reagan in general.[16] Noticing the discontent, the *Congressional Quarterly* suggested that the New Right secular conservatives might eventually bolt the Republican party and form a new party to the ideological "right" of the Republicans—talk that the secular conservatives encouraged.[17] Stan Hastey remarked as follows with reference to the divergent attitude toward the administration:

> The loyalty of the religious right leaders to Reagan is amazing. Almost from the first month of the Reagan Administration, the secular right leaders like Richard Viguerie, Howard Phillips and Paul Weyrich were carping at the President. They have complained continually about the agenda that has been acted upon, including the treatment the religious right has received. The religious right has not complained in any manner comparable to the secular right about the Reagan agenda.[18]

Hastey hit upon something that was rather ironic: the secular conservatives complained more about the treatment accorded the moral agenda of the Christian Right than did the movement itself. That unhappiness on the part of the secular conservatives probably stemmed in part from their ideological purity; their realization that pressure had to be kept on the administration; and their displeasure with not having received, or at least not having been satisfied with, the symbolic rewards that Reagan doled out to the fundamentalists.

Third, to some extent the fundamentalists simply outgrew the secular conservatives. That point was tacitly acknowledged by Paul Weyrich:

> When we began what is known as the New Right, you could keep track of all the conservative activity in Washington and nationally. If it was

happening, we knew about it, and in fact probably had a hand in it. [Now] the exponential explosion of activity is so great that we can't even keep track of some of the things our own operations are planning . . . It [the conservative movement] is now divided into spheres of influence and spheres of operation, and these operate . . . independently of each other.[19]

Metaphorically speaking, over time the "tail began to wag the dog." The Christian Right outgrew the ability of the secular conservatives to exercise control over it.

Concerning the theme of specification of alternatives, only one instance was found where a New Right leader played such a role analogous to that of congressional staff members. On the formulation of the school-prayer constitutional amendment, New Right operative Greg Butler, of Paul Weyrich's Committee For the Survival of a Free Congress, sat in on and contributed to the initial meetings where the precise proposal was hammered out.[20] Other examples may have occurred but remain undiscovered because interviews with certain key New Right leaders for this book did not transpire.[21] Other interviewees did not mention the role of those leaders in alternative specification, however, leading one to believe that it was modest.

If anything, the New Right leaders probably engaged more in agenda-setting than alternative specification. They received considerable attention during the early 1980s, granting many interviews to both the electronic and the print media. Richard Viguerie alone, for instance, appeared on the Phil Donahue talk show on several different occasions, published a book, and was quoted in such leading newspapers as the *Washington Post* with some regularity.[22] That finding is not inconsistent with the work of Kingdon. Recall that he found in his study of health and transportation policy that interest groups frequently moved between agenda-setting and alternative specification;[23] the available evidence suggests that, at least during the first Reagan term, the New Right was probably more involved with placing the moral concerns of the Christian Right on the systematic agenda than it was with alternative specification. Perhaps the seasoned political veterans of the New Right believed it was the prerogative of the Christian Right to work on the details of its own moral agenda.[24]

Interest-Group Activists: The Christian Right

For its part, the Christian Right was involved with every aspect of the moral agenda. Previous chapters pointed out that the the movement cultivated certain moral concerns and then placed them on the systematic and congressional agendas. It also helped specify alternatives with respect to those moral concerns. Numerous examples can be cited. In the 98th Congress (1983–84) alone, for instance, the Christian Right was actively involved in alternative specification with respect to the school-prayer, equal access, and abortion issues.[25] Because the ensuing chapters detailing the battles in Congress over those issues spell out the Christian Right's role in considerable detail, it will simply be noted at this juncture that alternative specification in fact occurred. The primary focus here is upon the key leaders and organizations of the movement who were responsible for placing and promoting the moral issues on the agenda during the first Reagan term.

National Christian Action Coalition

The National Christian Action Coalition (NCAC) was the outgrowth of an organization known as Christian School Action, which had been formed in 1977 by Bob Billings. The broad purpose of Christian School Action was to monitor legislation and regulations affecting the operation of private Christian schools.[26] In December 1978 its scope was broadened to include lobbying on Capitol Hill, and its name was changed to the NCAC.[27] Then, in 1979, a political action committee was added, known as the Christian Voter's Victory Fund. It provided some modest contributions to candidates in the 1980 election, but, more importantly, compiled a "Family Issues Voting Index" that rated members of Congress on ten controversial "family issues"; it was subsequently adopted by both the Moral Majority and the Religious Roundtable.[28] Following that, a non-profit, tax-exempt research foundation known as the Christian Education and Research Foundation (CERF) and a publishing arm known as the New Century Foundation were added. By the end of the first Reagan term, the NCAC was a multifaceted organization.

Despite the additions, the NCAC remained the umbrella organization that controlled the political action committee, the research foundation, and the publishing house. The primary task of NCAC was to publish a monthly newsletter named "Alert," which apprised an estimated 1,200 fundamentalist schools of legislation pending in the Congress that could affect their operations. The NCAC was funded through the contributions of churches and individuals, mostly through their subscriptions to the newsletter. In addition to the newsletter, the NCAC also produced a film starring conservative Senator Jesse Helms (R.-N.C.) that explained to apolitical fundamentalists how to become involved in politics. The film was used throughout the early 1980s as a recruiting tool. Toward the same goal, the NCAC also produced fliers and pamphlets.[29] The operations of the organization were summed up this way by its leader: "The main purpose of the NCAC is to help like-minded groups and to work on issues of concern to Christian schools."[30]

The founder and initial leader of the organization was Bob Billings, a former school principal and president of Hyles-Anderson College, a private institution. After attending a lecture in 1975 conducted by the Christian Freedom Foundation, an early though generally unsuccessful predecessor of the Christian Right, he was spurred to run for Congress in 1976 in Indiana's First District on the Republican ticket. He lost to popular incumbent Democrat Adam Benjamin in a 71 to 29 percent landslide. Unsuccessful in his bid, Billings went to Washington, D.C., to organize Christian School Action. As luck had it, he timed his move with the controversial Internal Revenue Service decision to examine the tax-exempt status of racially discriminatory private schools that was discussed earlier in this book. Billings used his contacts as a principal and college president to spur the dispatch of thousands of letters to the IRS on that issue. The outgrowth of the controversy was the institutionalization of Christian School Action and its subsequent envelopment by the NCAC.[31]

The NCAC remained under Billings's control until mid-1979, when he left it to become the first executive director of the newly formed Moral Majority. One source who requested anonymity suggested that Billings was never very happy with his new position, largely because Falwell usurped his role as the acknowledged leader of the Christian Right. Billings soon left that assignment to lead a fundamentalist voter turnout campaign for Reagan. Following the election, he accepted an offer from the Reagan White House to serve in the Department of Education—the only notable Christian Right activist to be offered an administration appointment. Yet, according to Evans and Novak, he was not well treated by the Reaganites.[32] He was initially offered the position of assistant secretary for non-public education, a key post that would enable him to formulate policy for all the nation's private religious (Catholic and fundamentalist) schools. The day he arrived at work, he was shocked to find that the position had already been filled by someone else. In lieu of the promised position, Billings was asked to accept one as a "special assistant" to Education Secretary Terrel Bell. Billings accepted the demotion, but was flabbergasted by it. Later, he found out that Bell, under pressure from the Catholic hierarchy to prevent the fundamentalist Billings from formulating policy for religious schools, had vetoed his appointment.

When Billings left the NCAC, his son William assumed the leadership. Bill Billings was a longtime conservative political activist, who had participated in such causes and organizations as the "Stop-ERA" campaign, the National Conservative Political Action Committee, and the American Legislative Exchange Council.[33] He basically ran the NCAC during the first Reagan term.

By the end of the first Reagan term, the NCAC had lost its position of prominence within the movement. Its staff dwindled to Billings and one assistant, plus some part-time assistance by family members. By then, it was headquartered some distance from Capitol Hill, in one of a series of offices above a Chinese restaurant in Alexandria, Virginia. Billings began to do political consulting in 1984 to supplement his income as head of the NCAC.

What caused the demise of the NCAC? It was due to a combination of Bob Billings's move to the Education Department and the related loss of hundreds of personal contacts in fundamentalist circles as well as the lack of a "big-name" preacher like Reverend Falwell who could attract attention.[34] The NCAC, in short, fell victim to the Moral Majority—an irony considering that Bob Billings was its first executive director.

This turn of events had to be difficult to accept. Bob Billings was not only displaced as the acknowledged leader of the Christian Right, but his NCAC was virtually driven out of existence. It must have been especially tough for Bill Billings and his staff assistant to be banished from the limelight because both were graduates of Bob Jones University—the bitter fundamentalist rival of Falwell and his Liberty University.

Religious Roundtable

The Religious Roundtable was probably the key Christian Right organization in existence in the period before the 1980 elections. It was formed during two days of meetings between such secular conservatives as Viguerie, Phillips, Weyrich, and Schlafly and such religious fundamentalists as Dr. Adrian Rogers and Ed McAteer, a salesman for the Colgate-Palmolive Company who was involved with the Christian Freedom Foundation and had extensive contacts in the Southern Baptist Convention.[35] The purpose of the Roundtable was to recruit prominent fundamentalist preachers into politics and instruct them in grass-roots political activity. McAteer was placed at the head of the Roundtable and, consistent with his retail background, dispatched to "sell" political activism to previously apolitical fundamentalist Christians. Reportedly, he personally recruited Falwell into politics; it is apparent that he introduced him to the secular conservatives who were trying to recruit fundamentalist preachers into politics.[36] According to Bob Billings, McAteer began the Religious Roundtable after he was not picked as the first executive director of the Moral Majority.[37] Feeling slighted, he headed off to form his own group.

Organizationally, the Roundtable was composed of an advisory board of fifty-six members who were drawn from the ranks of the secular conservatives; the National Religious Broadcasters; the Campus Crusade for Christ; the National Association of Evangelicals; and the Christian Voice plus the Moral Majority, both of which were in the process of being formally organized at that time. The number of advisory-board members was symbolic—reflecting the number of men who signed the Declaration of Independence. McAteer immediately recruited prominent fundamentalist minister James Robison as the Roundtable's vice-president in order to gain broader visibility and credibility within fundamentalist circles. McAteer then set out on a series of nationwide trips to recruit fundamentalist preachers into politics.

According to Viguerie's estimate, McAteer initiated nearly a hundred local Roundtable chapter affiliates and attracted an estimated 20,000 ministers to a series of conferences and briefings on the need to become involved in politics that were held from July through September 1980.[38] Those estimates were probably exaggerated, but they did reflect the attempted scope and mission of the organization. At the same time McAteer was traveling around the country, a lobbying arm known as "Roundtable Issues and Answers" began working the halls of Congress. Its existence was short-lived, but Roundtable lobbyist William Chasey gained considerable attention within at least fundamentalist circles when, at a major rally, he declared that, having been on Capitol Hill, he had "walked in the halls of the ungodly."[39]

The crowning achievement of the Roundtable was the 1980 "National Affairs Briefing" in Dallas. It was hosted by the Roundtable because the Reverend Robison was from the area and a proven crowd-pleaser. Almost overnight the rally made the Roundtable a well-known entity. Its name was pasted across the podium that prominent speakers used to relay their conservative messages to Americans via television.

The Roundtable vanished quickly after the 1980 elections, in part because of the tone and tenor of the "National Affairs Briefing." (Recall that anti-Semitic statements were made there.) More to the point, however, it was set up primarily to promote the Reagan candidacy among fundamentalists, a precursor of the ACTV organization that was to perform a similar task in 1984. As Stan Hastey remarked, "[The Roundtable] was begun to organize preachers to support the Reagan candidacy, after which it was interested in pursuing the legislative goals of the religious right."[40] After Reagan won, the mission was accomplished and the organization disbanded, except as a platform for conservative pronouncements by Ed McAteer. It eventually became completely defunct once he began his pursuit of the Tennessee U.S. Senate seat voluntarily relinquished by Howard Baker in 1984.[41] Once again, the words of Hastey are useful: "The Roundtable has almost no Washington presence. It has no staff presence here in the city . . . and it does not do any lobbying . . . From all accounts, there is nothing going on within the organization, largely because there is no national membership and no formal organizational structure."[42] By the end of the first Reagan term, the Roundtable existed only in the memories of Christian Right activists.

Christian Voice

The Christian Voice was commonly deemed to be the most overtly political of all of the conservative religious lobbies in Washington, D.C. It gained an early reputation as such because of its famous "morality report card" that rated members of Congress on such issues as school prayer, a balanced budget, recognition of Taiwan, abolition of the Education Department, abortion, busing, Rhodesia sanctions, and the Internal Revenue Service's regulations concerning private schools.[43] The reason that the "report card" gained so much attention compared to its dozens of competitors issued by other interest groups was that the results came out so skewed. Catholic Father Robert Drinan, for instance, received a zero "morality approval rating," but Richard Kelly (ABSCAM) and Bob Bauman (a self-admitted alcoholic and homosexual accused of soliciting sex with a teenage boy) received a 100-percent approval rating.[44] About 50,000 of the report cards were distributed by September 1980 for the upcoming election and they gained Christian Voice quite a reputation.[45] Legislative Director Gary Jarmin said as much in an interview: "We have been more visible than some groups because of our now famous 'morality rating' of members of Congress."[46]

Christian Voice had been created in 1979 at Pasadena, California, by the Reverends Robert Grant and Richard Zone. Both of them were active against gay rights, Grant possessing ties to the anti-gay Anita Bryant ministry in Florida and Zone opposing gay rights bill Proposition Six in California.[47] Their anti-gay-rights views were transferred into one of the major thrusts of the Christian Voice.

The organization received early publicity from the Reverend Pat Robertson on his Christian Broadcasting Network. He promoted the Christian Voice as an alternative to the Moral Majority in order to undercut the following of rival Virginia television evangelist Jerry Falwell. Aided by Robertson, the Voice grew quickly. Although reliable estimates are difficult to obtain, the total membership was probably somewhere between 126,000 and 190,000, roughly 37,000 of whom were clergy.[48] The annual budget was estimated to be about $3 million, the bulk of which was provided by Catholics, Mormons, and fundamentalists—a slightly more heterogenous group than the Moral Majority, whose membership came from the ranks of Independent and Southern Baptists.

The formal organization consisted of three separate parts: (1) Christian Voice, Inc., the lobbying arm active on the Hill; (2) Christian Voice Fund, a tax-exempt, non-profit educational wing; and (3) Christian Voice Moral Government Fund, a political action committee, whose subsidiary was known as "Christians For Reagan."[49] In 1980 "Christians for Reagan" spent some $50,000 on thirty-second television ads in key Southern cities which suggested that President Carter endorsed the gay life-style; additionally, it sent out an estimated 37,000 pro-Reagan packages of materials to ministers around the country.[50] Because those packages were not solicited, the actual number of clergy in the organization (37,000) was probably overestimated.

The Christian Voice underwent some fairly extensive changes shortly after it was formed in 1979. The impetus for them was the "moral report cards," which created an uproar. A number of conservative members of Congress who had consented to serve on the advisory board quit, the Reverend Richard Zone resigned, and the organization backed off from its "report cards" along the lines expressed by Gary Jarmin: "As we indicated from the outset, the report card was not intended to be judgmental, but rather was simply to express to conservative evangelicals around the country how various members of Congress voted."[51] Further evidence of the retreat was to be found in a subsequent report card, to which this caveat was added: "This rating is not intended, nor implied, to be a statistical judgment of a congressman's personal moral behavior or relationship with God. Only God can truly judge what is in the heart of man."[52]

Unlike the NCAC and the Roundtable, the Christian Voice prospered throughout the first term of the Reagan presidency. Following the initial shake-up, the organization retained its key personnel; maintained an office near the Senate Hart Building; and operated a California office, where most of the organizational activity (less lobbying) took place. Furthermore, the organization benefited from the expertise of Legislative

Director Gary Jarmin, who was a savvy and accomplished conservative lobbyist.

Moral Majority

The Moral Majority was formally incorporated in June 1979 and quickly became the symbol for the entirety of the Christian Right. When organized, it consisted of four parts: (1) Moral Majority, the lobbying and direct-mail wing; (2) Moral Majority Legal Defense Fund, the litigation arm; (3) Moral Majority Foundation, the tax-exempt educational and voter registration division; and (4) Moral Majority PAC, the political action committee.[53] The PAC raised only $22,089 by 1980 and was dismantled subsequently, but the other divisions remained in existence and prospered throughout the first Reagan term.[54]

Exactly how the Moral Majority began has never been clear because a variety of people have claimed credit for its creation, including Senator Jesse Helms; Ed McAteer, of the Roundtable; Falwell himself; and Bob Billings, of the NCAC. As Billings, the first executive director of the Moral Majority related its creation, he approached Falwell as early as 1977 to set up an organization like the Moral Majority.[55] At that time, Falwell was not interested. In lieu of his personal involvement, Billings borrowed $25,000 the following year for access to his "Old Time Gospel Hour" mailing list, which was used to send out what amounted to the first Moral Majority mailing. It raised some $400,000 from about 40,000 individuals and became the financial base of the organization. The profits and potential of such activity, coupled with growing sentiments that it was necessary to become involved in politics, convinced Falwell to take that step. Following a March 1979 meeting between Falwell, Billings, and key secular conservatives, it was agreed that an organization would be started, led by Falwell, and, at the suggestion of New Right activist Paul Weyrich, would be called the Moral Majority. Falwell subsequently proposed that the Moral Majority absorb the NCAC, which Billings declined.[56] He kept the NCAC autonomous, only to have it upstaged by the Moral Majority anyway.

The new organization enjoyed immediate success. According to its legislative director, Roy Jones, within six months after it was formally incorporated, it had a mailing list of 83,000; within twelve months, the list grew to 250,000 and more than $1 million was raised. The membership continued to rise: 500,000 (1981), 2,000,000 (1982), 4,000,000 (1983), and, according to Falwell, a projected 6,000,000 (1984).[57] Included in those numbers were an estimated 72,000 ministers.[58] In addition, the organization reportedly had a million regular contributors who received its *Moral Majority Report*; fifty state chapter affiliates; a lobbying office in Washington, D.C., staffed with eight people and an annual budget of $6 million; and a national headquarters in Lynchburg, Virginia, employing approximately sixty people.[59]

The accuracy of those statistics has been the focus of debate. Liebman has suggested that the Moral Majority in fact did have fifty state affiliates and an active Washington, D.C., office whose budget was approximately $6 million.[60] He also implied that the membership ranged between 400,000 and 3,000,000 at the time of the second anniversary of the organization, which is wholly consistent with Jones's stated estimates.[61] Along those same lines, Hadden and Swann pointed out that the *Moral Majority Report*, the official publication, claimed a circulation of 482,000 circa 1981.[62] That number is far less than the estimated more than 2,000,000 members Falwell publicly claimed during the 1980 presidential campaign, but again is reasonably consistent with Jones's estimates.[63]

On the other hand, Hadden and Swann found out from the executive director of the Washington state chapter that his affiliate had 12,000 members. After receiving confirmation from the national office of the Moral Majority that the Washington chapter was its largest state affiliate, simple extrapolation meant that the membership estimates were grossly exaggerated.[64] An analysis of the *Moral Majority Report* performed by a group of scholars also revealed that there may not have been fifty active state chapters.[65] Indeed, more than half of all state chapter reports on their activities filed with the national office came from Southern states.[66] Then too, as Liebman intimated, a healthy portion of the Moral Majority's membership may have consisted of people who simply were members of large independent Baptist churches whose pastors were involved with the Moral Majority.[67] The congregation's members, in other words, were counted into the membership estimates.

Whatever the actual numbers, which may never become clear, the central fact is that the Moral Majority enjoyed spectacular growth during at least its early years. The reasons are difficult to rank, but easy to identify: (1) the incredible energy of Bob Billings, who, in his capacity as the first executive director, traveled to all fifty states to set up chapter affiliates; (2) the organizational skills, personal following, and impeccable reputation of Reverend Falwell at the time the organization was formed, all characteristics made clear by his longtime successful ministry in Lynchburg, which had begun in an abandoned Donald Duck soda pop factory decades earlier; (3) the confluence of the Moral Majority with the shift to the political "right" in the 1980 elections, a correlation that made the organization appear extremely effective; (4) the clever use of direct mail, political symbols, and rhetoric; and (5) the appeal of the organization to the Independent Baptist clergy, who themselves were skilled in the arts of organizing and fund-raising and could help win support for it. Taken together, those factors served to make the Moral Majority a well-known public entity. They also made Jerry Falwell famous.

The early successes, according to several interviewees who asked to remain anonymous, led to substantial bickering within the movement. The focus of most of the infighting was control over the burgeoning resources, conflict that was said to have degenerated into fistfights at times. Circumstantial evidence buttresses those reports. Leading executive officials in the Moral Majority organization like Cal Thomas, Bob Billings, Tim LaHaye, Charles Cade, and Dick Dingman all left fairly quickly from an enterprise that was doing very well indeed. That fact suggested some bitter clashes were occurring.

On a different plane, the organizational essence of the Moral Majority changed over time. According to Bob Billings, the organization moved away from grass-roots work toward professional lobbying:

> Moral Majority has undergone a dramatic change from its original organization. When it began and I was active in it, it was a grassroots organization trying to identify people we felt were for us and against us, and to spur people at the grassroots level to defeat those people who were against us. Moral Majority went from that type of grassroots organization that I had set up to more of a full time lobbying outfit. Jerry could always excite people to write their elected officials on issues . . . [but] Moral Majority could not do such a thing. What Moral Majority could do was lobby, and they did change from a grassroots political organization to more of a professional lobbying organization.[68]

Although the Moral Majority changed in such a manner, it may have failed to do so effectively. A number of interviewees for this book, all of whom requested anonymity, suggested that the lobbying operation was at least questionable—headed by a young, relatively inexperienced, Liberty University graduate who was as much responsible for the public relations campaign as he was the lobbying effort. One of the interviewees even called the lobbying program a "paper tiger."

Division of Labor

From the outset, it was clear that the various Christian Right groups were all part of the same conservative movement that was composed of Christian fundamentalists. Personal and organizational rivalries occurred, but basically all the organizations were in pursuit of the same goals in essentially the same manner. Observing as much, Senator Orrin Hatch (R.-Utah) suggested that, in the division of labor between the four initial organizations, the NCAC served as a "think tank" to devise strategy, the Roundtable recruited fundamentalist preachers into politics, the Christian Voice lobbied, and the Moral Majority engaged in primarily grass-roots work.[69] That division of labor probably did exist, but it was by no means a conscious division. Rather, it simply grew out of the conditions and people involved at the time: the NCAC served as a "think tank" because it had been in Washington, D.C., the longest and its founder Bob Billings was out front on many of the issues; the Roundtable recruited fundamentalist ministers because of Ed McAteer's background as a salesman and his broad contacts within the Southern Baptist Convention; the Christian Voice concentrated on lobbying because Gary Jarmin had experience in that capacity at the American Conservative Union; the Moral Majority worked on grass-roots agitation because of Billings's travels and contacts as well as Falwell's visibility and excellent reputation.[70] By the end of the first Reagan term, no such division of labor existed. The Roundtable was defunct, the NCAC eclipsed by the Moral Majority, and the Moral Majority reoriented from grass-roots work toward lobbying Capitol Hill.

The fact that each of the Christian Right groups was "on its own" sometimes led to conflict between them as they lobbied on behalf of the moral agenda. What role did the various groups play? How successful were they in influencing the Congress? On what policy issues did they part company? Those questions are the focus of the next part of this book.

Part III

TAKING THE HILL

5. The Agenda

The political agenda of the Christian Right was a long time in coming. It began to take shape in the broadest of terms during the 1960s, in response to such trends as a more intrusive federal government and the rise of the counterculture. It was further molded in the 1970s at the hands of fundamentalist elites, who were able to place their concerns first on the systematic agenda and then on the institutional agenda of the Congress. By the 1980s, the painstaking process of specifying alternatives was underway. It was a slow process, but continuous. The amorphous discontent that existed within the fundamentalist community was given expression, focus, and serious consideration by the early 1980s.

Yet, in another respect, the battle was just beginning. No victories with regard to the moral agenda had yet been won on the Hill, and winning there was no easy process. The Congress had a knack for altering or dispensing with most everything that was placed before it. The struggle for agenda enactment on Capitol Hill was not an enticing prospect for any interest groups, including those of the Christian Right.

If that was not a welcome task, however, it was recognized as a necessary one. As early as the 1980 "National Affairs Briefing," even before the election of Ronald Reagan and a Republican Senate, movement elites recognized the need to channel their energies and those of their supporters toward the Congress.[1] New Right activist Paul Weyrich mentioned that he was going to work toward that end: "I'm going to make a substantial effort to refocus the efforts of those folks ['National Affairs Briefing' participants]. If you want to change America, you have to change the Congress."[2]

From a utilitarian standpoint, there was no better choice than the Congress. The interest groups of the Christian Right were fledgling organizations, most of which had been formed in 1979. They had to institutionalize themselves, and toward that end the Congress was the perfect choice. The permeability of the legislative process ensured the Christian Right groups at least some access to the institution, allowing them to claim credit to their supporters for any victories that were won. Influence could even be exaggerated if necessary because the immensely complicated legislative process—with its structure of standing committees, subcommittees, rules, floor calendars, and conference committees—was beyond the reach of fundamentalist constituents, who were relatively new to politics and lived outside the Washington, D.C., area. How would they ever know the difference if the truth were stretched just a bit? Besides, if for some reason that could not be done, the claim that the "good fight had been fought" was available. Important, too, was that any claims of influence or "fighting the good fight" could be made quickly; no delays characteristic of pushing issues in the Judicial Branch would occur. The Congress provided an avenue for prompt action.

The decentralization of the Congress in the 1970s made the strategy of heading to the Hill all the more compelling. The removal of several standing committee chairmen, the rise in the number of subcommittees, and the passage of a "subcommittee bill of rights" that institutionalized the importance of the subcommittees in relation to the full committees all meant that it was easier to gain access in the institution.[3] There were just more opportunities to do so. The decentralization also made it easier for interest groups to claim credit because a more intricate legislative process provided more opportunities for obfuscation. It was in recognition of the fact that a reformed, decentralized Congress provided so many opportunities for interest groups that they went to the Hill by the hundreds during that time, each pushing their own agenda.[4] The Christian Right was in that respect but part of a larger trend.

The move to the Hill on the part of the Christian Right was also a wise choice because it was an effective vehicle for raising money. What better way was there to obtain donations from bedrock conservative Christians than to send out appeals to "put prayer back in the schools" or "halt the murder of the unborn"? In Congress, opponents were easily identified and issues could be presented starkly, so as to arouse supporters. As Legislative Counsel Barry Lynn, of the American Civil Liberties Union, stated in an interview: "The money is there [for Christian Right groups] for the legislative struggles where they can whip up enthusiasm. It is pretty easy to get people whipped up . . . about social issues and things like that, but it is pretty hard to organize the masses to litigate in a superior court."[5]

As a practical matter, the Hill was the natural place to head because it was the Congress that had the power to redress or repeal offensive statutes, restrain offensive life-styles, narrow or overturn court decisions, and enact a moral agenda. It was recognized that the courts and the bureaucracy also "made laws" through opinions and regulations, respectively. Yet, the Congress possessed the ultimate lawmaking prerogative, and it made sense that a sizable social movement would head "right to the top" for redress of its grievances. It made even more sense that a burgeoning social movement would gravitate toward the "people's branch" of government for amelioration of its concerns.

Also, as a practical matter, there simply was nowhere else for the Christian Right to turn other than the Hill once it arose. The bureaucracy was no solution because it could be penetrated only marginally and incrementally at the lower echelons, and drastically at the upper echelons only with the support of a president who was willing to place ideology above administrative experience. Even if he were willing to do so, few qualified administrators were available within the newly formed social movement. Besides, how could fledgling interest groups excite and retain their adherents by claiming inroads into the bureaucracy? The proposition was ludicrous, made all the more so by the fact that the Christian Right agenda contained an anti-statist component.

The presidency was also no solution. It was filled after 1980 by a man who was generally sympathetic to the Christian Right agenda. Interest-group pressure was not much needed there, nor for that matter, much welcome. Anyway, a president could not change the law; he could only bring his prestige to bear upon the Congress to do so. It was wiser and more efficient to pressure the Congress directly rather than the president.

Like the bureaucracy, the courts could be penetrated only marginally and incrementally over time, and they were not a conduit for raising money. If that were not enough, the judicial system was also notoriously slow—hardly acceptable to a newly formed social movement anxious to flex its political muscles. Anyway, the courts were viewed as a fundamental part of the problem, not as a solution.

The various state and local governments presented somewhat more enticing prospects. They were more easily influenced and penetrated by grass-roots activity; they were also a means to raise money because supporters were interested in remedial solutions to perceived problems in their communities. Yet, the state and local arenas were not the perfect answer either. A single victory in the Congress could achieve the same result as fifty hard-fought victories in the states. Besides, the problems that existed were thought to be at the national level, not at state and local levels. The series of unfavorable court decisions and the conflicts with agencies like the FCC and the IRS, for instance, could not be settled in state and local arenas. Perhaps some day the political agenda of the Christian Right could be pursued at state and local levels, but now was not the time. A national movement had been organized and had placed items on the congressional agenda; it was not a propitious time to abandon the national focus and head off to fight in various states.

In the face of all these reasons why the Christian Right could not turn elsewhere, the Hill was all the more attractive and the movement consciously chose to focus its efforts there. Taking note of the focus, *U.S. News and World Report* suggested in the wake of the 1980 elections that the "main workplace [of the Christian Right] for their ambitions is Capitol Hill."[6]

The Priority Items

The moral agenda that the Christian Right took to the Hill encompassed such issues as abortion, school prayer, pornography, gay rights, and tuition tax credits.[7] Of those issues, several were clearly "first-tier" priorities. Although the legislative directors of the various Christian Right groups tended to prioritize them somewhat differently, the issues of abortion, school prayer, and tuition tax credits came through strongly in the interviews for this book as the major legislative objectives. Moral Majority Legislative Director Roy Jones spoke directly to two of those issues and alluded to the third (tuition tax) when he said that his group "was set up to move on school prayer and abortion legislation, as well as any measures affecting private Christian schools."[8] Bill Billings, of the NCAC, placed "anything having to do with parental rights in education" as his organization's overarching priority, but that "number two would be tuition tax credits, and number three school prayer . . . (while) below that would be issues like abortion and infanticide."[9] The Religious Roundtable grew out of Ed McAteer's efforts and Reverend Robison's Coalition for the First Amendment, a group specifically established to push school-prayer legislation.[10] Legislative Director Gary Jarmin remarked, "School prayer has been our number one priority at Christian Voice from the outset."[11] The "opposition" viewed those same three issues as the top legislative objectives of the movement. Both the Reverend Charles Bergstrom, of the Lutheran Council, and the Reverend Stan Hastey, of the Baptist Joint Committee, identified those issues, Hastey stating directly: "Their three big issues are abortion, school prayer, and tuition tax credits."[12]

Anti-abortion legislation on the Hill was of two types. The first consisted of constitutional amendments designed to overturn the *Roe* v. *Wade* (1973) Supreme Court abortion decision by claiming that nothing in the Constitution should be understood as guaranteeing a woman a right to an abortion. That approach was direct and a clear prerogative of the Congress, which, if the amendment were passed and ratified by the states, unambiguously overturned the Court's decision. The weakness of this avenue lay in the very fact that it was a constitutional approach, meaning that it had to win two-thirds majorities in both houses of Congress and ratification by three-fourths of the states. Only twenty-six amendments of the thousands presented before the Congress in the nation's history successfully ran that gauntlet.

The second type of anti-abortion proposal was statutory in nature, designed to restrict Supreme Court jurisdiction over the issue. Article III of the Constitution states: "The Supreme Court shall have appellate jurisdiction, both as to law and fact, with such exceptions, and under such regulations as the Congress shall make." That phrase was interpreted to give the Congress the power to restrict Court jurisdiction; if it did so, the legislatures were then free to pass anti-abortion measures. The obvious benefit of that approach was that it was relatively easy to enact, requiring only simple majorities in both houses of Congress and acceptance by the president. The problem was that it was enormously controversial because most lawyers and constitutional scholars believed the phrase from Article III could not be interpreted to mean that the Congress could "strip" the court of jurisdiction by simple majority vote. Even leading anti-abortion proponents like Congressman Henry Hyde (R.-Ill.), for whom the "Hyde Amendments" prohibiting the use of taxpayer dollars to fund abortions were named, and Senator Orrin Hatch (R. Utah) had intense reservations about the "court-stripping" approach.[13]

School-prayer legislation fell into the same two categories as abortion legislation: (1) constitutional amendments to allow voluntary, aloud prayer in the public schools by overturning the *Engel* v. *Vitale* (1962) Supreme Court decision prohibiting the practice; and (2) statutory proposals to strip the Supreme Court of jurisdiction over the prayer issue, after which the Congress would be free to reintroduce school prayer as it saw fit. A few bills were also introduced that provided for "moments of silence" during the school day during which time prayers could be said, as well as a few resolutions that merely expressed "the sense of the Congress" that prayer should be allowed. By and large, though, the focus was upon the amendment and the court-stripping approaches. Those interested the Christian Right anyway.

Tuition tax credit proposals were of one type and designed to do one thing: to allow the parents of children attending private (religious) schools to deduct the costs associated with that schooling from their federal income taxes. The proposals were intended to facilitate enrollments in private schools by moving them within the financial reach of a larger number of households. Because tuition tax credit proposals were designed to amend the tax law, only simple majorities in both houses of Congress and presidential acceptance were required for them to become law. As with the abortion and school-prayer measures, tuition tax credits were favored by President Reagan; what was needed was to push such measures through the Congress.

The Movement's Character

The moral agenda pursued by the Christian Right on the Hill revealed a great deal about it. Most fundamentally, it showed that the movement was not purely libertarian and bent upon decreasing to the maximum extent possible the amount of law in the land regulating individual citizen behavior. The Christian Right was a vital part of the conservative movement in American politics, but it was not part and parcel of the more libertarian right wing. It did not accept the libertarian principle usually associated with political philosopher John Stuart Mill that freedom from paternalistic authority (the state) was an end in itself; in fact, quite the opposite was true. The Christian Right accepted the view that it was often necessary and even desirable to bring the coercive power of the state down upon individual citizens in order to regulate their behavior. It was in that light that the movement sought to control the reproductive behavior of women and the religious practices of students through anti-abortion and school-prayer proposals, respectively. Although it remained true that the group sought less welfare statism and an end to state usurpation of functions historically associated with the family, and to that extent was libertarian, it was also the case that the libertarian element was highly selective in nature. The Christian Right was sympathetic to less government and less law in some areas, but in others it sought more of both.

The moral agenda also demonstrated that the Christian Right was not adequately understood within the context of "status politics," as some sociologists argued.[14] In a nutshell, the argument of the status-politics paradigm is that citizens whose social status or prestige has been devalued form right-wing political movements as a means of protesting their devalued status. Because it has been white, Protestant Southerners whose status has been devalued over time, it is they who have turned to right-wing movements.[15] Their protest may be more symbolic than substantive, though, serving mostly as a catharsis for those involved. Gusfield found in his study of the temperance movement, as did Zurcher and Kirkpatrick in their research on anti-pornography crusades, that the right-wing protest movement in question was a heavily "symbolic crusade."[16]

Over time, scholars expanded the status-politics framework to include struggles over life-styles, so that citizens whose cherished way of life came under attack were deemed likely candidates for right-wing protest movements.[17] Common to both the social-status/prestige and the life-style interpretations, however, were emphases upon symbolic politics and "status defense." In other words, concerned citizens were intent upon protecting and defending themselves, be it their social-status/prestige or their life-styles.

The moral agenda of the Christian Right suggests that it cannot be understood solely, nor perhaps primarily, as a symbolic crusade. Certain agenda items were narrowly drawn and self-interested, not broadly based and symbolic. A prime example was tuition tax credits, designed to give the parents of children attending private schools a specific tax advantage, with the ultimate hope that enrollments would rise in fundamentalist schools when it was made easier for parents to afford the costs of private education. A narrow constituency would have reaped economic rewards and fundamentalist schools would have prospered—hardly symbolic objectives.

A second example was the tax-exempt issue. Recall from an earlier chapter that the IRS promulgated guidelines designed to revoke the tax-exempt status of fundamentalist schools that it perceived to be racially discriminatory. The Christian Right, as will be discussed in more detail later in this volume, sought to overturn those guidelines in the Congress. Once again, the interested constituency was narrowly drawn and the motive self-interested.

Although it was not among the top legislative objectives, another example was the issue of Social Security taxation of the churches. As part of the 1983 Social Security "rescue" bill (P.L. 98–21), all churches were brought into the system on a mandatory, rather than a voluntary, basis. The fundamentalists, who were virtually alone among religious groups in their refusal to join the system voluntarily, bitterly fought against incorporation. In response, the Congress allowed churches an opportunity to opt out of the system as part of a 1984 budget deficit reduction bill (H.R. 4170).[18] The net effect was to decrease the fundamentalists' share of the nation's payroll-tax burden. Once again, a narrowly drawn and self-interested objective was pursued, not some grand symbolic one.

The moral agenda of the Christian Right also indicates that it cannot be understood adequately in terms of "status defense." Certain agenda items did not involve defense of values or life-styles, but rather entailed affirmative, "offensive" claims against the status quo. A prime example was again the tuition tax credit issue. The tax credits were designed to change the tax code in an affirmative way, so as to give parents whose children attended private schools a tax break they had not enjoyed previously. Abortion was another example. The movement pushed for a constitutional amendment that banned it as a matter of uniform national policy, a position that went beyond the pre-Roe period when the states were responsible individually for regulating the abortion procedure. In both the realm of tuition tax credits and abortion, the claim of the Christian Right went beyond a return to any status quo. There was nothing "defensive" about its claims.

Certainly the movement had some defensive element; it wished, for instance, to defend its institutions from secular society. Its legislative agenda, however, contained certain items that were not of a defensive nature. Along similar lines, as was discussed in an earlier chapter, the movement had a symbolic dimension to it, emphasizing symbolic artifacts and "enemies" like "secular humanism." Yet, its agenda also included certain items of a non-symbolic nature. The point, therefore, is not that the Christian Right wholly lacked either a defensive or symbolic element, but rather that it also contained a powerful offensive and non-symbolic component in conjunction. That fact calls into question the adequacy of the status-politics framework for understanding the Christian Right, or at least suggests that some refinement and differentiation is necessary.

Finally, the moral agenda revealed a major egalitarian dimension to the Christian Right. It was an egalitarianism quite unlike that of the political left, which emphasized the redistribution of wealth in order to gain a greater equality of living conditions and affirmative action in order to win greater equality of economic opportunity for historically less-advantaged citizens. The egalitarian dimension of the Christian Right was manifested in its attempts to institute a moral uniformity: to construct a nation within which abortion was illegal, pornography was unobtainable, and school children prayed. The effort to gain a "uniformity of moral conditions" might prove an unwise or intolerant undertaking, but it was nonetheless a very egalitarian aim. What could be more egalitarian than the attempt to use the power of the state to create moral uniformity? The equality of moral conditions was admittedly different than the equality of economic conditions or equality of opportunity stressed by the left, but it was no less egalitarian.

Certain of the policy positions of the Christian Right demonstrated a measure of egalitarianism. Take again the case of tuition tax credits. Although they might tend to favor the rich, as opponents frequently claimed, they might also bring a private school education within the reach of thousands of children hailing from less wealthy families. Similarly, although dismantling affirmative action programs might arrest the black movement toward equality, it might also end the unequal treatment received by whites who suffered from quotas that purposefully advantaged blacks.

The fascinating aspect about the egalitarian dimension of the Christian Right was that it demonstrated the inexorable drive toward equality in American society. Alexis De Tocqueville argued in *Democracy in America*: "There is hardly an important event in the last seven hundred years which has not turned out to be advantageous for equality . . . the gradual progress of equality is fated."[19] In the 1980s, the drive toward equality foreseen by Tocqueville was continuing: the left wing was seeking equality of living conditions as well as equality of economic opportunity, and the Christian Right was striving for equality of moral conditions.

What in retrospect did the moral agenda reveal about the Christian Right as a social movement? It showed that, at least in part, it was non-libertarian, non-symbolic, "offensively" oriented, and egalitarian. That was a far cry from an understanding of it as symbolic and status-defense oriented. Put another way, the moral agenda showed that the Christian Right was willing to use the coercive power of the state to enact narrowly drawn and self-interested measures that went beyond any notions of "status defense," some of which revealed a strong egalitarian element. The Christian Right was a complex social movement, not the "knee-jerk" reactionary one as it was all too often portrayed.

A Look Ahead

Having examined the reasons why the Christian Right headed to the Hill and the nature of its agenda, this study will now turn to an examination of its attempts to enact that agenda.[20] The discussion opens with the 97th Congress (1981–82), in part because no action took place in the 96th Congress. Yet, there are other reasons as well. For one, three of the four major Christian Right organizations formed during 1979, and throughout the next year they focused upon the coming elections rather than upon lobbying on the Hill. For another, the movement underwent considerable change during the period surrounding the 1980 elections, so much so that it is meaningful to speak of it in pre-97th Congress and 97th Congress (and beyond) terms. Specifically, the Reverend Jim Bakker and the Reverend Pat Robertson both dropped out of politics for a time. Bob Billings quit as executive director of the Moral Majority to take a position at the Department of Education, and the Reverend Richard Zone quit the Christian Voice group that he had helped form. Finally, the Reverend James Robison began publicly to rethink his participation in politics, and shortly thereafter also dropped out. The following account takes place after that shuffling occurred, at the time Ronald Reagan and a Republican Senate came into power.

6. Starting Out

Optimism abounded among the leaders of the Christian Right organizations at the start of the 97th Congress (1981–82). It was understandable, in view of the results of the 1980 elections. How often in recent decades had Republicans been able to gloat over national election returns? This time they were able to speak about the election of Ronald Reagan, the takeover of the Senate, and the gain of thirty-three seats in the House. Against that backdrop, Gary Jarmin euphorically exclaimed of the Christian Right, "We're the new wave in American politics."[1]

Journalists echoed that view. *U.S. News and World Report*, for instance, reported the 97th Congress might be "the beginning of a drive for a thorough overhaul of American laws on such issues as abortion, pornography, and prayer in schools."[2] Tom Minnery, of *Christianity Today*, believed that the 97th Congress might witness passage of school-prayer and tuition tax credit legislation.[3] The sentiment was summed up by one anonymous interviewee on the Hill at the outset of the 97th Congress: "Certainly the religious right had a cockiness to it when it came here [to Capitol Hill] in 1980. No one was really sure of its strength, but there was a real feeling that it had some clout. I am not a statistician and won't venture a guess on how it influenced the elections, but I do know it was feeling confident when it arrived here."

The Christian Right headed to the Hill with high expectations, certain that it had influenced the 1980 elections decisively and that it was well situated to influence the 97th Congress. This chapter will discuss how it fared, beginning in the House of Representatives.

House Action

The political party that controls the House is able to dominate its agenda. The majority party chooses the Speaker, possesses all the committee chairmanships, controls most staff allocations, and dictates the floor schedule. Since 1955, the Democrats have controlled the House. That fact was a serious problem for the Christian Right. Many House Democrats, particularly those who were non-Southerners, were opposed to the Christian Right's moral agenda. They not only wanted to prevent its enactment; they even sought to head off its serious consideration. Having controlled the chamber for several decades, they were well aware of the steps necessary to achieve that goal.

The election of Ronald Reagan and the Republican takeover of the Senate made the position of the Christian Right in the House even more difficult. Part of the difficulty stemmed from the fact that House Republicans adopted a relatively docile attitude toward the moral agenda, not from indifference, but in recognition of the political reality that action had to occur first in the Senate. After measures were pushed through the "other body," then pressure could be brought to bear upon the House to enact the moral agenda. Reagan was unlikely to weigh in on the House side until some action occurred in the Senate. He had no incentive to stake his prestige on possibly fruitless House struggles. Faced with a president reluctant to become involved on the House side and with a Democratic majority of 242–192, the Christian Right was in a difficult position.

Republican acquiescence should not be mistaken for silence, however, because some House members complained about the lack of attention to the moral agenda. Yet, the complaints were not made systematically nor passionately at this juncture, as they would be in the 98th Congress (1983–84), when the Conservative Opportunity Society was formed. The general sentiment in Republican circles in the House was to "close ranks" behind the president's budget and rearmament goals, after which the moral agenda was a priority.

For their part, House Democrats were not content to adopt a "wait and see" attitude. Having fared so poorly in the 1980 elections, they were nervous. Who knew what might happen in the next few years in American politics? Who ever would have thought that a Republican "hard-liner" like Ronald Reagan would be elected president, or that the Republicans would gain control of the Senate? Who would have believed that such prominent liberals as George McGovern, Birch Bayh, and Frank Church would all suffer defeat in the same election? It was no time to wait and wonder about what might happen with the moral agenda. It was a time for action.

The Democrats sought some action that would prevent the moral agenda from ever reaching the House floor. It could prove politically embarrassing to cast votes on issues like school prayer; Christian Right organizations had shown an ability in the recently completed 1980 elections to take such issues, place them within the context of "moral report cards," and then do some serious political damage. That type of situation had to be avoided. It would be avoided if the moral agenda were buried deep in the bowels of the legislative process.

House Democrats took an affirmative step in that direction. The Democratic Caucus "packed" the Judiciary Committee with confirmed social liberals at the outset of the 97th Congress, the committee where most of the moral agenda would be referred. Prominent among the additions to it at that time were gay Congressman Barney Frank (Mass.), black Harold Washington (Ill.), and feminist Patricia Schroeder (Colo.). All three of those members were dependable anti-school prayer and pro-choice votes. Taking note of the composition of Judiciary, Philip Kiko, the minority counsel of its Civil and Constitutional Rights Subcommittee, remarked: "However one looks at it, Judiciary is a very liberal committee. It is more liberal than most other House Committees, if not all of them. The Democratic Caucus prefers it that way, because they [House Democrats] prefer not to vote on the contentious social issues."[4] The liberal nature of the committee was the conscious design of a Democratic caucus intent upon burying the moral agenda.

In the upper echelons of the Judiciary Committee, the Democrats were already well prepared to bury the agenda. Full Committee Chairman Peter Rodino (N.J.), Civil and Constitutional Rights Subcommittee Chairman Don Edwards (Calif.), and Courts, Civil Liberties, and the Administration of Justice Subcommittee Chairman Robert Kastenmeier (Wis.) all stood steadfastly opposed to the moral agenda. They were the members who were the main recipients of agenda proposals. Taking note of the triumvirate, Republican Henry Hyde metaphorically referred to the three men as a "Bermuda Triangle" that swallowed up the social issues.[5] He addressed the situation in an interview:

> The Judiciary Committee has not only sought to bury the social agenda, but to cremate it and scatter the ashes. It is the designated vehicle to serve that role by the Democratic Caucus. Both the Civil and Constitutional Rights and the Courts, Civil Liberties, and Administration of Justice Subcommittees are interesting for their liberality as long as it is the ideas they

favor that are under discussion, but their "illiberality" when they are considering views not their own. . . . [The] Edwards, Kastenmeier, Rodino
triumvirate serves it [a burial function] quite well.[6]

Congressman Mike Synar (D.-Okla.), also a Judiciary Committee member, likewise claimed that the committee served as a burial ground: "It
is true that the Judiciary Committee has served as a block, or even a
mountain, to Christian Right proposals. Judiciary is composed of some
of the finest legal scholars in the country, and [I believe] the religious
right has been unable to justify intellectually, changing the laws to express
its views."[7]

When presented with Synar's assessment, Congressman Hyde retorted:
"We have never been given a chance to justify our stands intellectually
on the contentious social issues, because the Edwards, Rodino, Kastenmeier trio has proven impenetrable down the line. Everything we say
falls on deaf ears. Our proposals do not just fall on barren ground; they
fall on solid concrete."[8] Proof that the Judiciary Committee served the
burial-ground function was evident in the manner in which it handled
the school-prayer and abortion issues.

School Prayer

Twenty-nine school-prayer bills were introduced in the House in the
97th Congress, ten of which were designed to strip the Supreme Court
of jurisdiction over the issue and twelve of which were constitutional
amendments. The remaining seven bills were "sense of the Congress"
resolutions. All twenty-nine bills were referred to the Judiciary Committee, where they languished for the duration of the 97th Congress.

The main action that occurred was actually detrimental to the moral
agenda. Chairman Kastenmeier, of the Courts, Civil Liberties, and Administration of Justice Subcommittee, held hearings for three days in 1981
on the generic issue of "court-stripping."[9] He did so to lay the intellectual
groundwork to fend off any court-stripping initiatives. The hearings reflected the following view of the chairman: "If Congress can decide willy-
nilly that the Supreme Court and the federal appellate courts have no
appellate jurisdiction by a simple majority vote [in the Congress], then
we have arrogated to ourselves considerable power."[10]

The hearings were a clever ploy. In addition to laying the intellectual
groundwork against "court-stripping" proposals, they also served as an
issue-oriented means to defeat the moral agenda. Cobb and Elder have

demonstrated the strategies that opponents to an agenda may employ, several of which were used by the Democrats when they conducted the hearings.[11] First, the hearings served as symbolic reassurance to fundamentalists that their concerns were being addressed. Second, the hearings—held in the opening months of the 97th Congress—were a means of anticipating concern over an issue before the beginning of any public mobilization that was focused on the Hill. Third, the hearings were a form of "tokenism" that served as a means of acting on a limited concern (court-stripping) rather than on the larger issue (school prayer).

The hearings demonstrated that the Democrats took the Christian Right seriously. They were apprehensive about the clout of the Christian Right in the wake of the 1980 elections. They not only took the step of stacking the Judiciary Committee, but also followed several issue-oriented strategies intended to defuse the power of the opposition. The Christian Right was not very successful on the prayer issue in the House in the 97th Congress, but it was not taken lightly.

The only action on the prayer issue was an amendment proposed by Congressman Bob Walker (R.-Pa.) to the Fiscal Year 1982 State, Justice, Commerce, and Judiciary Appropriation. It barred the Justice Department from blocking voluntary prayer or meditation in the public schools and passed by a vote of 333–54 on September 9, 1981.[12] The overwhelming support for the amendment stemmed from the fact it was a symbolic rather than a substantive measure. It prohibited the Justice Department from doing something it was not doing anyway, namely blocking school prayer.[13] Consequently, Democrats backed the proposal in large numbers.

The Christian Right was ambivalent about such action. On the one hand, it was pleased that the school-prayer issue was raised in the House; on the other hand, it was not very interested in the amendment because of the mere symbolism. It was also concerned that Democrats were given an easy "pro-prayer" vote that they could take back to their constituencies. Passage of a constitutional amendment could be more difficult when Democrats were given opportunities like this one to lodge "pro-prayer" votes.

Abortion

The fate of abortion legislation in the House was virtually identical. A total of thirty-one anti-abortion bills were introduced, ten of which were court-stripping proposals and twenty of which were constitutional amendments. (One was a "sense of the Congress" resolution.) All those bills were referred to the Judiciary Committee, where they simply languished.

Somewhat more action occurred on the floor than with the school-prayer issue. The action involved the "Hyde Amendments," named after Congressman Hyde, which restricted the use of taxpayer dollars to pay for abortions. The first such amendment was offered in 1976, and in subsequent years others were attached routinely to authorization and appropriations bills. The Supreme Court affirmed the constitutionality of that practice.[14] In the 97th Congress, the Fiscal Year 1982 Foreign Aid Authorization (H.R. 3512) contained a provision prohibiting the U.S. Agency for International Development from using funds to perform abortions or sponsor abortion research; a bilateral aid bill (H.R. 4559) included a provision restricting the use of monies to train people to perform abortions; the Fiscal Year Treasury and Post Office Appropriations Bill (H.R. 4121) had a provision prohibiting federal employees from receiving abortion benefits under their health plan.[15] None of those struggles particularly involved the Christian Right. The "Hyde Amendment" approach predated it by several years, and passage of the amendments was institutionalized by the time the movement was involved on the Hill.

The realization that the Judiciary Committee was a hostile place prevented the Christian Right from much lobbying of its members in the 97th Congress. It was a waste of time, as Congressman Synar pointed out in an interview: "Essentially they [the Christian Right groups] have not lobbied Judiciary Committee members very much because they know there is little hope for their measures in Committee."[16] Minority Counsel Philip Kiko expressed a similar sentiment: "They basically feel House Judiciary is a lost cause, and do not concentrate much on it."[17] The Judiciary Committee performed its designated function for House Democrats as a "burial ground."

Tuition Tax Credits

The prognosis for the third of the Christian Right's top legislative objectives was favorable. Because tax law was involved, tuition tax credit proposals were referred to the Ways and Means Committee, not Judiciary. Ways and Means looked like anything but the "burial ground" that was Judiciary. Although Democrats outnumbered Republicans 23–12 on the committee, fourteen members serving on it in the 97th Congress had cast a floor vote in favor of a tuition tax credit plan when the issue had last been considered on the House floor in the 95th Congress (1977–

78).[18] Thus, a near majority of the committee already was on record on behalf of tax credits, and Democrats Kent Hance (Tex.), Robert Matsui (Calif.), and Don Bailey (Pa.) were possible supporters, though they had no established record on the issue as recent additions to the committee.

The situation with the chairmanship also differed drastically from Judiciary. Ways and Means Chairman Dan Rostenkowski (D.-Ill.) represented a heavily Catholic constituency in Chicago that supported tuition tax credits to boost its private schools. Whether he believed in tax credits in principle or out of necessity, he too was a supporter. He could see to it that a tuition tax bill would not languish in full committee, nor be lost in a subcommittee.

The political situation also looked better for tuition tax credits. In the 95th Congress (1977–78), a tuition tax bill had actually passed both houses. It died only when House and Senate conferees failed to agree whether to extend the credits down to the elementary schools.[19] Thus, the precedent for action existed. Then, too, when tuition tax credits made it through the Congress previously, the issue was primarily a "Catholic issue." Now, in view of the rise of the Christian Right, it was a fundamentalist issue as well. Anxious to be the sponsor of a tuition tax credit plan that would likely pass, members introduced twenty-five different bills in the 97th Congress, some of which were identical except for their sponsor. Anxious to defeat the bills, the public education lobby cranked up a serious lobbying effort in the summer of 1981, before there was even any indication that congressional action was forthcoming.[20]

As it turned out, tuition tax credit opponents did not need to worry so much. A new era in budget politics dawned on the Hill. Known as the "Reagan Revolution," it was marked by social-spending and tax cuts as well as a defense build-up. The "revolution" nixed tuition tax credits, which were estimated to cost the treasury as much as $7 billion annually in lost revenues once fully instituted.[21] How could members support tax credits for parents whose children attended private schools when they were cutting back on federal aid to the public schools? How could members justify a further drain on the treasury at a time when large tax cuts were likely to yield huge deficits?

Members could do neither, which was why they never seriously considered tuition tax credits in the House in the 97th Congress. Chairman Rostenkowski did not even include the credits as a "sweetener" for Republicans when he tried to rally House support for the Democratic alternative to the Reagan tax-cut package.[22] Tuition tax credits were removed from serious consideration by, of all things, a Republican president and his budget plan of 1981.

Senate Action

The Senate was the real target for Christian Right ambitions during the first two years of the Reagan presidency. Not only did the Republicans control it, but individual senators in key positions were sympathetic to the moral agenda. Judiciary Committee Chairman Strom Thurmond (R.-S.C.), for instance, was a firm proponent of that agenda, as was Judiciary Constitution Subcommittee Chairman Orrin Hatch (R.-Utah). That situation was in vivid contrast to that in the House Judiciary Committee.

Against the aura of high expectations in the Senate, however, lay the stark reality that the administration sought to delay the moral agenda until the president's budget and rearmament goals were in place. Even in the Senate, achieving those goals was going to be a formidable task. Reagan could not use up his bargaining chips over the moral agenda if he was to realize his other goals, upon which his administration would be judged and his pollster Richard Wirthlin said his 1984 reelection depended.[23]

If the administration's desire to delay consideration of the moral agenda was a secret, it was one of the worst kept in Washington. In the opening months of the Reagan presidency, White House aides like James Baker, David Gergen, and David Stockman worked avidly to keep the "social issues" from receiving serious consideration. The president broached them only when he was pressed to do so by reporters.[24] For that reason, journalists began to write articles with titles like "The Deferred Agenda" and "Putting the Social Issues on Hold: Can Reagan Get Away With It?"[25]

For his part, Senate Majority Leader Howard Baker (R.-Tenn.) was committed to carrying out the administration's wishes. He himself was a supporter of the moral agenda, but he, too, believed it was necessary to proceed first with the budget and rearmament goals. To some extent, he was even more committed to that position than the White House, made evident by his comment to CBS in August 1981 that he was frustrated that he was losing the battle to keep moral agenda amendments off pending legislation.[26] Not only did he seek to keep certain bills off the Senate agenda, but even amendments.

Delaying the moral agenda was no easy task for Baker. The flexible scheduling procedures of the Senate allowed all senators the opportunity to exert some influence over the floor schedule. The ability of a single, discontented senator to wreak havoc in the institution through use of the filibuster, and the acceptance of non-germane amendments that allowed senators to add unrelated prayer or anti-abortion proposals, vastly complicated the task of the majority leader. It was not like the situation in the House, where the leadership controlled the structure and, ipso facto, the content of the chamber. In the Senate, the situation was different.

Majority Leader Baker's problems did not end there. He faced a potentially rebellious group of newly elected conservatives within his own party, including John East (N.C.), Jeremiah Denton (Ala.), Steve Symms (Idaho), Don Nickles (Okla.), and Paula Hawkins (Fla.). They viewed their victories in 1980 as a mandate for conservative change. Their allies included such Republican incumbents as Jesse Helms (N.C.), Orrin Hatch (Utah), Paul Laxalt (Nev.), Malcolm Wallop (Wyo.), Roger Jepsen (Iowa), Gordon Humphrey (N.H.), and James McClure (Idaho). Together, those members constituted a powerful block within the Republican party. The proof was the outcome of the only GOP contested leadership race, over the chairmanship of the policymaking Senate Republican Conference. In that contest, conservative James McClure was chosen over moderate John Heinz (Pa.) by a 33–20 vote, despite the fact that Heinz had just served as chairman of the Senate Campaign Committee, which helped so many young conservatives into office.[27]

The weapons Baker had at his disposal to fight the insurgent conservative element within his own party were the support of the administration, the prestige of his position as majority leader, and the backing of his peers. The last of these was particularly important. Powerful Republican senators like Ted Stevens (Alaska), Robert Dole (Kans.), Mark Hatfield (Oreg.), Bob Packwood (Oreg.), and Charles Percy (Ill.) were moderates who were willing to support Baker in his efforts to delay the moral agenda. The battle lines were drawn. The struggle began.

School Prayer

The school-prayer issue received short shrift in 1981, a victim of successful administration attempts to keep the issue off the Senate agenda. Action commenced on May 6, 1982, when the president announced his intention to introduce a school-prayer constitutional amendment drafted by the Justice Department.[28] On May 17 he transmitted the bill to the Hill, where it was introduced by Judiciary Committee Chairman Strom Thurmond. The proposal read: "Nothing in this Constitution shall be construed to prohibit individual or group prayer in public schools or other public institutions. No person shall be required by the United States or by any state to participate in prayer."[29] The proposal was labeled Senate Joint Resolution 199 (S.J. Res. 199).

The timing of the Reagan announcement demonstrated that the administration did not yet wish to tackle the moral agenda. The president waited seventeen months from the time he took office to express genuine interest in a measure, after which he delayed briefly before sending a bill to the Hill. The late introduction virtually ensured that the issue was going nowhere in the 97th Congress. Time was running out.

Reagan's proposal did become the object of hearings. Congressional hearings serve a variety of functions for the institution. Among other things, they serve to disseminate facts to interested parties, provide a permanent record of the positions of members and the proceedings of Congress, furnish evidence that standing committees have scrutinized a bill before sending it to the floor for consideration, make possible evaluation of the competency of officials from the Executive Branch, and allow support to be rallied for a bill.[30] All those functions were important to the Christian Right with respect to school prayer.

Three days of hearings took place on S.J. Res. 199 in the Judiciary Committee over the course of four months. A total of thirty-two witnesses testified, including prominent Christian Right leaders. On the first day (July 29), Ed McAteer, of the Religious Roundtable, Gary Jarmin, of Christian Voice, and Ron Godwin, of Moral Majority, were all scheduled to testify. That three individuals were selected from the Christian Right revealed its power within Republican ranks. Although Godwin never testified, both McAteer and Jarmin did, arguing that prayer was a central part of the nation's heritage. They also argued that it was incumbent upon Congress to pass such legislation because the issue was widely backed in the country and it was an affirmative step toward reversing the moral decline that had occurred.[31] On the second day (August 18), the Reverend Pat Robertson testified for the proposal on a First Amendment basis, arguing that the Supreme Court overstepped its authority in finding school prayer an unconstitutional "establishment of religion."[32] No Christian Right figures testified on the third day (September 16), which was reserved for lawyers to debate the breadth of the language in the bill.[33]

Perhaps not surprisingly, the hearings were marked by a distinct lack of enthusiasm among the legislators. They realized that time was running out in the 97th Congress and that the administration was far from intent on winning floor consideration for its proposal. Only one or two committee members usually attended the hearings.[34] Their inattentiveness was well founded. S.J. Res. 199 died quietly in committee following the hearings.

One tussle occurred on the Senate floor over the prayer issue, though.

It began when Appropriations Committee Chairman Mark Hatfield offered an amendment to the Fiscal Year 1982 State, Justice, Commerce, and Judiciary Appropriation deleting the House language prohibiting the Justice Department from spending money to enforce the ban on school prayer. Senator Ernest Hollings (D.-S.C.) offered a motion to retain the House language and set aside the Hatfield amendment, which passed by a vote of 70–12.[35] From there, Senator Lowell Weicker (R.-Conn.) sought "clarification" of the House language by adding the word "constitutional" to those prayer programs the Justice Department was not allowed to block.[36] The Weicker amendment gave the Justice Department full reign because, according to the Supreme Court, there was no school prayer that was constitutional.

Debate over the Weicker amendment turned rancorous. In remarks later expunged from the *Congressional Record*, Hollings yielded the floor to Jewish prayer opponent Senator Howard Metzenbaum (D.-Ohio) by calling upon "the senator from B'nai B'rith."[37] Following an apology by Hollings, Weicker's amendment was turned back by a vote of 51–34.[38] The matter was set aside for the remainder of the day.

The next day, it was resurrected when Senator Weicker offered another amendment which affirmed that the prayer language should not be construed as running contrary to the First Amendment. It passed 93–0.[39] Added to the new Weicker amendment then was one by Helms which said that the Weicker amendment should not be interpreted as running contrary to the House-passed language. It, too, was accepted, by a vote of 58–38.[40] Where did the flurry of action lead the Senate? Back precisely to the status quo, before the amending process ever began on a matter that was symbolic in nature anyway.

Abortion

The abortion issue cut an entirely different path in the Senate from school prayer. Action began in the early months of the Reagan presidency, as newly elected New Right Senator John East convened hearings on abortion, as chairman of the Separation of Powers Subcommittee of Senate Judiciary. The hearings were on S. 158, a bill sponsored by East and Helms that was designed to restrict abortion by declaring that life began at conception, that a fetus was a person who deserved the full protections of the Fourteenth Amendment, and that the Supreme Court was not entitled to jurisdiction over the abortion issue. Eight days of hearings began on April 23, 1981.

The hearings were extraordinarily contentious. They were marked by medical and theological disputes over the beginning of life, the applicability of the Fourteenth Amendment, and the constitutionality of court-stripping.[41] They were also graphic, containing numerous exhibits of fetal development and the abortion procedure.[42] The media covered the hearings at length, raising the saliency of the abortion issue by the time the hearings ended in June.[43]

Following the hearings, East's subcommittee approved S. 158 by a 3–2 vote. New Right Senators East and and Jeremiah Denton supported the bill in principle; Senator Hatch backed it in order to encourage full Judiciary Committee hearings on the issue; Senator Max Baucus (D.-Mont.) opposed the bill because of its court-stripping provisions; and Senator Howell Heflin (D.-Ala.) described it as a "futile gesture" that would never pass the full Senate.[44] The proposal consequently just squeaked out of the subcommittee and was placed on the full Judiciary Committee docket.

Senator Hatch was disturbed that the bill was reported out. He believed he had to stand behind it to demonstrate his opposition to abortion, but he had serious reservations about it. The major one was that it was a court-stripping bill, which as chairman of the Constitution Subcommittee of Judiciary, he found unpalatable. In hopes of displacing S. 158, he began hearings in his subcommittee on his own S.J. Res. 110, a constitutional amendment proposal designed to give Congress and the states dual authority over abortion.[45] The proposal was structured to allow Congress to regulate the abortion procedure, but also allow the states to enact even stricter laws that went beyond the congressional standard if they so chose. It was a clever scheme by which Hatch hoped to win over senators who were not particularly enthusiastic about regulating abortion, but favored the provisions allowing the legislatures to set the policy within the federalist structure. The bill had particular potential because it was a relatively weak anti-abortion proposal, designed mostly to return abortion policy to the pre-Roe period, when the states were individually in control of the procedure.

Six days of hearings began on October 5, 1981. They were not contentious like those concerning S. 158 because the Fourteenth Amendment and court-stripping provisions were not relevant to a constitutional amendment approach. Hatch wrapped up the hearings December 16, moving directly to and completing subcommittee markup of S.J. Res. 110 within one hour after the hearings were completed.[46] The measure was reported out of subcommittee on a vote of 4–0; Senator Patrick Leahy (D.-Vt.) abstained because of the "material harm to the tradition of public participation in the lawmaking process" brought about by Hatch's prompt markup.[47] The bill was placed before the full Judiciary Committee.

Considerable conflict then ensued among the anti-abortion forces. The East/Helms bill was favored by American Life Lobby, the Ad Hoc Committee in Defense of Life, March for Life, and the Life Amendment Political Action Committee; the Hatch bill was backed by the U.S. Catholic Conference, National Right-to-Life, and the New Right and Christian Right.[48] The division was a very real one. Insurgent state chairpersons from eleven states within the National Right-to-Life organization, for instance, publicly called for the resignation of national director Jack Willke because he supported the Hatch bill.[49] Other advocates of the East/Helms bill held a March 1, 1982, press conference at which they called upon Hatch to withdraw his bill.[50]

Hatch withstood the pressure, as did the full Judiciary Committee, which chose to act upon S.J. Res. 110. Without holding any additional hearings, it approved the measure on March 10, 1982, by a vote of 10–7.[51] The bill never made it any further though because in September Hatch pulled it from the floor in response to a request from Majority Leader Baker to do so. Hatch acquiesced, but only after extracting a promise from Baker to take the bill up again the following year in the 98th Congress.[52]

Senator Helms was bitter. The constitutional-amendment forces had the audacity to supplant his (and East's) S. 158, and then not take further floor action on their own proposal. A frustrated Helms took his fight directly to the Senate floor, offering the gist of S. 158 as an amendment to a routine debt-ceiling bill (H.J. Res. 520) on August 16.[53] The response of pro-choice Senators Bob Packwood (R.-Oreg.) and Lowell Weicker was to filibuster the issue, which they did for some four hours per day for six weeks. Attempts to cut off the filibuster failed on several occasions by increasingly large margins, despite some lobbying by the president to cut off the Packwood/Weicker ploy.[54]

During the third attempt, tempers flared. In remarks later expunged from the *Congressional Record*, Senator Dale Bumpers (D.-Ark.) erroneously referred to Helms as the "senator from South Carolina" rather than North Carolina. He corrected himself, and then apologized to the state of South Carolina for naming Helms as its senator.[55] Finally tired of the protracted struggle, the Senate voted 79–16 on September 23 to return the debt-ceiling bill to the Finance Committee, to strip it of all amendments, and bring it back on the floor. The committee did so, and a "clean" bill was passed less than four hours later.[56] The Helms measure went down to defeat then, but it was the high-water mark for anti-abortion legislation during the 97th Congress. At one point, fifty-four votes were obtained to halt the Packwood/Weicker filibuster.[57]

The "politics of abortion" in the 97th Congress cannot be understood except within the context of the division over the proper approach. It was the central issue that came up during the interviews for this book. Laura Clay, legislative assistant to conservative Senator Don Nickles, stated: "I was quick to find out [upon coming to the Hill] that there was considerable dissension over what forms are best and proper to pursue [to restrict abortion]. It was a very real division."[58] American Life Lobby Director Gary Curran, a onetime consultant to Moral Majority, similarly noted that it was a serious division, caused in his mind by Hatch's refusal to acknowledge the political reality that a constitutional amendment did not have a chance.[59] The division delighted prochoice forces, of course, who really never had to become involved in halting restrictive abortion legislation in the 97th Congress. The anti-abortion forces accomplished that task themselves.

In some more minor battles the anti-abortion and Christian Right forces fared quite well. For instance, the Senate approved the nomination of C. Everett Koop, an avowed abortion opponent, to become surgeon general.[60] As part of a budget reconciliation bill, the Senate also approved the "teenage chastity provisions" of Senator Denton, which provided $30 million for research into the causes of teenage premarital sex and funding for nutritional counseling of pregnant adolescents.[61] Finally, the Senate approved the House's ban on the Agency for International Development from supporting private organizations that promoted or funded abortion.[62] The successes were welcome in Christian Right ranks, but they were not commensurate with what it hoped to achieve.

Tuition Tax Credits

As in the House, the prognosis for tuition tax credit legislation was favorable. It had passed the Senate before, was now a fundamentalist as well as a Catholic issue, and was favored by the president. Certain senators thought a bill would pass. When they introduced their own bill, sponsors Daniel Patrick Moynihan (D.-N.Y.) and Bob Packwood remarked, respectively, that "the 97th Congress . . . would finally come to grips with this issue of justice" and that "I expect the 97th Congress will see passage of this vital legislation."[63] Their assessment was echoed by Gary Jarmin, of Christian Voice.[64]

The Packwood bill (S. 550) was taken up by the Senate Finance Subcommittee on Taxation and Debt Management on June 3–4, 1981.[65]

The hearings included testimony from two Christian Right figures. The Reverend Jerry Falwell made a plea for tax credits on the egalitarian basis that parents who already were financing the public schools deserved a tax break with respect to the private schools in which their children were enrolled.[66] Bill Billings, of the NCAC, testified for the bill on the same grounds.[67] Their testimony was for naught, however, because S. 550 fell victim to a similarly drafted White House proposal.

The president first announced his intention to send a bill to the Hill on April 15, 1982, in a speech made before the National Catholic Education Association.[68] The forum was carefully chosen. Reagan had aroused the opposition of the Catholic church over assistance to the poor, the neglect of human-rights issues in foreign policy, and the military build-up.[69] The tuition tax credit announcement was designed to assuage a discontented Catholic hierarchy as much as was possible.

As with school prayer, the support of the president came very late in the 97th Congress. It once again suggested he was less than enthusiastic about a Hill fight. If he really wanted to see tuition tax legislation passed, why not rally behind the Packwood bill, on which hearings had been held ten months earlier? Further evidence that Reagan sought only to go through the motions on the issue was that he did not send up a formal proposal to the Hill until June 23, more than two months after his announcement before the Catholic community. The bill, S. 2673, was introduced by Finance Committee Chairman Robert Dole.

The administration bill called for credits of $100, $300, and $500 per child to be phased in over a period of several years. About three weeks after it was submitted, Chairman Dole began hearings in the Finance Committee. Prominent Christian Right figures again were brought in to testify. Ron Godwin, vice-president of the Moral Majority, spoke on behalf of a "free enterprise" system in education that he felt tuition tax credits would create, and which would prove beneficial to both public and private schools.[70] Ed McAteer, of the Roundtable, also testified, arguing that parents had the right to determine the proper education for their children, and that lessening the costs for private education was a boost for parental rights.[71]

Three contentious days of markup ensued during the months of August and September. Democrats David Boren and Ernest Hollings were unalterably opposed to tuition tax credits, believing that they undermined the entire public school system. They used every means possible to delay, weaken, and/or kill the proposal. Among other things, they managed to lower the credits from $100/$300/$500 to $100/$200/$300 per child, as well as prohibit the credits from being extended to any schools that were deemed racially discriminatory.[72] Following the changes, the Finance Committee voted out the measure on September 16, by a vote of 11–7.[73] It suffered the same fate as its predecessors. No action was ever taken on it on the Senate floor for the remainder of the 97th Congress.

An Inglorious Beginning?

The general perception was that the 97th Congress was not much of a success for the Christian Right. The movement went to the Hill with high expectations, only to find that, by the end of the first two years of the Reagan presidency, most of its agenda had either been beaten back or ignored. The bad news did not end there. Along the way, the Christian Right suffered two embarrassing defeats that undermined its power and prestige.

The first involved the nomination of Sandra Day O'Connor to the Supreme Court. The Moral Majority led the charge against her confirmation on the basis that she cast several "pro-abortion" votes as an Arizona state senator. The opposition proved costly, both because O'Connor whisked through on a 99–0 vote and because powerful conservatives were alienated along the way. Senator Barry Goldwater (R.-Ariz.), for instance, was prompted to remark in his characteristically blunt way, upon hearing that the Moral Majority opposed O'Connor: "Every good Christian ought to kick [the Reverend Jerry] Falwell right in the ass."[74]

The second defeat involved the "Family Protection Act," an omnibus measure supported by the Christian Right that contained provisions relating to school desegregation, gay rights, child abuse, school prayer, sex education, tuition tax credits, sex mingling in school athletics, contraceptives for minors, teachers' unions, and bloc grants, among other things.[75] Due to its omnibus nature, the various provisions of the bill were referred to as many as five different standing committees in each house. At the outset of the 97th Congress, the Moral Majority undertook the unenviable task of lobbying the relevant committees to report their provisions. Not surprisingly, the effort met with no success. The attempts to extract the provisions reflected poorly upon the Moral Majority. Few interest groups were foolish enough to lobby on behalf of controversial, omnibus measures sent to many different standing committees.

If the Christian Right looked like a loser in the 97th Congress, however, the reality was not so simple. Although it suffered some embarrassing defeats, it also enjoyed some notable victories. The most obvious ones were statutes passed that dealt with the moral agenda, though not with the top three agenda objectives per se. (Recall though, that victories of a minor nature were also won on two of the top three objectives.) One such statute involved a District of Columbia city-council decision to lighten the jail sentences for rapists, which proponents believed would lead to many more of them being convicted of their crime. The Christian Right lobbied hard against the new penalties, believing that it was simply bad policy to decrease the sentences for sex offenders. On three successive votes, the Congress sided with the movement and overturned the city-council decision.[76]

Second, the Christian Right helped kill a criminal code reform bill (S. 1630) that had provisions lessening the penalties for interstate transportation of pornographic materials. Ron Godwin, of Moral Majority, testified against the bill, arguing that lighter penalties increased the transmission of such materials through the mails and inhibited local community crackdowns on pornography.[77] With the help of the Christian Right, the bill was killed on the Senate floor in April 1982.[78]

Third, the Christian Right helped win support for an amendment sponsored by Congressman Larry McDonald (R.-Ga.) to the 1982 Legal Services Corporation (LSC) Reauthorization. As drafted, the amendment prohibited the LSC from spending funds to "promote, defend, or protect" homosexuality.[79] The amendment passed the House easily by a vote of 281–124, with the backing of the Christian Voice, whose anti-gay rights origins in California led it to take an active interest in the measure.[80]

Beyond those statutory wins, the Christian Right also made an impact on the legislative agenda of the Congress. In the House, for instance, the number of school-prayer bills introduced went up from twenty in the 96th Congress to twenty-nine in the 97th Congress, and the school-prayer and abortion issues were at least debated on the floor in the context of minor struggles like the "Hyde Amendments."[81] In the Senate, the influence of the Christian Right was really felt. The number of anti-abortion bills rose from four to fourteen and the number of school prayer bills from four to seven from the 96th to the 97th Congresses.[82] The number of hearings held on the top agenda objectives of the movement went from zero in the 96th Congress to five in the 97th Congress (two on abortion, one on prayer, and two on tuition tax credits).[83] A total of eight Christian Right leaders also testified before Senate committees and subcommittees on those issues.[84] How many other interest groups could claim a rise in bill introductions, five sets of hearings, and repeated testimony on behalf of their concerns in the *first* Congress in which they went to the Hill? It was no small accomplishment to just gain access to the congressional agenda, let alone action on issues. The only measure of success was not the number of bills actually passed into law.

Other goals were also served. The president was put on record on behalf of the moral agenda with respect to specific statutory proposals. Majority Leader Baker promised New Right senators their issues would be considered in the upcoming 98th Congress. Solid working relationships were established between the Christian Right groups and dozens of congressional offices.[85] Some practical lobbying experience by the groups was achieved. Enough was accomplished in substantive terms that the movement was able to claim credit to its constituencies, so money to finance operations would roll in. By the same token, enough remained to be done that supporters were unlikely to abandon ship, the mission having been completed. Thus, if the opportunity to enact the moral agenda in the immediate aftermath of the "Reagan Revolution" of 1980 was lost, at least there was much that gave the Christian Right hope. The movement appeared well positioned. It looked anxiously toward the 98th Congress.

7. The Struggle Intensifies

The determination of the Christian Right to continue the battle on the Hill in the 98th Congress (1983–84) was tempered somewhat when the 1982 mid-term election results were tallied. While the nation was in the midst of a recession and a Republican was in the White House, the Democrats gained twenty-six seats in the House of Representatives. That gain was not excessive by mid-term standards, but it was nonetheless an advance. Lilli Hausenfluck, who was then a legislative assistant to a New Right senator, remarked in an interview: "Essentially the tone [of the Christian Right at the outset of the 98th Congress] was pretty negative, and that was a direct outgrowth of the 1982 election returns."[1]

The bad news for the Christian Right did not end there. The House Democratic leadership seized the opportunity brought about by the election results to alter the partisan ratio on the Judiciary Committee from the 16–12 margin it had been in the 97th Congress to 20–11.[2] The change made the prospects for enactment of the moral agenda pretty slim. How could the Christian Right be successful in an institution that had already proven less than receptive, in light of a twenty-six-seat shift and an even more obstructionist Judiciary Committee? The situation in the House did not look good.

On the tuition tax credit issue, the pessimism was borne out. The tax credits were unacceptable to members in the 97th Congress because of cutbacks in federal aid to the public schools and high budget deficits. The credits were so unacceptable that they were never even given consideration in the House. Both the cutbacks and the deficits carried over to the 98th Congress, making any and all tax-credit proposals similarly unacceptable to members. Perhaps sensing that fact, members introduced only nine tuition tax bills, a drop of 64 percent from the preceding Congress.

The pessimism was also justified with respect to the abortion issue. The Judiciary Committee had served as a burial ground for court-stripping and constitutional amendment proposals in the 97th Congress; it was even better situated to play that role now. Again sensing that fact, members introduced only seventeen bills, down 45 percent from the preceding Congress.

Granted, some action still took place with regard to the "Hyde Amendments." The House voted restrictions on federal health employee benefits in the Fiscal Year 1984 Continuing Resolution (P.L. 98–151) and the Fiscal Year 1985 Treasury/Postal Services Bill (H.R. 5798), as well as on Medicaid funding of abortions in the Fiscal Year 1984 Labor/Health and Human Services/Education appropriations bill (P.L. 98–139).[3] Yet, those routinized struggles were only a sideshow in the context of broadly restrictive abortion legislation.

To show how the situation had changed in the House with respect to the abortion issue, certain members flirted with the idea of actually liberalizing abortion law. Health Subcommittee Chairman Henry Waxman (D.-Calif.) of the Energy and Commerce Committee, held hearings in 1983 on the wisdom of the "Hyde Amendments."[4] Since 1970, a total of twenty-one anti-abortion riders had been attached to authorization and appropriations bills.[5] The theme of Waxman's hearings was that the restrictions adversely affected the health of women. The impetus for the hearings was the Supreme Court's reaffirmation of its 1973 *Roe* decision in a series of test cases it had decided in 1983.[6] After the hearings, Congressman Vic Fazio (D.-Calif.) introduced a bill to restore abortion funding in numerous programs, including Medicaid, Indian Health Services, the Peace Corps, the Civilian Health and Medical Program of the Uniformed Services, and the Federal Employee Health Benefits plan.[7] The legislation went nowhere because the House continued to enact the "Hyde Amendments." The activity, however, was symbolic of the altered situation in the House with respect to abortion legislation.

School Prayer

Despite facing the same institutional obstacles as the abortion issue, school prayer traveled an entirely different route in the 98th Congress. It was an issue that enjoyed broad-based popular support, at least in the abstract.[8] For that reason, it had some solid congressional backing as well. It was also a matter that was pushed forcefully by President Reagan and the television evangelists. It was a good issue for them because it rallied the fundamentalist troops in a way that did not energize the liberal opposition as did other issues (for example, abortion and the women's groups). It also put Southern Democrats in an untenable position. Few of them were able to vote against school prayer, given their constituencies, especially with Ronald Reagan at the top of the Republican ticket again at the end of the 98th Congress.

The action did not come early in the session, but instead began in the spring of 1984. At issue was so-called Equal Access legislation, designed to allow voluntary, student religious groups in the public schools access to facilities on the same basis as other voluntary student groups. The idea for the legislation stemmed from the Supreme Court's decision in *Widmar v. Vincent* (1981). In that case, the Court forced the University of Missouri to allow student religious groups "equal access" to campus facilities.[9] The Court reasoned that, because the university had an "open forum" policy with respect to student groups, it could not discriminate against groups of a religious nature lest it be applying that policy in a non-neutral manner.[10] The gist of congressional efforts was to extend the Court decision down to secondary schools, and for many Republicans, down to elementary schools as well.

Opposition in the House came from liberal Democrats. The original equal access bill (H.R. 4996), introduced by evangelical Congressman Don Bonker (D.-Wash.), allowed student religious meetings during "non-curriculum" hours, so that a student who had a study hall could forgo it in favor of a Bible study, lecture, or prayer meeting. It was assumed that prayer would be a central element of all meetings, which led opponents to refer to equal access legislation pejoratively as "son of school prayer." They were deeply disturbed by the equal access concept because it was going to be an excellent tool for proselytizing. What better way to win converts than during school hours in school facilities? In that respect, it probably was better than a constitutional amendment that provided for voluntary, vocal prayer.

Various religious groups took a variety of official positions on equal access. Consistently opposed were a variety of Jewish organizations, the Unitarian church, the United Methodist church, and the Lutheran church. Reverend Charles Bergstrom elucidated the rationale for his denomination's opposition to equal access: "Equal access is either designed for the purpose of proselytizing or for the purpose of showing off religiosity. Religion should be far more than a school club. Furthermore, a prayer club is the opposite of the example Jesus gave to us. He was the one who said when you pray to your Father in heaven, you should do so behind a closed door."[11] If there was going to be some form of equal access, those religious groups were adamant that it not involve the elementary schools. They rightly believed students of that age were incapable of conducting their own periods of religious study, and feared the subjugation of students by proselytizing teachers.

A host of other religious groups favored equal access for the secondary schools only. Included were the National Council of Churches, the Southern Baptist Convention, and individual Catholic, Presbyterian, Episcopal, Quaker, and Seventh-Day Adventist churches. According to one source, the National Association of Evangelicals also fell into such a category.[12]

Independent Baptist churches and the Christian Right groups were supporters. Interestingly, they had initially been hostile to any form of equal access legislation—a point omitted in an otherwise fine study dealing with the entire issue.[13] They viewed equal access as a "sellout" on a vocal-prayer amendment. It was only after proponents launched an education campaign of sorts that the fundamentalists were convinced. They began to recognize that equal access provided not only proselytizing opportunities, but also openings for such diverse activities as guest lectures and Bible study, which went beyond vocal prayer. Forest Montgomery, counsel to the National Association of Evangelicals, noted the switch in sentiment: "There has been a real education given the evangelical/fundamentalist constituency on this [equal access] issue, and it has shifted the Christian Right away from an emphasis on state-sponsored and imposed school prayer toward the concept of equal access. The Christian Right has come to see that student initiated prayer is preferable."[14] Montgomery's assessment was also voiced by Reverend Jerry Falwell, who stated in 1984, "We knew we could not win on school prayer, but equal access gets us what we want."[15]

Christian Right support for equal access highlighted one of the glaring ambivalences of the movement. On the one hand, it continually wrote off the public schools as a total loss, filled as they were with "secular humanists" who taught "situation ethics" rather than moral absolutes.[16] On the other hand, the movement sought to institute "prayer clubs" in the public schools. Beyond that, it also sought influence over the formulation of school curricula; the content of textbooks; the teaching of creationism, which it wanted taught alongside evolution; and activities during the early minutes of the school day so that vocal prayer could be recited. The fundamentalists manifested a distinctly ambivalent attitude: should they cleanse the public schools or write them off? Uncertain which course to pursue, Christian Right leaders pushed for measures to reform the public schools while simultaneously lobbying for measures (for example, tuition tax credits) that were designed to pull students out of those schools.

The struggle over equal access, as Hertzke points out, was an act of "legislative sausagemaking, elaborate parliamentary maneuvering, and even human drama."[17] Consistent with its opposition to vocal-prayer legislation, the House Judiciary Committee was stacked against equal access. It sought jurisdiction over the issue so that it could be laid quietly to rest. Throughout the fight, Civil and Constitutional Rights Subcommittee Chairman Don Edwards (D.-Calif.) spearheaded the opposition.

Fully aware that Judiciary had to be circumvented if equal access was to see the light of day, proponents crafted a bill that contained an administrative rather than a judicial remedy in instances where equal access was denied to student groups. The specific punishment for non-compliance faced by school administrators was a cutoff of all federal aid to education.[18] That draconian measure was the brainchild of Congressman Carl Perkins (D.-Ky.), who realized that the use of such a remedy, rather than the traditional legal recourse, would mean that the equal access bill would be referred to his Education and Labor Committee rather than Judiciary. He was a solid supporter of equal access, eventually becoming the co-sponsor of the bill with Bonker.

The referral to Education and Labor was an interesting turn of events. Historically among the most liberal House committees, it was also highly sympathetic to school administrators and teachers. Yet, before it was a measure that undermined some discretion of administrators and injected religiosity into the public schools. The only explanation was that some committee members truly believed in equal access. Judiciary members complained loudly about being circumvented, particularly when ranking Republican Bill Goodling (Pa.), who stood solidly behind equal access, conceded that the administrative remedy had to be dropped eventually for a judicial remedy because it was too harsh.[19]

Once in Chairman Perkins's custody, the equal access bill was dealt with expeditiously. By then, the proposal was H.R. 5345, a "clean bill" incorporating Bonker's H.R. 4996. Hearings held on it were a genial affair, only a few members being opposed to the proposal. Even the appearance of Congressman Edwards before the committee, protesting the circumvention of Judiciary, was mild-mannered. The exchanges between Edwards and Perkins made evident that they were longtime allies and close friends, not foes.[20]

Congressman Gary Ackerman (D.-N.Y.) was the only member who "grilled" witnesses. He was one of only several sitting on the committee who were opposed to equal access. He used the "Socratic method" with respect to witnesses who were proponents, first asking if main-line Protestant and Catholic denominations were entitled to equal access as legitimate religious groups. After witnesses assented, he then asked them whether the followers of the Reverend Myung Moon or other groups considered by many people to be "cults" were also eligible. The replies generally involved invocation of administrative discretion, saying that school principals would be empowered to sort out the legitimate religious groups from those that were not.[21]

The equal access bill passed out of the Education and Labor Committee on April 5, 1984, by a vote of 30–3, with Ackerman, Paul Simon (D.-Ill.), and Sala Burton (D.-Calif.) in opposition. Perkins then asked Speaker O'Neill to place the measure on the "suspension calendar," which required a demanding two-thirds vote for passage, but which also allowed the bill to bypass the Rules Committee and restricted the amount of debate on the House floor. The Speaker, looking at the lopsided committee vote, agreed to place the bill on the suspension calendar. Edwards then petitioned him to delay a floor vote, contending that the Democratic party should be careful about "heavy politicization" of the religious issue heading into the 1984 elections.[22] The Speaker was persuaded by the plea, and agreed to delay the floor vote until May 7.[23] During the ensuing weeks, Edwards collected the signatures of eighty Democrats who requested that the issue be discussed in the party caucus before it was taken up on the floor.[24] The Speaker also acceded to that request, making May 7 the date of the caucus discussion rather than the floor vote. Edwards then failed in a further attempt to garner a second set of signatures, designed to force the equal access issue back into the Judiciary Committee.[25]

House Democrats decided in caucus to proceed to the floor with the equal access bill, which was then scheduled for a May 15 vote. Because the bill enjoyed substantial Republican support, it appeared as if the two-thirds vote was no problem. At that point, however, Conservative Opportunity Society member Newt Gingrich (R.-Ga.) entered the fray in a spectacular manner.

Gingrich chose May 15 as the day to respond to Democratic criticism of him. Several days prior, he had launched an acerbic verbal assault upon ten Democrats who wrote an open letter to the Sandinista government of Nicaragua. The letter contained advice on how to influence American public opinion. In his speech, Gingrich questioned the wisdom of such a letter; in the minds of the ten Democrats, he impugned their patriotism as well. In the days prior to May 15, the Democrats struck back forcefully at him, claiming that he had no right to criticize them in such a manner and/or that he was obligated to inform them in advance so they could be on the House floor to respond. He rose on May 15 at the start of the legislative day on a motion of "personal privilege," a high-priority motion in the House. He subsequently was given sixty minutes to respond to his Democratic counterparts, as well as to clarify his own earlier criticism of them, which he claimed had been misinterpreted.

The next sixty minutes were marked by "partisan pyrotechnics" of the first order. Gingrich attacked the Democrats for being soft on communism, suspiciously unpatriotic, and arrogant about the wisdom of their policy regarding Central America.[26] At the end of his sixty minutes, he received a spontaneous chorus of cheers from the Republican side of the aisle. These members even crowded around to shake his hand, similar to the way that members positioned themselves to shake hands with the president as he headed down the House aisle to deliver his annual State of the Union message. The Republicans, both moderates and conservatives, were enthralled with Gingrich's performance.

Sharp partisan exchanges then ensued between Gingrich and such Democrats as Ron Dellums (Calif.), Tom Downey (N.Y.), David Obey (Wis.), Charlie Rangel (N.Y.), Majority Leader Jim Wright (Tex.), and even Speaker Thomas O'Neill (Mass.), who stepped down from the Speaker's chair to enter into the fray. Wright and O'Neill had some of the most vituperous exchanges with Gingrich. O'Neill said that Gingrich's criticism impugning the patriotism of the ten Democrats was the "lowest thing" he had seen in his thirty-two years of public service. Republican Whip Trent Lott (Miss.) immediately rose to object to O'Neill's use of the term "lowest," which he claimed was by House rules an unparliamentary expression when used in a personal sense. He requested that the Speaker's words formally be "taken down," or ruled unparliamentary. After tense moments of consultation with the House parliamentarian, presiding Speaker Joe Moakley—a fellow liberal Massachusetts Democrat and close friend of O'Neill—sheepishly stated that O'Neill's words were indeed "unparliamentary" and that such expressions were to be avoided in the future. That was the first time in the twentieth century that a Speaker's words were "taken down," and the Republicans cheered "en masse." Following the exchanges between O'Neill and Gingrich, Majority Leader Wright rose on his own motion of "personal privilege." For the next sixty minutes, he blasted the Conservative Opportunity Society, Gingrich, and the House Republicans. The intense partisan bickering thereby continued for yet another full hour.

For Chairman Perkins, floor manager of the equal access bill, the situation was a nightmare. The very *first* item of business on the legislative agenda, following the two hours of acrimonious debate, was consideration of the equal access bill under the "suspension procedure." Throughout the short debate that ensued, Perkins and ranking Minority member Bill Goodling attempted to lessen the partisan atmosphere. Perkins knew full well that the bill was not going to pass without major Democratic support because a two-thirds vote was needed; and, as the debate unfolded, he moved from member to member pleading with them to set aside their partisan feelings. Virtually the entire Democratic membership was on the floor at the time, drawn there by Gingrich's novel maneuver. Democrats, though, were in no mood to stand behind a measure that Republicans backed so strongly, even if it meant offending Perkins. The equal access bill went down to defeat, the Republicans voting for it 147–17 and Democrats against it 123–134.[27] It fell just a handful of votes short of the required two-thirds, with many Democrats changing their minds as a result of the day's proceedings.

One month after the defeat of equal access, Forest Montgomery, of the National Association of Evangelicals, lamented:

> The [O'Neill/Gingrich] episode still haunts us because it occurred the same day as the equal access vote. Gingrich really polarized the House doing what he did, and possibly cost us the equal access vote. One person said to me that Gingrich's statements cost us about forty votes among the Democrats, who were not going to vote for something all the Republicans favored. Even if that was not the case, I knew that [original equal access sponsor Congressman Don] Bonker had six votes who were willing to change and vote for equal access if Bonker really needed them. The measure lost by only eleven votes, so if Gingrich swayed only a handful of votes, it still made a difference. That was clearly a variable beyond our control, but next time I see Gingrich, I am going to tell him of our unhappiness over the timing of his action.[28]

The setback proved only temporary. On June 27 the Senate attached an equal access proposal to H.R. 1310, a popular math and science education bill already passed by the House. The vote was a lopsided 88–11.[29] After several weeks with no movement, President Reagan held a July 24 news conference, at which he criticized the House Democrats for not acting on the equal access bill now before them.[30] The very next day, the House voted 227–77 to pass H.R. 1310 as amended, proof that the first time equal access had come to a vote the Democrats had simply wanted to make a point. Democratic opposition dropped by 50 percent the second time around.

The final version of the equal access bill mandated that the student religious groups be allowed to use only secondary, but not elementary, public schools and that they be restricted to non-curricula (before or after school) rather than non-instructional (study-hall) periods. The bill also required that all religious meetings be student initiated and that all teachers/supervisors play only a monitoring, but not an active, role. Finally, the bill permitted school authorities "to protect the well-being of students and faculty," a provision whose congressional intent was to allow administrators some discretion over what groups constituted legitimate religious groups eligible for equal access.

The final bill, then, contained constraints upon the extent of equal access that made it more acceptable to Democrats than it might otherwise have been. The Christian Right's role in the struggle was that of an ally to pro-equal access forces. It was not the principal player in the struggle, a point noted by Stan Hastey:

> The victory on equal access would not have been achieved without the support of the mainline churches. The work of the National Council of Churches and those of us here at the Baptist Joint Committee was instrumental in bringing the issue to the floor on the House side under the "suspension of the rules" procedure. The Christian Right was a junior partner in that success. In fact, it was important to keep individuals like Falwell in the background on the second equal access vote in the House . . . The equal access measure fell short the first time of the necessary two-thirds vote because of the Falwell statement about equal access [being what he wanted].[31]

James Dunn, a colleague of Hastey at the Baptist Joint Committee, even stated that the Reverend Falwell was "off the wall" at one point.[32]

Hastey's view that the first equal access vote was lost because of intemperate remarks by the Reverend Falwell was surely correct, especially coupled with the exchanges initiated by Gingrich. Likewise, Hastey's assessment that the Christian Right was a junior partner in passing equal access was entirely correct. It was an assessment that came through strongly in interviews for this book and was verified by the author's experience on the Hill during that time. Recently, Hertzke provided a similar evaluation in his detailed treatment of the role of a number of the religious lobbies in the equal access struggle.[33] A clear Christian Right legislative objective was obtained, ironically, with the help of many tra-

ditionally liberal religious organizations and in spite of the activity of
Conservative Opportunity Society leader Newt Gingrich.

The very next day, the House took one other step with respect to the
school-prayer issue. On the floor that day was an omnibus education bill
(H.R. 11), to which Republican Steve Gunderson (Wis.) offered an
amendment prohibiting any state or school district from denying individuals in public schools the opportunity to participate in moments of
silent prayer. The amendment probably was aimed at the Supreme Court,
signaling it that the House backed the concept of a "moment of silence"
at the beginning of the school day—a matter the Court had not yet
considered fully. The amendment was innocuous in the minds of most
Democrats. How was voluntary silent prayer ever restricted in the
schools, or any other facet of life, short of some form of Orwellian mind
control? The amendment was simply a confirmation of an undeniable
reality. For that reason, the Democrats voted heavily in favor of the
Gunderson amendment, and it passed by the lopsided tally of 356–50.[34]
The Christian Right was uninterested and unimpressed by the proceedings; despite the fact that six people were interviewed for this book after
the Gunderson amendment passed, it was never mentioned by any of
them. It was the type of symbolic struggle in which the Christian Right
was not particularly interested.

Senate Action

The mid-term elections were not as detrimental to Republicans in the
Senate as they were in the House. In a night that otherwise belonged to
the Democrats, the Senate Republicans actually gained one seat. They
thereby retained partisan control of the chamber and reinforced the Christian Right strategy of the preceding Congress: to win action first in the
Senate on the moral agenda, after which pressure could be brought to
bear upon the House. That was the situation which ultimately occurred
with respect to equal access; the Christian Right hoped to follow it as
well with anti-abortion, tuition tax credit, and school-prayer legislation.
The struggles were often intense.

Abortion

Nine major anti-abortion bills were introduced in the Senate, three of
which were court-stripping bills and six of which were constitutional

amendments. Anti-abortion forces were still deeply divided over the proper approach to restrict abortion, but the dynamics of the situation were different this time around. The court-stripping advocates had raised a furor in the preceding Congress, but gained little support. Their approach having been discredited in principle and rejected in practice by the Senate, the way was paved for the constitutional amendment forces.

Once again, Senator Hatch led the way. In the previous Congress, he had submitted a proposal which said that the right to an abortion was not guaranteed by the Constitution, and which gave the Congress and the state legislatures dual authority over regulating the practice. In an attempt to bring the court-stripping forces on board, he altered his approach at the suggestion of Senator Tom Eagleton (D.-Mo.). The new proposal, which became S.J. Res. 3, was a simple ten-word constitutional amendment: "A right to abortion is not secured by this Constitution."[35] Hatch hoped that proposal might allay the concerns of court-stripping proponents who believed that dual authority constituted an acknowledgment of the legitimacy of the abortion procedure. His bill was a straightforward attempt to overturn *Roe* v. *Wade*; it was a proposal of the lowest common denominator, which he hoped would unify anti-abortion forces.

Court-stripping forces were not impressed. They still believed a constitutional amendment approach was fatally flawed because it was impossible to realize; they also felt that a return to the pre-Roe days was no answer because abortion flourished when the states controlled it. Women were able to obtain an abortion by simply crossing into states that allowed it.

Hatch proceeded nonetheless, hoping that a consensus would be built along the way. Under his guidance, S.J. Res. 3 received prompt action. Two days of hearings (February 28 and March 7) were held in the Constitution Subcommittee in 1983, just weeks after the beginning of the 98th Congress.[36] Because the proposal was direct in its effect, it was not hotly debated. In fact, on March 24, when the subcommittee reported out the bill, it did so with no debate. The full Judiciary Committee then split 9–9 on whether to report out the measure when it considered it several days later.[37] On a subsequent motion, members agreed to send the bill to the floor without a committee recommendation. Anti-abortion legislation was on a fast track, in part because of Majority Leader Baker's promise to take up a bill in return for Hatch pulling S.J. Res. 110 from the floor near the end of the 97th Congress.

The treatment S.J. Res. 3 received in Judiciary was neither surprising nor enlightening. The committee members had well-established records on the issue, and were not swayed by the specifics of the Hatch proposal. The vote lent credence to the observation of Gary Curran: "The precise wording of a constitutional amendment [on abortion] makes very little difference . . . virtually all members have positions on government funding, human life statutes and human life amendments and few members are going to be swayed by slight differences in wording. If Eagleton and Hatch thought they were going to pick up votes by changing the wording, they were wrong."[38] If the Judiciary vote indicated one thing, it was that the bill faced a difficult time on the Senate floor.

Ten hours of floor debate transpired from March through June 1983. In all, thirty-two senators spoke on the amendment, in a "debate" that was characterized by *Congressional Quarterly* as a succession of lackluster, perfunctory statements.[39] Sensing the floor vote was a forgone conclusion, the senators did not call forth their best oratorical or debating skills.

The proposal was defeated June 28 by a vote of 49–50, some eighteen votes shy of the two-thirds needed for a constitutional amendment.[40] (Helms voted "present" in objection to the entire constitutional amendment approach.) Following the vote, he threatened to resurrect his court-stripping proposal, but never did so.[41] The defeat of S.J. Res. 3 meant the end of major restrictive abortion legislation in the 98th Congress. The only satisfaction the Christian Right received was the garnering of a floor vote on a constitutional amendment.

Tuition Tax Credits

In contrast to his timing during the preceding Congress, President Reagan weighed in early on the tuition tax credit issue. He sent his proposal (S. 528) to the Hill on February 16, 1983, just days after the 98th Congress convened. Virtually identical to the one reported out in the 97th Congress by the Senate Finance Committee, it provided for phased in tax credits of up to $300 per child.

The judiciary helped shape the battle over tuition tax credits. On May 24 the Supreme Court handed down its decision in *Bob Jones University* v. *U.S.* (1983).[42] The Court ruled that racially discriminatory schools were not eligible for tax-exempt status, which meant that tuition tax credits were not to be extended to such schools. Shortly thereafter, on June 29, the Court ruled in *Mueller* v. *Allen* (1983) that a Minnesota tuition tax credit plan consistent with its holding in the *Bob Jones* case was in fact constitutional.[43] The twin decisions simplified the issue. Tuition tax credits were deemed constitutional in principle, contrary to claims that they violated the "establishment clause" of the First Amendment, but were not available to racially discriminatory schools. Debate over tuition tax credits was therefore centered on the economic, not constitutional, aspects. Given the cuts in federal aid to education and the high budget deficits, it was not surprising that members found the tax credits unjustified.

The full Senate disposed of the gist of S. 528 when it was offered as an amendment to a minor House tariff bill on November 16. The vote was a fairly lopsided 59–38. Throughout the debate, bill sponsor and Finance Committee Chairman Robert Dole (R.-Kans.) apologetically pushed the proposal, claiming he was bringing it forth to honor a commitment to the president.[44] Yet, it was clear that he was lukewarm on the issue, a point made in an interview with fellow Finance Committee member and avid tuition tax opponent, Senator Boren: "Senator Dole was twisting arms to get the tuition tax bill out of Committee because the White House wanted it to get to the floor. Dole did not appear to push it as hard once it got to the floor, and neither did the Senate leadership."[45] Such was indeed the case, for even Majority Leader Baker voted to table the bill.[46] The White House apparently wanted a bill on the floor to help win over its Catholic constituency and to energize its fundamentalist one heading into the 1984 elections. The White House got its wish.

As mentioned in an earlier chapter, the tuition tax credit issue highlighted a selfish element within the Christian Right that sought a narrowly drawn, tangible benefit without much regard to the impact such credits would have on the public schools. According to Senator Boren, this attitude of the fundamentalists set them apart from the Catholics, whose desire for the tax credits diminished somewhat in light of the problems faced by the public schools.[47] For a movement that claimed a strong theological underpinning, the Christian Right's social conscience was remarkably absent on the tuition tax issue. The point was made in a general sense by Congressman Bob Edgar:

> I would be pleased if they [the religious right] would put anywhere near the effort into advancing the quality of life for humanity that they put into getting prepared for the Second Coming and the next Kingdom. . . . If I may use an analogy, the [religious] right has tended to want to save a person before they give him the medicine to help himself; the [religious] left has tended to give him the medicine first to help himself, and then

asked him to think about why it was given. The right has made things more immediate to the people, but I would say at the expense of the intent of the larger social gospel.[48]

In the absence of a strong social conscience, the Christian Right staked a claim no stronger than one voiced by a variety of secular interest groups that were pursuing similarly self-interested goals.

Perhaps sensing that tuition tax credits were not enough to hand Catholics heading into his 1984 reelection, President Reagan also announced in December 1983 his desire to appoint a formal ambassador to the Vatican.[49] Previously, envoys had been assigned there, but never a duly-authorized diplomatic mission. The move to appoint such an ambassador was opposed by virtually all non-Catholic religious groups, including those of the Christian Right. They all believed that an ambassadorship unfairly recognized Catholicism over and above other denominations. Not surprisingly, civil-liberties groups like the American Civil Liberties Union also opposed a diplomatic mission, but on church/state separation grounds. The Christian Right was thus a partner with the civil libertarians, who were wholeheartedly against the moral agenda. It was a strange twist to events. It was also proof that the Christian Right was willing to work with a variety of groups to achieve desired objectives.

The president prevailed on March 7, 1984, when the Senate voted to confirm William Wilson as ambassador.[50] (The matter did not involve the House because confirmation was a constitutional function of the Senate.) The only apparent casualty from the struggle was the prestige of the Reverend Jerry Falwell, according to one interviewee who requested anonymity:

> Jerry has done some rather silly things that have taken away from his credibility. For instance, when an ambassador was appointed to the Vatican, which some fundamentalists had real problems with, he joked that if Reagan was going to send a Catholic ambassador there, he should send a Baptist one to [Falwell's home town of] Lynchburg. He said it jokingly, of course, but he said it a number of times and it put some people off.

The Senate addressed one other issue on the moral agenda in the 98th Congress. It considered the request of the Christian Right to pass a constitutional amendment permitting voluntary, aloud prayer in the public schools. The fascinating odyssey of the prayer amendment is the focus of the ensuing chapter.

8. The High-Water Mark

The prognosis for passage of a school-prayer constitutional amendment in the Senate was excellent. It was definitely the more receptive of the two chambers to the moral agenda, and the school-prayer issue was easily the most popular item on that agenda among senators. It was perfectly obvious that a majority of senators could be persuaded to support a prayer amendment. The only question was: Could the two-thirds vote required to pass a constitutional amendment be obtained? There was no clear answer.

The genesis of the prayer-amendment struggle was a set of meetings between Gary Jarmin, of Christian Voice, and Stephen Markman, who was Senator Hatch's top assistant on the Constitution Subcommittee of Senate Judiciary.[1] For several years, Jarmin had been involved with the prayer issue through Christian Voice and "Project Prayer," an umbrella organization representing some 110 individuals and groups.[2] As Hatch's head lieutenant on the Constitution Subcommittee, Markman was a key player in any prayer fight. His boss was the likely floor manager of any prayer amendment.

Following general discussions of strategy and wording, Jarmin and Markman held another set of more inclusive meetings that involved Dick Dingman and Roy Jones, of the Moral Majority, Forest Montgomery, of the National Association of Evangelicals, and Greg Butler, of the New Right organization Committee for the Survival of a Free Congress.[3] At the second of those meetings, Markman floated the idea of a prayer amendment containing provisions for silent (rather than vocal) prayer, coupled with equal access, which yet had to be considered.[4] In backing that dual approach, Markman pushed a constitutional amendment (S.J. Res. 212), already introduced by Hatch and residing in his Constitution Subcommittee.

125

Hatch introduced S.J. Res. 212 at the opening of the 98th Congress out of a conviction that a vocal-prayer amendment was unobtainable. He thought a silent-prayer amendment, coupled with equal access, stood a chance. He correctly sensed that the equal access provisions had substantial backing across party lines as well as the ideological spectrum, and that only the most liberal Democrats were opposed. He believed that, because of the silent—rather than the vocal—prayer emphasis, many moderates and liberals could be persuaded to support S.J. Res. 212. In the past, liberal concern over school prayer had focused on two aspects: (1) that it placed the state, school, or teacher in the business of composing a suitable prayer, which could lead to one that was "too Protestant" or "too Catholic" or even "too generic" to be meaningful; (2) that students of minority religions and/or agnostics and atheists were compelled, via peer pressure, to participate in prayer.[5] A silent-prayer approach alleviated both concerns. No one was responsible for drafting a prayer and no one was forced to say one. It was all unspoken.

At that juncture, however, the Christian Right organizations were not amenable to a silent-prayer/equal access measure. In any scenario, they were hostile to the silent-prayer provisions, both as a matter of principle and as a reflection of the fact that they had long agitated their constituencies about the need for a vocal-prayer amendment. How could they back away from it now? To them, anything less than vocal prayer was a "sellout." For the same reason, they were not interested in the equal access provisions. That too was a sellout, at least at this point. Gary Jarmin summed up the sentiment felt within the Christian Right at the time: "I was in it to win [a vocal-prayer amendment], having invested three years of my life into the school prayer issue and having been the recipient of other people's money and efforts given through Christian Voice."[6] It was an understandable position. Why concede defeat on a vocal-prayer amendment before the waters were even tested?

Then too, as a matter of strategy, it seemed best to proceed with a vocal-prayer amendment and to use a silent-prayer/equal access amendment as a "fall-back" measure. Common sense dictated that, though a silent-prayer/equal access proposal might be considered in the wake of a vocal-prayer amendment, the reverse was not true. Regardless of whether the Senate passed a silent-prayer/equal access proposal, it was unlikely to move to a stronger version of prayer legislation. Gary Jarmin again summed up the situation: "We knew that if we brought up equal access first, we would never get a vote on a constitutional amendment. Morton [Blackwell, White House liaison to the conservative religious community] and I agreed on that matter, that equal access would serve as a fall back following a vote on a vocal prayer amendment."[7] For both policy and strategic reasons then, the Christian Right sought to bury Hatch's S.J. Res. 212. It tried to talk Markman out of advocating it.

With the White House as an ally, the Christian Right was able to compel Hatch to delay consideration of his S.J. Res. 212. The administration's motive for siding with the Christian Right was both that it recognized the strategic value of considering a vocal amendment first and that it was good politics to side with the movement in an election year. Out of deference to the White House, Hatch agreed to the delay, at least until such time as the administration sent a vocal-prayer proposal to the Hill. Yet, despite the agreement, he vented his anger at the Christian Right for sending the White House after him: "All I can say is that some of our right-wing friends continue to badger and fight and cause difficulties and disruptions and animosities and bad feelings because they can't get their most extreme approach on a lot of these issues."[8] The tone of the comments demonstrated the extent of Hatch's displeasure.

The White House then began work on a vocal-prayer amendment. It was drafted originally by University of Texas Law Professor Grover Rees, and then reworked by Justice Department and White House officials, including Ed Meese.[9] It then read simply: "Nothing in this Constitution shall be construed to prohibit individual or group prayer in public schools or other public institutions. No person shall be required by the United States or by any state to participate in prayer."[10] The language was simple, but not at all popular on the Hill because of the absence of a safeguard prohibiting the state from composing an official prayer that students would be asked to recite. Without that safeguard, pro-prayer senators were reluctant to "sell" the proposal to the moderates, who were likely to determine the final outcome.

Frances Zwenig, lobbyist for the anti-Christian Right "People For the American Way" remarked, "Hatch thought S.J. Res. 73 was terrible as drafted . . . Both Thurmond and [Constitution Subcommittee Republican Senator Charles] Grassley were purported to wonder about it as well. I was told off the record that Thurmond actually opposed it [the president's proposal] as written."[11] Jarmin echoed Zwenig's comments: "Thurmond and Hatch did not like the language, and they were the chief sponsors of the bill."[12] It was astounding that the White House came up with such unacceptable language after drafting and redrafting the proposal. It led one to wonder whether the poor language was intentional, designed to assuage the Christian Right while simultaneously undercutting support for a prayer amendment.[13]

If it was an attempt to assuage the Christian Right, it did not work particularly well. Unhappiness with the White House language led to a fissure within Christian Right ranks. Sharing the concerns of Judiciary Committee Chairman Thurmond and Constitution Subcommittee Chairman Hatch, Gary Jarmin, of Christian Voice, tried to convince White House liaison Morton Blackwell to change the language: "My recommendation to Morton was to get the President, Hatch, and Thurmond all together on some version of a vocal prayer bill and then push it. Morton said 'no' to that recommendation, saying we had to fight for the President's language."[14] In pushing for the language change, Jarmin moved Christian Voice away from the other Christian Right groups. He stated as much in an interview: "There was a split about appropriate strategy between the White House where Morton was working and Christian Voice, with many of the other [interest] groups around town siding with the White House since it was after all, *the White House*, and they felt obligated."[15]

For his part, Blackwell was clearly intent on retaining the president's language. As he viewed the issue: "We needed an entire coalition to get the prayer amendment passed, and so had to have the support of Falwell, Robertson, and all possible Southern Baptists. They were supportive of the President's language."[16] As Blackwell saw it, Christian Voice was simply out of step with the other groups, and in any case was not as important an ally as were the Southern Baptists and major groups headed by television evangelists. This assessment was shared by one Christian Right supporter involved in the issue who requested anonymity: "In short, Christian Voice were mavericks on this issue, out of step with others who favored the [president's unamended] prayer amendment."

Divisions over language apparently created some hard feelings at the time between Jarmin and Blackwell. Jarmin believed the White House language was poor and that he was unfairly frozen out of the issue: "The bottom line is that my role as leader [in the school-prayer fight] was usurped by Morton Blackwell at the White House. He took the lead on the issue [with the president's proposal] and in a sense, froze me out of it. . . . Morton and I were at odds over strategy on the matter, and he got rather nasty about it which he shouldn't have since he was never organized."[17]

When presented with Jarmin's assessment, Blackwell replied: "When one deals with organizational entrepreneurs like Mr. Jarmin, one sometimes suffers from their desire to claim credit. In the case of the school prayer amendment, Jarmin came up with a number of different variations which he pushed, hoping his version could be adopted so that he could claim credit."[18] Blackwell's evaluation was shared by one other individual who requested anonymity: "They [Christian Voice] came to the Hill with one amendment after another, some of which repudiated parts of Reagan's proposal. It confounded the issue, and weakened the position of those prayer proponents who were standing by the Reagan version and trying to build a coalition around it." Apparently, throughout the course of the struggle, Jarmin in fact did offer a number of versions of a prayer amendment that served to confound the issue. At the same time, he was correct that the president's language needed work. It was soon altered.

In terms of Kingdon's dichotomy, discussed earlier, it was clear that such "hidden" actors as academics, bureaucrats, interest-group activists and congressional staff members played a definite role in specifying alternatives with respect to school prayer. They not only provided the initial language for the prayer amendment, but also shaped the cleavages that developed within the Christian Right and between pro-prayer forces in the White House, on the Hill, and interest groups off the Hill. In that sense, they "specified alternatives" and also shaped the entire prayer struggle that ensued. What conclusion is to be drawn from these facts? Kingdon's dichotomy, in some instances, may understate the importance of the "hidden" actors in actually shaping and structuring policy debates.

The White House Proposal

Out of courtesy to the president, Judiciary Chairman Thurmond introduced the White House proposal formally on March 23, 1983. It was labeled S.J. Res. 73. At the time he presented it, Thurmond pointed out his concern about the language of the bill, telling his Senate colleagues that he would "welcome their thoughts on how we can improve its specific provisions."[19] The prayer amendment was then promptly referred to the Judiciary Committee. From there, it moved on to Hatch's Constitution Subcommittee, where it lay alongside his own silent-prayer/equal access proposal.

Hatch's Quandary

Senator Hatch faced a difficult choice. His Constitution Subcommittee had jurisdiction over both the president's prayer amendment (S.J. Res. 73) and his own (S.J. Res. 212). If he chose to act on the former proposal, he was placed in the unenviable position of pushing a bill that he believed was poorly drafted and was unlikely to pass. Moreover, he risked incurring the wrath of moderate Republicans and some Democrats who preferred his silent-prayer/equal access approach to a vocal-prayer approach. On the other hand, if he chose to act on his own proposal, he would incur the wrath of both the White House and the Christian Right, which had teamed up to persuade him to delay consideration of his bill until a vocal-prayer amendment was drafted by the White House. Whichever bill he took up, he stood to lose.

Realizing that Hatch was ambivalent about what to do, the administration again applied pressure, this time in the form of direct phone calls from Ed Meese and the president.[20] They argued that S.J. Res. 73 was the preferred alternative and the proper focus of subcommittee action. This time, however, Hatch was not so acquiescent. Although he was willing to consider the president's proposal, he was not willing to move on it at the expense of his own. Consequently, he pushed both proposals through his subcommittee on June 9, 1983.[21] After doing so, he remarked: "If I had my preference, I would put one [proposal] out, but who am I to say that I am right and the President is wrong? I will give him that deference."[22] The deference, of course, extended only so far.

The Christian Right was taught a valuable lesson by Hatch's action: It was unproductive to pressure a key senator to forgo his convictions. This was a lesson that was evident to most interest groups, but one that was apparently necessary for the Christian Right groups because of their inexperience in politics and specifically in the legislative process. Their tactic of using the White House to pressure Hatch to recant on his own prayer proposal, without regard to the difficult position that placed him in, backfired. It was a reflection of a lack of political sophistication that surfaced again before the fight ended.

Thurmond's Quandary

Hatch escaped his predicament, but only by "passing the buck" to full Committee Chairman Thurmond. That placed Thurmond in a bad position. Like Hatch, he did not wish to contravene the White House or the Christian Right; by the same token, he, too, believed that the president's language was poor and that his prayer amendment was unlikely to pass. In fact, an informal canvass of the full Judiciary Committee revealed that the prayer amendment was unlikely to be reported out favorably.[23] Was it best to act on the president's proposal? Was it best to act on Hatch's proposal? Should the language of the president's bill be altered? Those were the questions Thurmond faced.

At that juncture, the lack of consensus among prayer proponents was evident. The White House and most of the Christian Right groups wanted action on the original proposal of the president; Senator Hatch, on his S.J. Res. 212 silent-prayer/equal access proposal; and Senator Thurmond and Christian Voice, on the president's proposal after the language was altered. Gary Jarmin noted the fissures and the view of Christian Voice: "People had too many reservations about the President's language to push it unreconstructed . . . I gave up working with the White House on language, and worked exclusively with the Judiciary Committee people at that juncture."[24] As if those cleavages were not enough, recall that the White House, Senator Thurmond, and all the Christian Right groups were allies on the question of action on a vocal-prayer amendment before action on an equal access proposal. Hatch dissented on that question. The alliances cut many different ways.

In an attempt to resolve some of the differences of opinion and difficulties, Senator Thurmond went to see the president in July 1983. He brought with him the results of his informal canvass of Judiciary, which showed that Reagan's proposal was unlikely to make it out of committee with a favorable recommendation.[25] The decision was made to bury Hatch's proposal and to proceed with the president's, but also to alter its language. Originally, the president's language read: "Nothing in this Constitution shall be construed to prohibit individual or group prayer in public schools or other public institutions. No person shall be required by the United States or by any state to participate in prayer." Thurmond's desire was to add a third sentence that read: "Neither the United States nor any state shall compose the words of any prayer to be said in public schools." This was designed to alleviate concern that the state would be involved in the formulation of a prayer. It was an attempt to rework the White House proposal in order to get it out of Judiciary.

Following his meeting with the president, Thurmond held one day of hearings on July 14. The third sentence was added at that time by voice vote.[26] Nevertheless, prospects in Judiciary were not good. A head count conducted by staff members found eight firm votes against and for the proposal, with Senators Robert Byrd (D.-W.Va.) and Howell Heflin (D.-Ala.) leaning against it and for it, respectively.[27] In other words, it looked like a tie. Senator Byrd broke the tie when he drafted a proxy for use against the proposal. Heflin's vote was then irrelevant in a sense. At best, Judiciary was deadlocked.

The attempt to add a third sentence failed to help, perhaps confirming the initial view of the White House and most of the Christian Right groups that the president's proposal was best left unchanged. (Also, the effort lent credence to Hatch's view that a vocal-prayer amendment was a lost cause, and he was alienated because a deliberate effort was made to bury his amendment proposal.) The change highlighted the divisions within the ranks of pro-prayer forces and provided the opposition with ammunition. They were able to pose the following question to senators: Why support a constitutional amendment concerning prayer over which the White House and its chief Senate sponsors disagreed? It was a reasonable question.

Lacking the votes to report out the measure with a favorable recommendation, wily Chairman Thurmond also decided to "pass the buck," just as Hatch did to him. Following the addition of the third sentence, Judiciary voted 14–3 in favor of Thurmond's suggestion to report out both the president's proposal (S.J. Res. 73) and Hatch's (S.J. Res. 212) with no favorable or unfavorable committee recommendation.[28] The problem was thus put in the hands of Majority Leader Baker (R.-Tenn.). Interestingly, Hatch's proposal ended up on the floor after all, despite several concerted attempts by the White House to quash it.

The Mobilization Begins

The fortunes of the prayer amendment plummeted during the first seven months of 1983. It went from a reasonable chance of passing to barely squeaking out of Judiciary, and then lacking a recommendation. The majority leader was acutely aware of the declining fortunes of the amendment and the divisions that had arisen among pro-prayer forces. In an attempt to put momentum back on the side of that group and to elevate his own standing among the conservatives within the Republican party, in January 1984 Baker brought forth his own proposal (S.J. Res. 218). It was similar to the one his father-in-law, former Minority Leader Everett Dirksen, had introduced in an earlier Congress. It read: "Nothing contained in this Constitution shall abridge the right of persons lawfully assembled, in any public building which is supported whole or in part through the expenditure of public money, to participate in voluntary prayer."[29] The proposal was designed to overturn the *Engel* v. *Vitale* (1962) Supreme Court decision banning prayer, without providing an affirmative mechanism for instituting it, as did the Reagan and Hatch proposals. It was a watered-down approach in an attempt to build a Senate consensus on some prayer bill.

Unfortunately for him, the majority leader's bill was not well received. The White House, the Christian Right, and Senators Thurmond as well as Hatch were all displeased with it. For one thing, they did not like the approach of simply overturning the Court decision without putting something affirmative in its place. What was the point of working for a constitutional amendment that was not the embodiment of what was desired? Secondly, they had labored long and hard on the prayer issue and did not appreciate a late entry. Thirdly, they were placed in an even more difficult position than when only two competing proposals existed. Now there were three prayer amendments sponsored by three key Senate Republicans (Baker, Thurmond, and Hatch). How could any of the prayer proponents ask senators to support a prayer amendment in view of that divisiveness? The majority leader's miscalculation cost him some prestige among pro-prayer forces, even though his S.J. Res. 218 was never acted upon. Despite his good intentions, he further muddled the picture and fractured pro-prayer forces.

After being rebuffed in January, the next month the majority leader announced that the president's proposal (S.J. Res. 73) was going to be the focus of Senate action in March. (Hatch's amendment was again to be quashed.) The decision to proceed with the White House proposal was both political and tactical. It was done in deference to the president and out of recognition of two realities with respect to school prayer: (1) that the only way an amendment would pass was if the popular president was completely behind it, which meant consideration of his own proposal; (2) that the vocal-prayer amendment had to precede a silent-prayer/equal access amendment.

As the date of the impending floor vote approached, pro-prayer forces swung into action. At the White House, lobbyist Robert Cable began trying to line up support; various cabinet members made some thirty calls directly to senators; the president and vice-president made twenty calls to senators who were thought either to be undecided or committed only to some form of silent prayer.[30] Then, too, in what turned out to be an embarrassing episode, Reagan invited fifteen undecided senators to the White House for some personal lobbying. Only Senators Dennis DeConcini (D.-Ariz.) and John Chaffee (R.-R.I.) showed up.[31] Senators apparently decided that having their "arms twisted" on this issue was undesirable. Evidently, it was easier to avoid Reagan than say "no" to him, or else it was considered wise to keep a low profile while deciding how to vote.

The president also made two public appeals for support. In one of his weekly radio addresses to the public (February 25, 1984), he said with respect to the prayer amendment: "If ever there was a time for you, the good people of this country, to make your voices heard, to make the mighty power of your will the decisive force in the halls of Congress, that time is now." On March 6, 1984, he repeated his call for a prayer amendment in a highly publicized speech before the annual gathering of the National Association of Evangelicals in Columbus, Ohio.[32] Although the public lobbying was real, there was some question about the "behind-the-scenes" activity of the president. Senator Boren suggested in an interview that neither Reagan nor his administration made a wholehearted effort: "Certainly they [the administration] did not make a 'full court press' on the school prayer vote similar to their efforts on AWAC's or Central America. If they went 100% on AWAC's, they probably went 75–80% on school prayer . . . I should add though, that the President did call me on the school prayer vote, encouraging me to support it. I was also in contact with the Vice-President on the matter, so certainly they did put forth some effort."[33] At least some of the Christian Right groups never fully appreciated the fact that the administration did not lobby wholeheartedly, again because of their inexperience in the congressional milieu. One interviewee who requested anonymity bluntly declared: "The Christian Right was unable to recognize sincere from half-hearted Administration efforts."

Apparently believing the White House was doing all that it could, the Christian Right did only limited direct lobbying of members. This was a rational choice. What was to be gained, for instance, by the personal lobbying of Roy Jones, of the Moral Majority, when the president himself was engaged in such activity? It seemed more productive to concentrate on drumming up grass-roots support in senators' states as a means of lobbying them indirectly, thereby supplementing the personal efforts of Reagan. The main evidence of personal lobbying from the Christian Right at the time came in the form of phone calls from the Reverend Jerry Falwell to Senate offices, most of which were not taken by individual senators.[34] It was in that context that anti-prayer amendment lobbyist Frances Zwenig remarked: "Moral Majority did not turn up anywhere that I ran across them. They certainly weren't hanging around in the hallways."[35]

If the personal lobbying of the Christian Right groups was limited, however, their grass-roots agitation was considerable. The Reverend Pat Robertson, of the 700 Club, for instance, devoted entire programs to the issue.[36] During them, he flashed on the screen the names and addresses of undecided senators, asking constituents to write them. The television preachers apparently had some effect on the sheer volume of contact with the Hill. Senator Boren, for example, received more than 3,200 letters for and 1,400 letters against school prayer in the space of a few weeks.[37] Those numbers did not include the phone calls made either to Washington or to district offices. According to the *Congressional Quarterly*, Senator Lloyd Bentsen (D.-Tex.) received approximately 1,500 calls on the prayer issue on February 27, 1984, alone; Senator Pete Wilson (D.-Calif.), some 2,000 calls in the last two weeks of February and some 400 calls per day in March, compared to 5,400 total calls on all issues during the entire preceding year.[38] Examining large states, the *Congressional Quarterly* probably overestimated the volume. Still, looking at the sheer number of postcards, letters, and calls generated by the television evangelists on the issue, Episcopal minister and prayer opponent Senator John Danforth (R.-Mo.) was prompted to remark: "With all the calls and the mail we're receiving, you would think this is the most important issue facing the country."[39] Frances Zwenig, of People for the American Way, agreed about the volume of communication drummed up by the television evangelists: "They organized an amazing outpouring of communication and put pressure on the Hill."[40]

Nevertheless, the effectiveness of the effort was limited because it was clearly stimulated by the television evangelists. Members of Congress were impressed by spontaneous grass-roots outpourings, but were less influenced by mass-produced campaigns, in part because they signaled the possibility of many repeaters. As Stan Hastey noted: "My wife Bettie [who works for a senator] could always tell when the 700 Club broadcast was over . . . because the switchboard into the office was flooded. Bettie said she could tell the 700 Club callers because they all said the same thing in the same way."[41]

The mass-produced pressure campaign was a serious mistake on the part of the Christian Right. Again because it was relatively new to politics, it did not fully recognize that legislators were not particularly swayed by pressure campaigns involving "look-alike" postcards and "sound-alike" telephone calls. Campaigns of that type made members ask themselves the following questions: Just how many repeaters were there? What level of intensity was present, given that constituents were acting on cue? How many phone calls came from out-of-state viewers of the television evangelists? How much of an electoral threat was presented by citizens who were unaware of the cardinal rule of pressure campaigns: the need to make them appear at least somewhat spontaneous? The quality of the Christian Right campaign was lacking particularly in comparison to that of the opposition, which consisted of many more handwritten, personal letters.[42] Members asked themselves whether even half as many of those letters did not mean as much as twice as many mass-produced postcards.

Meanwhile, House Republicans contributed to the mobilization effort in two particularly colorful ways. First, the conservative House Republican Study Committee brought a number of famous sports personalities to Washington to "testify" before their committee on the virtues of school prayer. Because the House Democrats never held hearings on the issue, the Republicans decided to stage their own as a means of winning attention and support for a prayer amendment. Among others appearing before the committee were: Dallas Cowboy football coach Tom Landry and quarterback Roger Staubach, Washington Redskin football coach Joe Gibbs and placekicker Mark Moseley, former New York Giant football player Rosey Grier, and former Harlem Globetrotter "Meadowlark" Lemon.[43] The net effect of their appearances was unclear. On the one hand, their presence did raise the salience of the issue, which was a prime objective of pro-prayer forces, who did not want a prayer amendment quietly disposed of. On the other hand, the staged "testimony" delivered on February 29 served to trivialize the issue. Senator Nancy Kassenbaum (R.-Kans.) demonstrated this when she quipped that she would be happy to have the debonair Roger Staubach stop by her office.[44]

Second, the Conservative Opportunity Society staged an all-night vigil on March 5—the day the Senate began consideration of the prayer amendment. Inside the House chamber, Republicans began to make long pro-prayer speeches that began at 1:30 p.m. and did not end until about 9:00 a.m. the next day.[45] The speeches filled dozens of pages in the *Congressional Record*.

"Average" citizens also lent their support to the mobilization effort. On the night the Conservative Opportunity Society held the all-night vigil inside the Capitol, about 500 people gathered on the steps overlooking the Mall to listen to an hour of pro-prayer speeches and vocal prayer. These were followed by some two hours of singing of such religious songs as "Onward Christian Soldiers" and such patriotic ones as "America the Beautiful" and "The Star-Spangled Banner." The singing occurred during a driving rainstorm on a cold March night.[46] Concurrently with the gathering on the steps and the all-night vigil within the House chamber, another 150 people held a twelve-hour prayer session in a nearby House office building.

On March 7, two days later, pro-prayer citizens also tried to gain attention and mobilize support for the prayer amendment by forming a human chain stretching from the Supreme Court Building to the Capitol.

The chain was designed to symbolize the fact that the Court created the prayer controversy with its 1962 *Engel* decision and that Congress now had the opportunity to reverse it. All this activity led *Congressional Quarterly* to observe in its weekly report that, as the Senate began debate on the prayer amendment, there was "the atmosphere of a revival meeting around much of the Capitol."[47]

Buying Time

From the very beginning, the central goal of opponents to the prayer amendment was to extend the debate. They realized that the pro-prayer forces had the jump on them. President Reagan was making speeches, the White House lobbying operation was geared up, the House Republicans were staging events, and the Christian Right groups were fully mobilized and were drumming up grass-roots support. In contrast, prayer opponents had no ready-made constituency apart from some liberal Protestant churches, minority religions, civil libertarians, and teachers. An effective constituency could be built from those groups, but it would take a little time. Barry Lynn, of the ACLU, summed up the dilemma faced by prayer opponents: "The key element for us was to buy a little time because we knew it would take some time to defeat it [S.J. Res. 73]. The Christian Right was out months ahead of us preparing the groundwork, and the rhetoric they used was in place. They kept talking about how God had been 'kicked out of the schools,' how kids weren't allowed to pray, and how they knew of one little girl who was not even allowed to say grace over lunch."[48]

The opposition bought some time through the efforts of Senator Lowell Weicker (R.-Conn.). A self-proclaimed civil libertarian and defender of the Constitution, he began what amounted to a Senate filibuster in early March. He went on at length about the dangers inherent in amending the Constitution and the insensitivity of prayer supporters to the plight of students from minority religions. While he tied up the Senate, prayer opponents furiously counterattacked.

Senators Weicker and Danforth began the assault with an elaborate "education" campaign. They personally lobbied their Senate colleagues, read statements into the *Congressional Record*, submitted "op-ed" pieces to newspapers, and led several press conferences and marches opposing a prayer amendment.[49] Barry Lynn fondly recalled their efforts: "Weicker and Danforth did a remarkable job in . . . giving the public an education as good as any that I have ever witnessed."[50] Frances Zwenig also spoke warmly of the efforts of the two senators, saying "Weicker was instrumental" and "Danforth was just great" in the battle to defeat the prayer amendment.[51] Outside the Senate, organizations like the ACLU, People for the American Way, and various Jewish, Methodist, and Lutheran groups began lobbying moderate Republican senators like Andrews (N.D.), Chaffee (R.I.), Kassebaum (Kans.), Evans (Wash.), Gorton (Wash.), Rudman (N.H.), and Specter (Pa.). They were perceived as the "swing votes," and were thought to be disturbed by a prayer amendment despite the heavy backing for it within the Republican party. The opposition groups also held a series of widely publicized news conferences at which they reiterated their position.[52] In the House, Judiciary Subcommittee Chairman Don Edwards announced two days after the Senate began debate on the prayer amendment that he would soon hold hearings on the issue in his Civil and Constitutional Rights Subcommittee.[53] His offer was disingenuous, of course, intended only to divert and divide the attention of pro-prayer forces.

The counterattack was not only broadly based, but also well timed. For weeks, senators had heard from pro-prayer forces only, but, in the days just preceding the floor vote, they began to hear from the opposition. As a vote drew closer and closer, it was clear that the momentum was shifting away from the pro-prayer forces. Senator Patrick Leahy (D.-Vt.) summed up the shift: "The longer the debate goes on, they'll lose votes."[54] Weicker succeeded in delaying a floor vote until March 20, just over two weeks from the date the Senate opened debate on the issue. At that point, he was content to proceed with a vote, which he believed his side would win.

The Floor Vote

The floor debate over S.J. Res. 73, which lasted about a dozen days in March, was unspectacular. It was often perfunctory and rambling. Senators realized that the battle was to be won off the Senate floor and that scoring debating points was of little use. Apart from some sharp exchanges between Hatch and Weicker, the debate was, according to the *Congressional Quarterly*, "desultory."[55]

Sensing they were losing ground as the debate dragged on, pro-prayer forces launched two "eleventh-hour" efforts to salvage some sort of victory. First, Majority Leader Baker again actively intervened, offering an idea that was an amalgam of the president's S.J. Res. 73, Senator Hatch's S.J. Res. 212, and his own S.J. Res. 218. The idea never materialized, but it again divided prayer forces and befuddled the issue. Baker's efforts were unappreciated by Gary Jarmin, who was then personally lobbying on behalf of the prayer proposal, sensing it was in trouble: "Baker's attempt to forge a compromise at the last minute made my job impossible as a lobbyist. The language was changing virtually every hour, and not only was that no way to draft a constitutional amendment, but it made me look silly . . . I could not in good conscience go to a senator when I wasn't even sure about the final language, but that was what resulted."[56]

Second, Senator Alan Dixon (D.-Ill.) attempted to revive Hatch's silent-prayer/equal access proposal. Like a number of moderate senators, he was unhappy that the White House vocal-prayer amendment was chosen by the majority leader as the only one to receive Senate attention. After all, Hatch's proposal had been reported out with it at the same time and received the same "no recommendation" Judiciary Committee endorsement. Unhappy that his alternatives were structured by the majority leader, Dixon offered the gist of the Hatch proposal as a substitute amendment to S.J. Res. 73 on March 15. It was defeated overwhelmingly by a vote of 81–15, through an unlikely alliance of anti-prayer and pro-prayer senators who sought an "up or down" vote on the vocal-prayer amendment.[57]

The Dixon substitute placed Hatch in a particularly awkward position. Despite repeated administration efforts to bury his own amendment proposal, he graciously agreed to serve as the floor manager for the president's S.J. Res. 73. The White House asked him to serve in that key capacity as a way of simultaneously apologizing and winning him over— as well as recognizing that, as chairman of the Constitution Subcommittee of Judiciary, he was the appropriate person to manage the prayer amendment. In any case, the Dixon substitute placed him in the position of serving as the floor manager for S.J. Res. 73 at the same time that his own proposal was being considered. In an ironic twist to events, he voted against the Dixon substitute. In so doing, he was opposing the very prayer amendment that he had drafted and clashed over repeatedly with the White House and the Christian Right. His vote typified the strange twists and turns the prayer fight took as it played out.

On the day of the final vote, a certain aura of excitement prevailed, even though it was assumed that the prayer amendment was headed to defeat. The excitement stemmed from the fact that under consideration was a twenty-seventh amendment to the Constitution—an unusual circumstance in any year. Then, too, until the votes were actually cast, the outcome remained undetermined. About one hour before the floor vote began, the Senate gallery filled to capacity. The observers were cautioned against making any noise during the last hour of Senate debate, lest they be removed from the gallery. For its part, the media was present in large numbers, with network artists busily sketching the unfolding drama.[58] As the excitement heightened, Vice-President Bush arrived to preside over the floor debate, in a symbolic show of administration support for the prayer amendment. Even Democratic presidential hopeful Gary Hart (Colo.), who was then riding a wave of success in the 1984 primary season, was present. He left the campaign trail to fly back for a vote that involved all 100 senators.[59] It was a rare vote and it attracted each and every senator, which was unusual in an election year.

In the waning minutes of the debate, floor manager Hatch sat by himself on the Senate floor, perfunctorily calling upon pro-prayer senators to deliver their endorsements of S.J. Res. 73. He clearly sensed defeat. His counterpart, Senator Weicker, moved from colleague to colleague, though with no sense of urgency. After Judiciary Committee Chairman Thurmond's closing remarks that constituted a ringing defense of the prayer amendment, the Senate bells sounded and the final vote began. Over the next fifteen minutes, senators casually ambled into the chamber from the adjoining cloakrooms and cast their votes when their names were called. As numerous spectators and senators kept a running tally, the Senate defeated S.J. Res. 73 by a vote of 56–44. The prayer amendment won a majority, but fell eleven votes short of the required two-thirds for a constitutional amendment. As soon as he received word of the outcome, House Judiciary Subcommittee Chairman Edwards promptly canceled the promised hearings on the prayer issue.

Despite the defeat, the vote was the high-water mark for the Christian Right on the Hill during the first Reagan term. The movement convinced the Senate to entertain one of its top agenda objectives; it persuaded a majority of senators to amend the Constitution of the United States in a manner it thought appropriate. Furthermore, the vote paved the way for passage of an equal access bill, which was considered on the House floor less than two months later. Those were no small accomplishments.

9. A Term of Accomplishment

In September 1984, near the end of the first Reagan term, the *Congressional Quarterly* concluded that the Christian Right had failed on the Hill: "The political tide that helped elect Reagan and a more conservative Congress in 1980 did not lead to a sweeping enactment of the New [Christian] Right agenda, which includes criminalizing abortion, legalizing organized school prayer, and enacting tuition tax credits for parents who send their children to private schools."[1] This was a reasonable assessment if final passage of top moral agenda objectives was considered to be the only measure of influence. If other forms of influence were counted, however, a summary assessment of failure was overstated, if not actually misleading.

The reality was that the Christian Right was quite successful on the Hill during the first Reagan term. Its success came in two related forms: (1) in the enactment of items on the moral agenda other than top objectives; (2) in inroads into the congressional agenda. Together, those two forms of influence represented accomplishment, not failure.

Passing Bills

Certainly the Christian Right enjoyed success with respect to the enactment of items apart from top objectives. In the 97th Congress (1981–82), its position prevailed on various anti-abortion riders, a school-prayer rider restricting Justice Department activities, a vote to halt criminal-code reform, a measure prohibiting the District of Columbia from lessening its rape penalties, and a rider stopping the Legal Services Corporation from defending gay rights causes. In the 98th Congress, the Christian

Right's cause was advanced in various anti-abortion riders, a silent-prayer amendment to an education bill, an equal access bill, a measure allowing churches to opt out of the Social Security system, and a test vote on the Equal Rights Amendment. Granted, some of those victories were more symbolic than substantive (for example, the rider restricting the Justice Department from blocking school prayer), but that was not the case with all of them. At the end of the first Reagan term, taxpayers' money was not being used to fund abortions, the Legal Services Corporation was not backing gay rights causes, the penalties for interstate pornographers were not lessened, the Equal Rights Amendment was turned back, the fundamentalist churches were able to withdraw from the Social Security system, and voluntary student religious groups in the secondary schools were given access to school facilities. Those were substantive legislative victories involving the moral agenda, not token, pyrrhic ones.

Whether the Christian Right was the driving force behind those victories, an ally in them, or mostly the beneficiary of others' efforts varied by issue. In the cases of the Legal Services Corporation and Social Security, the movement seemed to be the driving force, but with equal access and the Equal Rights Amendment it was more of an ally. In the case of anti-abortion riders and criminal-code reform, it was mostly the beneficiary of others' efforts ("right-to-life" groups and law enforcement officials, respectively).[2] To some extent, however, the influence of the Christian Right relative to other groups in particular policy struggles is irrelevant, though not uninteresting. What mattered was that on certain issues where it made some lobbying effort the movement and its preferred position prevailed. Whether it received some, or even considerable, assistance from like-minded groups, did not detract from its aggregate record of success.

Agenda Inroads

The Christian Right also exerted significant impact on the congressional agenda. The most obvious manifestation was the time spent by the Congress debating and voting on the issues just mentioned. Another was the increase in the number of bills, hearings, and testimony that concerned the top objectives of the moral agenda in the 97th (1981–82) and the 98th (1983–84) Congress compared to the 96th (1979–80), when the Christian Right was just arising and not yet lobbying actively nor regularly on the Hill.

Recall the statistics comparing the 96th to the 97th Congress that were presented in an earlier chapter: the number of anti-abortion bills in the Senate rose from four to fourteen and the number of school-prayer bills in the House increased from twenty to twenty-nine, as well as in the Senate from four to seven; the number of hearings rose across-the-board from zero to two on anti-abortion, one on school prayer, and two on tuition tax credit legislation; and the number of Christian Right figures who testified before congressional committees and subcommittees rose across-the-board from zero to eight (one for anti-abortion, three for school prayer, and four for tuition tax credit legislation).

In comparing the 98th with the 96th Congress, the numbers are fairly similar: anti-abortion bills in the Senate rose from four to nine and school-prayer bills in the House from twenty to twenty-eight, as well as in the Senate from four to nine; hearings increased across-the-board from zero to one on anti-abortion, two on school prayer (or four if equal access is included), and one on tuition tax credit legislation; and the number of Christian Right representatives who appeared before committees and subcommittees rose across-the-board from zero to four (one for anti-abortion legislation, two for school-prayer legislation, and one for tuition tax credit legislation).[3] Unquestionably, the trio of issues received more attention from the Congress after the rise of the Christian Right. As was pointed out in preceding chapters, the movement was undoubtedly a major force behind congressional consideration of those issues.

Cobb and Elder have argued that simply placing an issue on an institutional agenda like that of the Congress is a significant accomplishment because such agendas tend to be clogged with issues carried over from preceding years.[4] Against that backdrop, the Christian Right's accomplishments were considerable and its power apparent. It placed several major issues on a crowded congressional agenda, proof of which was evident by the objective criteria of the number of bills introduced, hearings held, and testimony given.

Yet, the achievements and influence of the Christian Right did not end at the point of mere placement of issues on the congressional agenda. The movement also obtained substantive action on those issues, a form of influence rightly recognized by Cobb and Elder as exceeding that of agenda placement.[5] In what manner did it do so? As was noted earlier, it helped obtain hearings on its issues in subcommittees and committees, as well as arrange for debates and votes on the floor. The latter achievement was especially impressive when it is recalled that two of the issues that were voted upon (abortion and school prayer) were constitutional amendments, not routine bills. One of those amendments (school prayer) even won a clear majority of senators.

This line of reasoning may be carried yet another step. When it helped obtain floor votes, the Christian Right stimulated action on basically dormant issues. When the Senate held a floor vote on tuition tax credits in 1983, for instance, it was the first time that either chamber had voted on a tuition tax bill since 1978. Similarly, when the Senate held floor votes on school prayer and anti-abortion constitutional amendments in 1984 and 1983, respectively, it was the first time that either chamber had voted on a prayer amendment since 1966 and the first time since the Supreme Court's 1973 abortion decision that an anti-abortion amendment was voted upon. Put another way, the Christian Right helped bring about action on issues that had received no analogous treatment for a period ranging from five to seventeen years. Hence, in addition to obtaining action on issues, the movement did so on those that were essentially dormant.

This line of reasoning may be pursued one last step. Besides ultimately winning consideration of its issues, the Christian Right also obtained fairly prompt action. Kingdon has shown that years of agitation are often required to even *place* an issue on the congressional agenda.[6] He cites Medicare as an example, which had to overcome the stigma of "socialized medicine" before it won serious attention on the Hill.[7] Against that background, consideration (and not mere placement on the agenda) of the top objectives of the Christian Right within one presidential term was impressive—all the more so when it is again recognized that constitutional amendments were involved.

In sum, during the relatively short span of some four years, the Christian Right placed its issues on the congressional agenda, helped obtain substantive action on them, and in so doing reignited those that had been moribund. Those were no small accomplishments in the realm of agenda-setting and influence. They were testimony to the movement's power on the Hill during the first Reagan term.

Two interviewees were cognizant of the agenda accomplishments of the Christian Right. Senator Boren remarked: "My view is that the Christian Right has been quite influential. Certainly it has been active here in the Senate."[8] Forest Montgomery echoed that view: "Without Christian Right pressure, the moral issues probably would have been moot. What made the issues was the work of the Christian Right and the Library Court people, and without their work those issues would not have gone very far."[9] Those qualitative observations buttress both the crude empirical evidence cited earlier (that is, bills, hearings, testimony) as well as the line of reasoning pursued with respect to agenda influence.

Other Benefits Derived

The inroads made by the Christian Right into the congressional agenda served other objectives as well. First, the movement's organizations were placed in a relatively advantageous position. They were able to claim some credit to their constituencies for "opening up" the Congress to the moral agenda, though not too much could be made of issues where final votes were lost lest the faithful become disheartened rather than agitated and hopeful. Second, in Gary Jarmin's words, the inroads "made politicians think about the moral quotient [in politics] before casting their votes."[10] In other words, members were made to think twice before contravening the Christian Right, given its apparent power. Who could say what future electoral danger the movement presented in view of its contemporary agenda successes?

Third, the advances provided the Christian Right and the larger conservative movement with ammunition to use against liberals in campaigns. As Lilli Hausenfluck explained it in an interview: "We need votes [on the moral issues] to get people elected. Only by putting liberals on record on the social issues can we win elections because otherwise liberals like [former Iowa Democratic senator] Dick Clark can be duplicitous, saying one thing in Iowa and another in Washington."[11] Tom Ashcraft, legislative assistant to Senator Helms, similarly remarked: "Tripartite government sometimes makes it difficult for the public to assign responsibility for government policy. However, roll call votes in Congress are an exception to that rule and what Senator Helms . . . [and others have] done is to obtain many recorded votes on the so-called social issues . . . and then let the people make personnel changes."[12]

Finally, the access gained by the Christian Right to the congressional agenda helped bump off a competing set of liberal issues. Obviously, the congressional agenda has a saturation point at which new issues can be added only at the expense of other ones—a notion made painfully evident in recent years by members and legislative scholars who have lamented the enormous workload of the institution.[13] In practical terms, when the previously dormant issues of the Christian Right were taken up during the first four years of the Reagan presidency on that "zero-sum" agenda, competing liberal issues were knocked off.

Roy Jones, of Moral Majority, summed up the point and provided some examples:

> The liberal thinkers and practitioners have begun to sweat in recent years because they realize their agenda is being displaced by an alternative agenda.

> For that reason, they have taken to countering and discrediting the con-
> servative movement exemplified by people like Falwell . . . The liberal
> agenda clearly has changed. For instance, they no longer are talking about
> national health insurance, or feeding hungry people at government expense
> because the government owed them something. They now speak of finding
> the hungry people jobs so they can feed themselves . . . The liberals are
> abandoning the welfare state and are speaking to conservative principles.[14]

Other examples of the liberal agenda gone awry—at least during
the Reagan era—would be full-employment legislation (for example,
Humphrey-Hawkins), affirmative action quotas, "comparable worth,"
national health insurance, and a national child day-care policy. Congressional inaction on those issues was as much of an accomplishment for
the Christian Right as was action on its moral issues.

The other factor that must be remembered in any discussion of Christian Right influence was its ability to shift public discourse. Many pieces
of evidence suggest that it made changes in the nation's systematic agenda.
First, the movement and its issues were the focus of much media attention
for a number of years, which by itself was evidence of a shift. Second,
the Republican party incorporated many of the concerns of the Christian
Right. Likewise, the Democratic party moved closer to it symbolically
and rhetorically (and perhaps even substantively). That point was aptly
made by Roy Jones in an interview the day after Governor Mario Cuomo's
speech at the 1984 Democratic national convention: "At the Democratic Convention last night, you had a keynote speaker talking about
issues of the New Right like the importance of the family. It was astounding to those of us associated with the Christian Right that at a
Democratic Convention, the topic of discussion was essentially . . . [our]
issues."[15] Although admittedly anecdotal, those examples demonstrated
the power of the Christian Right in shaping the nation's systematic
agenda.

Other evidence, a part of which was mentioned in an earlier chapter,
affirms that point. The *Reader's Guide to Periodical Literature*, for example, had only two references under the subtitle "Religion and Politics"
from March 1979 through February 1980 when the Christian Right was
forming, but sixty-eight, thirty-eight, twenty-seven, and nineteen references under the same subtitle in the ensuing years.[16] Similarly, the *Social
Sciences Index* carried no listings under its "Christianity and Politics"
subtitle from 1978 through 1980, but four such references in each of the
next three years.[17] Finally, the platforms of the two major political parties
emphasized Christian Right issues much more in 1980 and 1984, after

the movement arose. To cite just one example, the Republican platforms in both 1980 and 1984 had new sections (compared to the 1976 platform) devoted to the strengthening of the traditional family. In short, an analysis of leading indices of the nation's systematic agenda reflected a shift toward the issues and concerns of the Christian Right.

Four Successful Years

The movement made impressive strides during the first Reagan term. In 1979 it was just beginning to take shape; as late as early 1980, it was still little more than a compilation of "letterhead" organizations. By the end of the 98th Congress in October 1984, however, a whole host of bills had been passed dealing in some way with the moral agenda; the number of bills and hearings on the top legislative objectives had risen dramatically; floor votes had been cast on previously dormant issues, including two votes on constitutional amendments; and liberal issues had been displaced at least somewhat on both the systematic and congressional agendas. This was not a bad track record for a set of groups that were new to the machinations of the Hill and that were led by previously apolitical fundamentalist ministers.

The accomplishments were all the more impressive in view of the clogged nature of the congressional agenda and the fact that literally thousands of other interest groups were competing for access at the same time. The Christian Right fared well in the rush for congressional attention brought about by the decentralization of the Congress.

The Christian Right failed on the Hill during the first Reagan term only if final passage of top agenda objectives is deemed to be the sole measure of success. Tom Bovard provided some perspective in an interview: "I think it is a bit narrow to view the 'defeats' in the legislature as defeats . . . The goals of any major group take a generation to come to fruition, and it is my belief that if the Christian Right is patient, its goals will come to fruition and the country will be changed."[18] In that context, the movement's success in obtaining the enactment of moral agenda items and making inroads into both the congressional and systematic agendas was impressive. Most interest groups lobbying on the Hill would be pleased with a track record even approaching that of the Christian Right during the first Reagan term.

Part IV
A New Era?

10. Reputation Problems

The waning months of 1984 were a pleasant time for most Americans. The nation was at peace, basking in the glory of the successful invasion of Grenada a year earlier. The economy was booming: the inflation rate was substantially lower than it had been in the late 1970s, the unemployment rate was down from where it had been during the 1982 recession, and the stock market was rising to new heights. Energy shortages seemed to be artifacts of the past, and problems like the AIDS virus were mostly in the future. Americans watched proudly as their Olympic athletes won medal after medal at the Los Angeles Games. Even esoteric things like national Scholastic Aptitude Test (SAT) scores showed improvement. It was understandable that the Reagan reelection campaign saw fit that year to run a series of "morning in America" ads that reinforced citizens' perceptions of peace and prosperity.

In the nation's capital, however, it was not a sanguine time for the Christian Right. Rather, it was a time for reassessment. Despite the successes the movement had enjoyed during the first term of the Reagan presidency, ending with the equal access victory in the summer of 1984, it faced some troubling questions as it looked toward the 99th Congress (1985–86). Would that body reconsider the Right's major legislative objectives, given that it had just defeated them? If it reconsidered certain issues, were they likely to pass this time around? If not, what would grass-roots supporters think? Were they likely to become disenchanted? By themselves, those questions necessitated reassessment of a strategy focused on the Hill.

Yet, this reassessment was also motivated by the realization that the movement's many successes there came at considerable expense to its reputation. The fight over the school-prayer amendment highlighted some of the things that hurt its reputation. For one, it ran a "look-alike, sound-alike" pressure campaign, not realizing that members discounted the importance of such campaigns because of the likelihood of repeaters and the lack of original effort on the part of those citizens initiating the contact. The movement also did a poor job of inciting elites in the states and districts to contact members, according to a legislative director of one of the Christian Right organizations who requested anonymity. Instead, the pressure campaign was centered around the mass followers of the television preachers. Running a simplistic pressure campaign to bolster a top legislative objective under consideration was a costly error.

Second, the Christian Right was "heavy-handed" during the prayer fight. When it failed to get its way in Hatch's subcommittee over whether a vocal-prayer amendment or a silent-prayer/equal access amendment should be reported out, it sent the White House after Hatch to pressure him to forgo action on his own legislative proposal. That was by no means the only instance where bullying tactics were used. For instance, when Republican Congressman Mickey Edwards (Okla.) failed to sign a discharge petition designed to extract a "court-stripping" school-prayer bill from the Judiciary Committee, the Religious Roundtable saw to it that he was castigated by name and issue on local religious broadcasts back in his Oklahoma City district.[1] Despite his impeccable conservative credentials as former chairman of the American Conservative Union and the fact that he was "with us ninety percent of the time" according to one Christian Right leader, he was pressured into signing the discharge petition.[2] A small victory was won, but a close friend was alienated. In a more general sense, the mere idea of "moral report cards," which gave members of Congress an "approval rating" on the basis of a handful of roll-call votes, struck many members as heavy-handed, if not outright arrogant.

Third, the Christian Right was at least somewhat disunited during the prayer fight. The White House had its proposal, Senator Thurmond sought to push that proposal with some language changes, Senator Hatch sought to advance his own silent-prayer/equal access measure, the Moral Majority sided with the White House to push its proposal unamended, and the Christian Voice generally backed Thurmond, though it had its own ideas about the language at different times. Thus, a major division existed between the two major Christian Right organizations that was easily visible to interested parties.

Fourth, the Christian Right cast the prayer amendment in such strict theological terms that it bred an overreaction among supporters. Elites regularly asserted that "God had been kicked out of the schools" by the secularists and that "God was on their side" in the battle to reinstate vocal prayer. That rhetoric so permeated the struggle that Senator Danforth was prompted to remind people that "the debate on school prayer is not between the godly and ungodly," and Senator Weicker was the recipient of numerous telegrams congratulating him on his fine work in defeating the prayer amendment that were signed "your pal, Satan."[3] Barry Lynn, of the ACLU, was extremely critical of the quality of political participation by the Christian Right: "There was a lot of hate mail during the school prayer debate written by people that they [Christian Right elites] had freaked out. The fight over S.J. Res. 73 [the prayer amendment] was a very nasty thing, as nasty a fight as I have been involved in. I think it is incumbent upon them to moderate that sleazy type of behavior."[4] When members realized that excesses on the part of the political neophytes acting in support of the Christian Right organizations were fed rather than tempered by elites, the stock of those organizations and elites dropped.

Together, those incidents sullied the Christian Right's reputation on the Hill. Members wondered if it was not prone to factionalism, and certainly believed it was belligerent and somewhat irresponsible. By themselves, all those things might not have been sufficient to discourage the movement from heading back to the Hill. Unfortunately, for the Christian Right, other incidents and episodes led to even further reputation problems.

A Lack of the Sophisticated Touch

One of the factors, in addition to those mentioned, that tarnished the Christian Right's reputation on the Hill was its quixotic attempts to win patently unwinnable legislative struggles. A celebrated case in point was the "Family Protection Act," which, as mentioned in an earlier chapter, contained provisions dealing with such diverse topics as gay rights, teachers' unions, tuition tax credits, sex education, bloc grants, and birth control. The Moral Majority in particular worked hard on that omnibus measure, attempting to extract its various constituent elements from as many as five different congressional committees in both houses (for a total of ten committees). Eventually, the Moral Majority surrendered on that hopeless task, but not before it wasted precious time and resources.[5] Similarly, the organization squandered those precious commodities when it opposed the nomination of Sandra Day O'Connor to the Supreme Court. Opposition in the Senate to her nomination was nonexistent and any attempt to create some was futile. No senator was going to pass up the historic opportunity to place a woman on the Supreme Court. An undaunted and unwise Moral Majority, however, lobbied hard against the nomination.

Another thing that tarnished the movement's reputation on the Hill was its early failure to apply pressure on members with much precision. Rather than identify key junctures in the legislative process such as committee hearings and put pressure on relevant members at the appropriate time, the Christian Right used a broad-based approach. A onetime Moral Majority consultant remarked in an interview: "When I was at the Moral Majority, it did not have its impressive mailing list coded by congressional district. It has that capacity now [in 1984], but it was a long time in coming."[6] That point was acknowledged by Roy Jones:

> Initially, we used a "shotgun" approach to stimulating grassroots pressure. When an issue came up we sought to generate pressure, and we did so in virtually every congressional district by every means we could. Now we utilize our mailing lists much more by congressional district, being more selective about districts where we try to generate pressure. Targeting key districts where we believe we have the chance of getting a member's vote is more cost effective than the shotgun approach, results in far less mailing, and has proven more effective and productive.[7]

Lacking a district mailing capacity, the Moral Majority initially wasted some of its resources. This deficiency also signaled to members on the Hill that it lacked some requisite political skills, which made it somewhat less feared than it was in the aftermath of the 1980 elections. Then too, it consumed some goodwill among supporters, who were continually asked to contact members, even when it was not an appropriate time to do so. The legislators hastened to point that fact out to their constituents, which worsened the reputation of the Moral Majority.[8]

Third, the Christian Right sometimes exhibited a less than complete understanding of the issues, as well as of legislative strategy. The abortion struggle nicely illustrated that point. Gary Curran, of American Life Lobby, noted:

> They [the Christian Right] are the new kids on the block, and they do not fully understand the issues in all circumstances. For instance, Falwell went on national television making the case for a constitutional amendment restricting abortion except in cases of rape and incest. His very suggestion of loopholes provided the pro-abortion movement with the leverage to attack the anti-abortion efforts of Congressman Hyde, since Falwell had

opened up that possibility. In that particular case his efforts were misguided, and the outgrowth of a less than full understanding of the issue.[9]

The abortion issue was not the only example. As pointed out previously, the Christian Right did not at first fully comprehend the virtues of equal access legislation, and did not support the concept until an "education campaign" was undertaken after the defeat of the prayer amendment by other prayer advocates. Then, too, at some points the Christian Right was enthusiastic about some court-stripping bills as short-cuts to constitutional amendments, not fully appreciating the fact that an institution filled with lawyers had serious concerns about such an approach.

Fourth, the Christian Right sometimes acted as if inroads into the nation's systematic agenda automatically translated into victories on the congressional agenda. Any sensitivity to the incongruities between the two agendas was often not apparent, especially on the part of the Moral Majority. Gary Jarmin noted the problem, though pointing out that it was endemic to virtually all of the conservative lobby groups:

> There are two views of what constitutes success. One measure is the amount of money and media time one is able to garner, while another is the number of wins and losses in the legislative and electoral realms. Although money and attention are necessary to achieve some sort of success, it does not follow that legislative and electoral success will follow . . . the second measure . . . is more important . . . [It does not matter whether] I had 7,000 newspaper articles written about me this year compared to 5,000 last year.[10]

The insensitivity to the incongruities between the two agendas again showed that some political skills were lacking, and also indicated to members that the Christian Right might not have much of a stomach for the day-to-day grind of the legislative process. It appeared all too content at times to flit off the Hill to gain some press coverage.

What was the common theme to all the problems discussed? It was a relative lack of political sophistication on the part of the Christian Right. Time and time again, the movement exhibited this weakness: it ran simplistic pressure campaigns, bullied friends and allies, failed to unite behind legislative proposals, squandered valuable time and resources on quixotic tasks, applied pressure with imprecision, failed to exhibit a thorough understanding of issues and of legislative strategy, and neglected to appreciate the difference between the systematic and congressional agendas.

The lack of sophistication was acknowledged by one leading Christian Right activist, who stated optimistically in a personal letter: "As in all things, experience accrues in time and with it, hopefully, our effectiveness as well."[11]

The lack of sophistication was perfectly understandable. After all, the individuals involved in the Christian Right were for the most part new to politics, even at the level of leadership of the interest groups lobbying on the Hill. Roy Jones, of the Moral Majority, for instance, was a twenty-four-year-old graduate of Falwell's Liberty University when he was named the legislative director of an organization consisting of millions of members and handling millions of dollars. Then too, the groups themselves were new. It was understandable that they underwent a period of transition, during which mistakes were committed. That was especially true with respect to groups lobbying on the Hill, with its informal folkways and its complex procedures. It was not only understandable that new groups would make mistakes in that environment; it was highly probable.

One interesting question is why the Christian Right did not turn to more experienced political activists when it first went to the Hill in order to avoid some of the mistakes it was likely to commit. There is no single answer to that question; it seemed to have been a combination of several things. One was the dearth of individuals available who possessed the necessary political expertise, coupled with beliefs in conservative politics and fundamentalist Christianity. People like Gary Jarmin were a rarity. For another, at some point Christian Right activists needed to "learn the ropes" themselves. Why not do so at the very beginning? For a third, the Christian Right had enough hubris so that it thought (at least initially) it could win its objectives outright on the Hill, even with inexperienced people. It was not an irrational belief. The movement catapulted from nowhere to a spot on the nation's systematic and congressional agendas in a short time. Finally, in a more philosophic vein, the fundamentalist leaders were not anxious to leave the task of realizing the moral agenda to the experienced politicos of the secular state, whose sins were best cleansed by committed fundamentalists new to politics and unwilling to compromise away their values.

The Case of the Moral Majority

The lack of sophistication that occurred during the first Reagan term did not hold evenly across the Christian Right. As the examples indicated, the Moral Majority in particular was beset by legislative mistakes. It was the group that squandered resources on the "Family Protection Act," bullied Senator Hatch, applied pressure with imprecision, exhibited a less than thorough understanding of strategy and issues, and was insensitive to agenda incongruities. Why was the Moral Majority so afflicted? It may have been idiosyncratic or due to the youthful inexperience of Roy Jones. More likely, it was the Reverend Falwell's fault for spreading the Capitol Hill operation too thin. In addition to running the lobbying effort and Hill office, for example, Jones was also a regular contributor to the *Moral Majority Report*, the group's national newsletter. Regardless of whom or what was to blame, the fact that the Moral Majority made so many legislative mistakes hurt the reputation of the entire Christian Right on the Hill because it was the acknowledged "flagship" of the movement. Its errors reflected poorly upon the other groups.

In the 99th Congress (1985–86), the Moral Majority was abandoned in effect by Falwell, who created the Liberty Federation as his new organization for the advancement of his political goals. The demotion of the Moral Majority was interpreted widely as the beginning of the decline of the Christian Right as a political movement; in reality, its demotion was as much a recognition of the reality that it had a distinctly unfavorable reputation on the Hill. A relatively recent study made a similar argument on the basis of a content analysis of the *Moral Majority Report*, adding too that Falwell sought to broaden his focus beyond the moral agenda: "The creation of a new organization [the Liberty Federation] with a new image and a broader mission can be seen both an initiative to rid himself of the negative sentiments that have accrued to the name Moral Majority as well as an effort to form a new conservative Christian alliance that he could move beyond the issues of personal morality."[12] During the 100th Congress (1987–88), Falwell disassociated himself from the organization, handing what was left of it over to a longtime friend, Atlanta businessman Jerry Nims.

In a strange way, the lack of sophistication demonstrated primarily by the Moral Majority, but also the other groups, testified to the power of the Christian Right during the first Reagan term. It was able to win some legislative victories and make inroads into the congressional agenda though it failed to present its case to members very effectively. How many other groups could make a similar claim? The deficiency, however, was a contributory factor in the movement's inability to realize passage of its top legislative objectives.

In any case, a curious situation arose out of the first Reagan term: all the while the Christian Right was faring quite well on the Hill in pursuit of its legislative goals, it was undermining its position for future congresses. Even as it was winning some votes and consideration of its major objectives, it was committing serious legislative mistakes that sullied its reputation and made it less welcome on the Hill to friend and foe alike. On the flip side, precisely because it enjoyed some success there, the Christian Right undercut support for its issues. Why should the Congress reconsider a prayer amendment, for instance, after defeating one in 1984 *and* passing equal access legislation? The Christian Right was damned on the Hill both by its failures and its successes.

The Reagan Revolution

The 1984 election results removed any lingering doubts the Christian Right may have had about returning to the Hill with gusto. The election institutionalized the "Reagan Revolution" when the president swept forty-nine states en route to a landslide victory. However, the election generally diminished Republican fortunes in Congress and, with them, those of the Christian Right as well.

In the House, the Republicans won a meager fourteen seats, hardly a triumph given the president's margin of victory. The gain left the Republicans twelve seats short of the number they had lost in the 1982 mid-term election and seventy seats short of what the Democrats held. Thus, little was new in the House for the Christian Right. All it could expect in that institution was frustration at the hands of the Democratic majority and some "bomb-throwing" on its behalf by the Conservative Opportunity Society.

In the Senate, the Republicans actually suffered a two-seat loss, decreasing their margin of control to 53–47. Moreover, some changes in personnel were masked by the aggregate numbers, which made the Senate a more liberal institution. Among the new senators elected were liberal Democrats Paul Simon (Ill.), Albert Gore (Tenn.), John Kerry (Mass.), and Tom Harkin (Iowa). At the same time, conservatives John Tower (R.-Tex.) and Jennings Randolph (D.-W.Va.) stepped down, and New Right Senator Roger Jepsen (R.-Iowa) lost his reelection bid.

The bad news did not end there. The Christian Right faced the reality that never again would President Reagan stand for election to any office. Although it was unlikely that he would abandon the Christian Right agenda, he no longer had an electoral incentive to push it. He needed to think about his place in the history books, which was not going to be gained from potentially futile struggles over the moral agenda on the Hill. Then too, the Christian Right had to face a period of transition in the once receptive Senate. Majority Leader Baker voluntarily retired at the end of the 98th Congress, ostensibly to run for the presidency. His retirement suggested a period of factionalism within the Republican party, as members jostled to succeed him, and a period of transition while the entire leadership hierarchy was shuffled. Eventually Bob Dole emerged from a five-man race to succeed Baker.

In short, the November 1984 elections provided no good news for the Christian Right. The prognosis for the enactment of the moral agenda on the Hill was at its lowest ebb since the movement had been founded in the late 1970s. Its period of intense activism on the Hill appeared over.

11. The Transition Period

Taxes were always a high-priority item on Ronald Reagan's political agenda. His 1980 campaign was centered heavily around a call for lower taxes; the massive tax cuts put into effect in 1981 were the backbone of the "Reagan Revolution." After he defeated Democratic presidential nominee Walter Mondale in the 1984 election, in which taxes were a major issue, the president turned his attention to reforming the existing tax structure. In fact, he made it one of his top legislative priorities in the 99th Congress (1985–86). Aided by many members of Congress, the Tax Reform Act of 1986 was enacted into law.

Tuition tax credits were included in the administration's tax-reform package when it was first sent to the Hill in 1985. They were only a bargaining chip, though, designed to be traded away. Treasury Secretary James Baker testified before the Senate Finance Committee as the tax-reform debate opened that the administration was willing to drop tuition tax credits as part of a larger tax-reform package.[1] The credits in fact were summarily dropped. They fell off the congressional agenda.

The abortion issue similarly lost its place of prominence on the congressional agenda. The usual scuffles occurred in the 99th Congress over anti-abortion amendments tacked on to other legislation, but even those were lackluster. In the Senate fight over the Fiscal Year 1987 Labor/Health and Human Services Appropriations bill, an amendment was even added in the Appropriations Committee that provided for federal funding of abortion in cases of rape or incest. (The mere fact that abortion funding was added symbolized how far the fortunes of anti-abortion groups like those of the Christian Right had fallen.) Senator Helms angrily challenged the amendment on the floor. He eventually prevailed, but in turn agreed not to attack the $145 million contained in the bill for federal family planning programs and not to offer any school-prayer or busing proposals.[2] In contrast to abortion struggles in preceding congresses, this matter was worked out behind the scenes by Helms and Appropriation Committee Chairman Mark Hatfield (R.-Oreg.).[3] Thus, there was no public debate, nor the intensity and visibility of earlier abortion fights. The abortion issue, too, was basically off the congressional agenda.

In the case of school prayer, some movement occurred. As before, a division still existed among prayer proponents whether to pursue a court-stripping or constitutional amendment approach. This time around, the Christian Right largely abandoned its support for a vocal-prayer amendment, believing that, in the wake of its defeat and the passage of equal access in the 98th Congress, it was an unobtainable goal. The movement instead put its support behind a court-stripping measure, for the simple reason that it thought it stood a better chance than an amendment. Gary Jarmin justified the switch: "I think the burden of proof is on them [amendment advocates] to show us the 67 votes [needed to pass an amendment in the Senate]."[4]

The switch in position showed that the Christian Right was willing to adapt to the new realities. It had helped shape the political environment on the Hill during the preceding congresses; its switch in position demonstrated in turn that it was shaped by that environment. It was sensitive to the less-favorable situation on the Hill and adjusted itself accordingly.

At issue was S. 47, a court-stripping bill introduced by Senator Helms and placed directly on the Senate calendar. The bill would probably have lingered there except for the Supreme Court's decision in *Wallace* v. *Jaffree* (1985). A 6–3 decision handed down June 4 struck down an Alabama statute authorizing a one-minute period of silence in public schools for "meditation or voluntary prayer."[5] Within two days after the decision, the Moral Majority cranked out an estimated 500,000 fund-raising letters urging contributors to back the Helms bill, and the Reverend Falwell flew to Washington to meet with the senator.[6]

All the furor was for naught. The Senate considered S. 47 on September 10, 1985. After a debate described as "short and desultory," it was defeated by a vote of 62–36.[7] Helms and the Christian Right knew they were fortunate to win consideration of the bill alone, harboring few illusions about victory. After S. 47 was defeated, Helms conceded that he pushed the bill simply to "fulfill my responsibility" of putting members on record.[8]

Less than a month after this bill was defeated, Senator Hatch pushed a prayer amendment (S.J. Res. 2) through the Judiciary Committee. His amendment was designed to overturn the *Wallace* v. *Jaffree* decision, allowing "silent prayer or reflection" in the public schools.[9] Consistent with its disdain for silent-prayer measures, the Christian Right took no active interest in the bill, and Roy Jones, of Moral Majority, even publicly stated that the Hatch amendment was at most "an incremental step."[10] Even though Hatch was able to report the amendment out of Judiciary by a 12–6 vote on October 3, 1985, it never received floor action.[11]

The only appreciable floor success for the Christian Right in the first session of the 99th Congress (1985) was a provision written into the National Science Foundation reauthorization (P.L. 99–159). The provision directed that monies spent by "magnet schools" be used for the improvement of "core academic courses." Magnet schools were set up to provide special curricula to attract minority students; the requirement that they spend their money on core academic courses was intended to ensure that no money was spent to teach "secular humanism."[12] It was a small victory, and one in which the Christian Right was an observer as well as beneficiary of conservative senators' efforts.

The results of the first session really brought home to the Christian Right what it had sensed at the close of the first Reagan term: its attempts to obtain enactment of the moral agenda were fruitless. Its reputation on the Hill was in tatters; its agenda was no longer welcome. Recognizing those realities, President Reagan left both the abortion and school-prayer issues almost entirely out of his January 1986 State of the Union speech. He chose instead to transmit his support for those issues to the Hill as part of a legislative "laundry list."[13] For the first time in a number of years, the top moral agenda objectives of the Christian Right basically failed to make it into a State of the Union speech. Discouraged by all these factors, later in the year the Reverend Falwell reconstituted the Moral Majority into the Liberty Federation, and the Reverend Pat Robertson disbanded his Freedom Council lobby group that had been formed at the end of 1984. For the groups like Christian Voice that remained, it was time for a new strategy—a defensive rather than an offensive one.

On the Defensive

The transition from an offensive to defensive strategy on the part of the Christian Right vis-à-vis the Hill was shaped by the realization that it was in no position to win enactment of the moral agenda anytime soon. Because of its damaged reputation and a passé agenda, what other choice did it have than to try and thwart liberal initiatives? Beyond that, there was good reason to believe that the 100th Congress (1987–88) would be even less sympathetic to the moral agenda. History demonstrated that the sitting president's party almost always lost seats in mid-term elections.[14] Further gains on the Hill for the Democrats meant only bleaker prospects for the Christian Right and its agenda.

The decision to adopt a defensive strategy was a wise one. It provided an opportunity for the various organizations to regroup after the flurry of activity during the preceding couple of years. It also gave their supporters some respite from contacting their members on the Hill. It made possible the training of people in the art of politics—something sorely needed after the performance in preceding congresses. Then, too, as Roy Jones, of Moral Majority, stated in an interview when queried about the virtues of a defensive strategy: "Being on the defensive is not what we want at this point, but it is not all bad either. It is an effective strategy for raising money and it tends to get otherwise uninvolved people interested and involved."[15] Thus, some advantages were to be gained via a switch in strategy.

The new strategy was cemented when the 1986 election results rolled in. The Democrats gained only five House seats, a modest gain by mid-term standards, but they won a hefty eighty-one seat overall edge (258–177). In the Senate, they scored an impressive eight-seat gain, catapulting them into majority-party status there for the first time in six years. For the Christian Right, the Senate results were even worse than the new 55–45 Democratic majority indicated; it lost such staunch Republican supporters as Mack Mattingly (Ga.), Paula Hawkins (Fla.), Jeremiah Denton (Ala.), and Jim Abdnor (S.D.). Its prospects were enhanced only marginally when a Republican member was appointed to fill a Democratic seat, which decreased the margin to 54–46.[16] The outlook was dismal.

Concurrent with the election results was the rise of a new set of issues far removed from those of moral reform: the farm crisis, the trade imbalance, the budget deficit, and the lack of an arms-control agreement. The voters thus dictated the continuation of a defensive strategy on the Hill by the Christian Right in the 100th Congress, a point readily conceded by a leader in the movement as it convened: "Others will be setting the agenda, and we'll be reacting."[17]

Prospects on the Hill

The rise of new issues on the systematic agenda, coupled with the 1986 election results, guaranteed the end of substantive struggles over the moral agenda on Capitol Hill for the remainder of the Reagan presidency. Throughout the first session of the 100th Congress (1987), no action occurred on school prayer or tuition tax credits; the only movement on abortion was in the context of routine "Hyde Amendment" struggles.[18] By the time of the summer conventions in the second session (1988), when only a few more legislative weeks remained in the 100th Congress, the Democratic-controlled chambers showed no predilection to entertain the moral agenda.

Events that transpired off Capitol Hill during the 100th Congress reinforced the dismal prospects for the Christian Right on the Hill. Two incidents in particular were devastating. The first was the claim of the Reverend Oral Roberts in March 1987 that, if he did not raise an additional $8 million for his ministry, he would be "called home" by God.[19] The money was intended for a noble enough purpose: to subsidize the costs of medical students at Oral Roberts University so that upon their graduation they were able to take their skills abroad as medical missionaries, free of the burden of medical school debts. The means of raising the money, however, was something less than exemplary. Soliciting money based on a threat to die struck many people as a form of psychological extortion.

The whole incident was confounded when a Florida dog-track owner, who made his fortune via the gambling misfortunes of others, traveled to Tulsa to present Reverend Roberts a $1.3 million check—the remainder needed to reach the $8 million goal. The payment complicated matters because, when he presented the check to Roberts, seventy-nine-year-old Jerry Collins freely offered his opinion that the minister was in dire need of a psychiatric evaluation. The issue was aggravated still further when the Reverend Richard Roberts, the son of Oral and heir to his religious empire, initially declined to admit that the $8 million figure had been reached. He was later forced to concede that it had.

This incident raised the specter of greed among the evangelical and fundamentalist television preachers, some of whom were involved heavily with the Christian Right. Those preachers, such as Jerry Falwell and Pat Robertson, were deemed to be guilty by association.

The second incident, which occurred at virtually the same time, raised the same concerns to new heights. In a saga that unfolded throughout the year, it was revealed that the Reverend Jim Bakker, of the PTL (Praise the Lord) Club, agreed to pay $265,000 in "hush money" to a young church secretary named Jessica Hahn after a tryst in a Florida motel room in 1980. The story was uncovered and apparently leaked by the Reverend Jimmy Swaggart and the Reverend John Ankerberg, competing evangelists who were contemptuous of the Bakker ministry.[20] Further allegations followed that Bakker was a bisexual and that his wife Tammy had an affair to "get even" with her husband for his tryst with Jessica Hahn.

Amidst the allegations, Bakker resigned from PTL and moved to California. In doing so, he claimed that his resignation was motivated by a "hostile takeover" attempt by an unnamed rival television evangelist and not by the Hahn affair. Further, he purportedly asked the Reverend Jerry Falwell to assume temporary custody of the PTL ministry, which Falwell did. He promptly reconstituted PTL's board of directors and installed Bakker's top assistant, the Reverend Richard Dortch, as its president.

The full-blown national scandal made the covers of *Time, Newsweek,* and *U.S. News and World Report* that same week (April 6, 1987). Matters degenerated still further during the ensuing months. Among other things, it was revealed that: the Reverend Dortch participated in the "hush money" scheme (he was forced to resign); the Bakkers paid themselves salary and bonuses in the range of $1.9 million for 1986 alone; the PTL Club spent millions in homes and cars for the Bakker family; the massive PTL operation was bordering on bankruptcy; and Tammy had undergone treatment for drug dependency. Further allegations were also made: Falwell claimed that Bakker had engaged in rampant financial and sexual misconduct; and Bakker contended that, under the pretense of helping him, Falwell and lawyer Norman Roy Grutman conspired to "steal" PTL. Bakker also claimed that Jessica Hahn was a prostitute who knew the "tricks of the trade," rather than the innocent virgin she claimed when her tryst with him became public information.

Over the course of the next several months, the allegations gave way to revelations: that key aides at PTL under the Bakkers received six-figure salaries annually; that the Bakkers paid $4,500 for an air-conditioned doghouse; and that, upon resignation from PTL, they submitted a severance settlement list that included requests for a $400,000 annual lifetime salary for the two, hospitalization insurance, bodyguards, all proceeds from books and records, a furnished PTL-owned home, secretarial help, maid service, and a year's worth of free telephone calls. The financial troubles at PTL prompted Falwell to claim a "May emergency" fund-raising drive to raise $10 million. Later that summer, he promised to plunge down PTL's sixty-foot waterslide in his clothes if 1,000 people pledged $1,000 toward the ministry. He took the plunge in mid-September.

During the waning months of 1987, the Bakkers tried to stage a comeback. They moved from California and settled near Heritage USA, in Fort Mill, South Carolina, in an attempt to work their way back into the PTL ministry. Failing in that attempt, they scheduled a nationwide tour to tell their side of the PTL story; it was subsequently canceled due to low advance ticket sales. They then tried a telephone fund-raising scheme, where the Bakker faithful were able to call a "900" number to hear a daily taped message from Jim and Tammy, who gleaned a percentage from each call.

Also, in the waning months of 1987, Jessica Hahn posed nude for *Playboy* magazine and in it told of forcibly losing her virginity at the hands of Bakker. Rival *Penthouse* magazine then produced Roxanne Dacus, an ex-madam who claimed that Jessica Hahn was a professional prostitute who had worked for her in 1977–78, several years before she supposedly lost her virginity to Bakker.

Last but not least, Reverend Falwell resigned from PTL after a bankruptcy judge ordered that Bakker loyalists be placed on a board to determine a reorganization plan. Falwell's resignation in October after an approximately six-month reign over PTL was followed by a rather startling announcement in mid-November: that he was quitting politics to go "back to the pulpit, back to preaching, back to winning souls."[21] Meanwhile, at PTL, the Internal Revenue Service staked claims on the ministry's assets, claiming it owed thousands of dollars in back taxes. By the end of 1987, the Bakkers were disgraced and living in relative seclusion in Tennessee, Falwell was back full time in Lynchburg and avowedly out of politics for the first time since 1979, and the Internal Revenue Service was thoroughly investigating the situation at PTL. At the beginning of 1988, the IRS revealed that payments to Jessica Hahn were underestimated by about $100,000.

The improprieties involving Reverend Roberts and Reverend Bakker severely tarnished television evangelism. The Reverend Jerry Falwell and Reverend Jimmy Swaggart reported sizable declines in viewer contributions to their ministries, as did the Reverend Pat Robertson, of the Christian Broadcasting Network. Midway through 1987, Robertson laid off nearly 500 employees.[22] The "holy war" among television evangelists, as it was dubbed by the mass media, was devastating to all of them.

While still reeling from the events of 1987, the world of television evangelism was dealt a further blow in early 1988. In February it was revealed that the Reverend Jimmy Swaggart had paid a prostitute to pose nude for him in a Baton Rouge motel room. He publicly confessed to unspecified sexual improprieties after his Assemblies of God denomination began to investigate the allegations. The national headquarters of the organization subsequently ordered Swaggart to step down from the pulpit for one year. Rather than risk the permanent damage to his ministry that such a suspension was likely to engender, he chose to defy the order. He was later defrocked by Assemblies of God.

Those separate events, in addition to tarnishing television evangelism, were also devastating the reputation of the Christian Right on the Hill, which was already suffering. In August 1987 Congressman J. J. Pickle (D.-Tex.) announced plans to hold hearings in his House Ways and Means Subcommittee on the tax-exempt status of the television ministries.[23] The fact that such a proposal was even made, given the explosiveness of that issue, was a reflection of sentiment on the Hill.

The irony of the damage to the Christian Right was that the scandals embraced preachers who for the most part were only tangentially involved with the movement. All three individuals—Roberts, Bakker, and Swaggart—lent their names to such organizations as the American Coalition for Traditional Values and provided rhetorical support to the moral agenda as part of their ministries.[24] Unlike other television preachers, however, they did not form lobby groups nor consistently campaign for enactment of the moral agenda on Capitol Hill. One interviewee, who requested anonymity, spoke contemptuously of Bakker: "Bakker was a vacillator from the outset. One day he would want on board and the next day he would try to distance himself from the statements he made the day before. I know of one time in particular when he rode around with Reagan for a day [during the 1980 election] and the next day rode around with Carter. He has a very strong ego and likes to be around people with power." Despite their peripheral involvement with the Christian Right, the three preachers did it considerable harm.

Near the end of the Reagan era, then, the Christian Right was in poor position vis-à-vis the Hill. Most of its formal lobbying organizations had been disbanded (for example, the NCAC, the Roundtable, and the Freedom Council) or informally abandoned (for example, the Moral Majority); its reputation on the Hill, as with large segments of the public, had been badly damaged; it faced a House of Representatives where the Democrats enjoyed a substantial eighty-one seat majority; and, given the perennially high incumbent reelection rates usually bordering around 90 percent, seemed likely to retain control well into the 1990s; and it had to deal with a Senate where the Democrats enjoyed an eight-seat majority, and would need to defend only a little more than a half (34 of 64) of the seats in the next two elections. Not until 1992, when the Democrats would need to protect twenty of thirty-four seats, did Republican prospects appear bright in the Senate. Until that party gained control of one of the two chambers of Congress, prospects for the moral agenda were bleak.

The second Reagan term, in short, was a period of transition for the Christian Right, first from an offensive to a defensive strategy; and then, in the wake of the television evangelist scandals, to an emphasis off Capitol Hill. Even looking as far ahead as the 1990s, barring something unexpected and dramatic, the prospects for the Christian Right in Congress were nonexistent.

12. Off the Hill

It was founded in 1971, though it did not catch the attention of the mass media until about a decade later. Today, it has a strict ninety-two-page "code of conduct" that mandates formal dress and bars such activities as drinking and dancing. The vision of its chancellor is that it will grow from its current enrollment of about 7,000 to 50,000 by the turn of the century.

What is the entity in question? It is Liberty University, originally known as Liberty Baptist College, whose progenitor is also its chancellor, the Reverend Jerry Falwell. It is a fully accredited institution of higher education nestled on 4,400 acres in Lynchburg, Virginia. It offers a wide range of undergraduate majors as well as a small selection of graduate programs. It has a museum devoted to proving the biblical account of creationism and a shrine in memory of aborted fetuses.

Liberty University, like nearby CBN University, in Virginia Beach, founded by the Reverend Pat Robertson, is misunderstood by the mass media, which regard those institutions solely as artifacts of "empire-building" television preachers. Although that perception may be partly correct, another purpose is behind the founding of the schools. The Reverend Jerry Falwell stated it plainly: "As far as I'm concerned, Liberty University is one of the best ways that I can [have an] impact [upon] the course of the country. I foresee creating for political conservatism what Harvard has done for political liberalism."[1] In other words, Liberty University is Falwell's long-term vehicle to achieve the political objectives of the Christian Right.

The quest to revamp American politics through the university is an ambitious one. The hope is that graduates of Liberty will disseminate themselves throughout all the various professions of secular society, bringing with them their bedrock biblical values; the expectation is that society will be remade with opinion leaders in the arts, humanities, social sciences, and physical sciences. Already the dissemination of graduates is being felt within religious circles: about seven hundred former Liberty students are serving as pastors of their own churches—a number that is growing by about three hundred annually.[2] Reverend Falwell views Liberty as much more than a seminary, though, hoping that it will be to fundamentalists much like Notre Dame has been to Catholics and Brigham Young has been to Mormons: a center of education, organization, and inspiration.

The creation of institutions like Liberty and CBN University are long-range undertakings designed to complement the short-term efforts of the Christian Right to realize its political objectives. Whether such ambitious long-range pursuits will yield benefits commensurate with those expected is unclear. In the meantime, however, the Christian Right is engaged in a range of political activities "off the Hill" in pursuit of its agenda. Realizing that its opportunities in Congress are limited for the foreseeable future, it has vigorously pursued its other political activities.

Infiltrating the Public Sector

In 1972 an organization was formed by conservatives known as the Committee for Responsible Youth Politics (CRYP). Although its name was later changed to the Conservative Leadership Political Action Committee (CL-PAC), its purpose remained the same: to mobilize young conservatives, especially on college campuses, on behalf of candidates for public office. In 1979 longtime conservative activist Morton Blackwell created the Leadership Institute to supplement its efforts. It was established as a non-profit, non-partisan public education foundation devoted to "free enterprise, national defense and traditional family moral values."[3] The newly created institute held several seminars during the early 1980s, when Ronald Reagan was elected as president and Blackwell agreed to serve as a White House liaison to the conservative religious community.

In 1984 Blackwell left his position at the White House in order to work full time with the institute, which then consisted of four separate divisions: (1) a "youth leadership seminar" intended to identify and train young conservatives on college campuses; (2) a "job and talent bank" that tried to match conservative activists with job openings in the Reagan administration; (3) a "student publications seminar" designed to train college students in the basics of beginning a conservative publication;

and (4) a "leadership training service" that served as a clearinghouse for some four hundred conservative speakers who were willing to deliver lectures and hold training sessions in their areas of expertise. The institute, including all its subdivisions, was quartered in rented offices in the National Right-to-Work building in Springfield, Virginia.

The Leadership Institute is a principal means by which the Christian Right now pursues and advances its political agenda. Much like Liberty University, the institute attempts to place religious conservatives in various key positions, though it has restricted its efforts to politics and government. A partial listing of its alumni is evidence of its success in placing people in the political process: Lilli Hausenfluck (legislative assistant to former New Right Senator Jepsen), Stephen Markman (Senator Hatch's top aide on the Constitution Subcommittee and more recently an assistant attorney general), and Grover Rees (University of Texas Law Professor, originator of the first draft of the Reagan school-prayer amendment, and now Chief Justice of American Samoa). Some of the individuals listed in the institute's "leadership training service" to speak at conservative gatherings included Roy Jones (Moral Majority), Dick Dingman (Moral Majority), Bill Billings (NCAC), and Gary Curran (Moral Majority and American Life Lobby).[4] The era of overt Christian Right activity on the Hill is probably over, but the Leadership Institute continues to train and place its students in the political process, awaiting future battles over the moral agenda.

The impact of the Leadership Institute is impossible to estimate at this juncture. Interestingly, its activities are virtually unnoticed by the mass media and the community of scholars. The neglect is reminiscent of the manner in which the fundamentalist mobilization was not recognized until the movement literally exploded on the scene. The systematic infiltration of the public sector by religious conservatives is similarly unnoticed; over the long term, the impact of the infiltration may be pronounced.

Heading to the Courts

Another avenue pursued by the Christian Right off the Hill is litigation. From the very outset, the movement has viewed this technique as a means of achieving its agenda. One of the initial divisions of the Moral Majority, for instance, was the Legal Defense Fund. The Christian Right did not pursue litigation in earnest during the first Reagan term, however, while it focused on Capitol Hill. Besides, at that time the judiciary was considered more of an adversary than an opportunity. Over time, the Judicial Branch has been remade in a manner that opens up litigation as a viable strategy for the Christian Right.

Since Ronald Reagan assumed the presidency in January 1981, he has substantially influenced this branch. He has appointed some 333 of 761 (44%) federal court judges, more than any other president in the nation's history; and he has elevated conservative Associate Justice William H. Rehnquist to the position of chief justice of the Supreme Court, as well as appointed Associate Justices Sandra Day O'Connor, Antonin Scalia, and Anthony M. Kennedy. This reconstitution of the judiciary mostly went unnoticed by the media in the furor over the unsuccessful nominations of Robert Bork and Douglas Ginsburg to the Supreme Court.[5]

The various appointments by no means ensure Christian Right victories in the judiciary. During the second Reagan term, for instance, the Supreme Court struck down a law allowing public school instructors to teach secular subjects in parochial schools, an Alabama law providing for a "moment of silence," and a Connecticut law requiring employers to give workers their Sabbath day off.[6] In the summer of 1987 alone, the Court ruled against a Louisiana law requiring the teaching of "creation science" alongside evolution, and the 6th Circuit Court of Appeals overturned a district-court decision that seven fundamentalist families were entitled to damages because the public school textbooks their children used offended their Christian beliefs.[7]

On the other hand, the Supreme Court refused in 1986 to consider a challenge to the constitutionality of the equal access law passed by the Congress.[8] Then, too, the Court's 7–2 decision in Roe v. Wade (1973) that a woman is entitled to an abortion based upon a constitutional right to privacy was affirmed by only a 5–4 margin in 1986.[9] More to the point, the simple fact that Reagan was able to "pack" the judiciary virtually ensures that the concerns of the fundamentalists will retain prominence on the systematic agenda, even if victories prove elusive. The Christian Right can marshal test cases in the jurisdiction of Reagan appointees.[10]

The possibilities for litigation are endless, and might include attempts to overturn (or modify) the Supreme Court's school-prayer and abortion decisions, to prohibit sexually explicit cable and satellite television programming, to end surrogate motherhood, to force medical care for newly born handicapped infants, to stop "gay" from being defined as a classification deserving of constitutional protections, and to prohibit RU 486—the "abortion pill" already available in Europe—from being marketed in the United States.[11] One final area ripe for litigation is "secular humanism." In October 1986 Judge W. Brevard Hand, of Mobile, Alabama, ruled that "secular humanism" constituted a religion that was illegally advocated in the textbooks of Alabama public school children.[12] Some 130 challenges in forty-four states have already been made to curriculum content in the public schools.[13]

Back to the Grassroots

Although litigation is an attractive possibility because of a revamped judiciary and the endless opportunities that presents, it suffers from two major drawbacks. It is both slow and expensive. For those reasons, the Christian Right may place more emphasis on state and local struggles. The benefits of such activity are numerous: (1) It keeps the moral agenda visible to the public; (2) It indirectly pressures the Congress, whose members must stay responsive to grass-roots constituencies; and (3) It attracts new supporters, to whom the struggles in Washington, D.C., are psychologically distant, but to whom local struggles are highly significant.

Some of this activity is issue-oriented, where results have already been achieved. For instance, after fundamentalist boycotts of neighborhood Seven-Eleven stores because they sold *Playboy* and *Penthouse* magazines, Southland Corporation, the parent company, ordered them to remove the magazines. Other similar boycotts aimed at stores still carrying the magazines were successful for a time, including two prominent chains in New England.[14] In Oklahoma, fundamentalist picketing convinced Cox Cable to remove the Playboy channel from its cable television programming.[15] In Maine, the heavily fundamentalist Christian Civic League managed to have an anti-pornography referendum placed on the ballot in 1986; and in 1988 its leader, Jaspar Wyman, opened his bid to unseat Democratic incumbent U.S. Senator George Mitchell.[16] In Indiana, fundamentalists weakened child-abuse laws out of a conviction that the discipline of children was a prerogative of the parents; in Illinois, they nearly convinced the legislature to loosen rules against corporal punishment at day-care centers.[17] In Louisiana, as was noted earlier, fundamentalists convinced the legislature to pass a measure allowing the teaching of "creation science" alongside evolution.[18]

In addition to those activities, it is important to point out that there are other state and local issues that have yet to be pursued with vigor by the Christian Right: the dispensation of contraceptives in some of the nation's public high schools, the breadth of permissible equal access activities in the schools, and the rights of fundamentalist schools that refuse to submit to state accreditation. In 1984 the accreditation issue rose to the forefront in Nebraska, when the state arrested the fathers of children who attended a fundamentalist school in Louisville that refused to submit to accreditation. To avoid arrest, the Reverend Everett Sileven, who headed the school, fled across state lines. Fundamentalist pastors from all over the nation traveled to Louisville in support of the school, and after weeks of negotiation a compromise was worked out that allowed it to remain open and submit to a relaxed form of accreditation. Because seventeen other states have mandatory accreditation laws similar to those of Nebraska, the issue is likely to surface elsewhere.[19] It is one that can give vigor to the Christian Right in select locales.

Other Christian Right local activity is oriented toward elections. The movement is trying to turn out fundamentalist voters, recruit people to run for political office (for example, Donald J. Lynch in Indiana's Second District, Jim Golden in Tennessee's Third District, Stuart Epperson in North Carolina's Fifth District, all of whom were unsuccessful in 1986), and assume control of the Republican party apparatus in various localities. The *Congressional Quarterly* noted that the last of these processes began in 1986 in such states as Arizona, South Carolina, Tennessee, Michigan, Oregon, Nebraska, Indiana, and Minnesota.[20] According to that source, challenging for control "is an increasingly organized and politically sophisticated network" of conservative Christians.[21] Similar battles may be expected in North Carolina, Alabama, Idaho, Iowa, Oklahoma, and Florida—all states that elected New Right senators in the 1980s. Those states will be the fundamentalist electoral battlegrounds in the 1990s.

The major story of Christian Right electoral activism at the state and local levels, however, was the mobilization on behalf of the Reverend Pat Robertson for the 1988 Republican presidential nomination. On September 17, 1986, he announced that he would run for the presidency if three million registered voters signed petitions backing his candidacy. In 1987 he scored victories over five Republican opponents in delegate selection contests in South Carolina and Michigan and in straw polls in Iowa and Maine. During the primary/caucus season, he placed first among the Republicans in the Washington and Alaska caucuses, second in the Iowa and Michigan caucuses, second in the South Dakota and Minnesota primaries, and third in the New Hampshire primary.

Reverend Robertson's campaign fizzled on "Super Tuesday," the day in March when seventeen Republican caucuses and primaries were held simultaneously. That day, he won only in Washington, losing races all across the South to Senator Robert Dole and Vice-President George Bush, including states like South Carolina, where he had initially predicted victory. What caused the demise of the Robertson campaign? Arguably, it was a function of the mistakes he had committed heading into "Super Tuesday." Among other things, he intimated that the campaign of Vice-President Bush had leaked the information about Jimmy Swaggert's misconduct in an attempt to undercut his campaign, that the Soviet Union had placed missiles in Cuba, and that the Christian Broadcasting Network had informed the State Department of the precise location of American hostages in Lebanon.[22] All those charges led to vehement Reagan administration denials and undercut the credibility and viability of the Robertson campaign. The mistakes he committed in the campaign, like those made by the Moral Majority on Capitol Hill in pursuit of its moral agenda, tarnished his reputation. The collective mistakes were evidence of the lack of political sophistication exhibited by relatively new entrants into politics.

Whether the Christian Right will be successful in state and local arenas in the coming years is unclear. Gary Jarmin thinks so, remarking perhaps prophetically, "If I had to guess, I would say it is at the local level where our future lies and where our successes will be found. Grassroots successes will not be seen on the front page of the newspapers, but they will be there to the careful observer."[23] In view of the early successes of the Robertson campaign, this is a reasonable prognostication.

A Squirt Gun

All the activities of the Christian Right in the 1980s suggest that the motivation within its ranks is high. It worked for the election and reelection of Ronald Reagan. It lobbied on the Hill with vigor. More recently, it tried to infiltrate the bureaucracy, exploit the courts, and carry the moral agenda to various states and locales. It even ran one of its own for the presidency. At the time the Christian Right formed, Bill Billings remarked that, though fundamentalists were not very sophisticated politically, they were willing "to charge hell with a squirt gun."[24] Many of them are still willing to do so, which portends a period of intense conflict between the Christian Right and the secular state over the shape of the nation's political agenda.

Notes

Introduction

1. Roger W. Cobb and Charles E. Elder, *Participation in American Politics: The Dynamics of Agenda-Building*, 2nd ed. (Baltimore: Johns Hopkins University Press, 1983), 14.
2. Ibid.
3. Ibid.
4. Ibid., 89.
5. John W. Kingdon, *Agendas, Alternatives, and Public Policies* (Boston: Little, Brown & Co., 1984), 15–16.
6. Albert J. Menendez, *Religion at the Polls* (Philadelphia: Westminster Press, 1977), 104.
7. Bill Keller, "Evangelical Conservatives Move from Pews to Polls, But Can They Sway Congress?" *Congressional Quarterly Weekly Report*, September 6, 1980, 2630.
8. To date, only two scholars have treated Christian Right activities on the Hill: James L. Guth, "The New Christian Right," in *The New Christian Right*, ed. Robert C. Liebman and Robert Wuthnow (New York: Aldine, 1983), 34–35; and Allen D. Hertzke, *Representing God in Washington* (Knoxville: University of Tennessee Press, 1988). Neither of these works greatly impinges upon this study. Guth's treatment was only four paragraphs in length and Hertzke's discussion of the Christian Right was but one part of a broader study of the role of religious lobbies in American politics.
9. Anson Shupe and William Stacey, "The Moral Majority Constituency," in *The New Christian Right*, ed. Robert C. Liebman and Robert Wuthnow (New York: Aldine, 1983), 111. More recent scholarship suggests that the constituency of the Christian Right has become

more upwardly mobile over time. See Wade Clark Roof and William McKinney, "Denominational America and the New Religious Pluralism," in *The Annals of the American Academy of Political and Social Science*, ed. Wade Clark Roof, 480 (July 1985): 32. See also Wade Clark Roof, "The New Fundamentalism: Rebirth of Political Religion in America," in *Prophetic Religions and Politics: Religion and the Political Order*, ed. Jeffrey K. Hadden and Anson Shupe (New York: Paragon House, 1986), 26–27.

10. Robert Wuthnow, "The Political Rebirth of American Evangelicals," in *The New Christian Right*, ed. Robert C. Liebman and Robert Wuthnow (New York: Aldine, 1983), 168–174.

11. Shupe and Stacey, "The Moral Majority Constituency," 106.

12. Clyde Wilcox, "Evangelicals and Fundamentalists in the New Christian Right," *Journal for the Scientific Study of Religion* 25 (September 1986): 357.

13. Wuthnow, "The Political Rebirth of American Evangelicals," 167.

14. Albert J. Menendez, "Religious Lobbies," *Liberty* 77 (March/April 1982): 5.

15. Wilcox, "Evangelicals and Fundamentalists in the New Christian Right," 357.

Chapter 1. Politicizing the Faithful

1. Frye Gaillard, "Right Wing Religion," *The Progressive* 44 (April 1980): 13.

2. Interview with Bob Billings, July 26, 1984.

3. Eileen Ogintz, "Evangelists Seek Political Clout," *Chicago Tribune*, January 13, 1980, 5.

4. Kenneth Briggs, "Evangelicals Hear a Plea: Politics Now," *New York Times*, August 24, 1980, 33.

5. Ibid.

6. Ibid.

7. Bruce Campbell, *The American Electorate* (New York: Holt, Rinehart & Winston, 1979), 70–109.

8. A good study is Arthur Miller, "Political Issues and Trust in Government, 1964–1970," *American Political Science Review* 68 (September 1974): 951–972.

9. The figures are reprinted in Abner J. Mikva and Patti B. Saris, *The American Congress* (New York: Franklin Watts, 1983), 258.

10. Interview with Phil Crane, May 31, 1984.

11. Interview with James McKenna, May 18, 1984.

12. Ibid.

13. Included in this group were Tom Daschle, Bob Edgar, Charles Bergstrom, John Buchanan, Barry Lynn, and Robert Drinan.

14. Interview with Barry Lynn, June 1, 1984.

15. *McCollum* v. *Board of Education*, 333 U.S. 203 (1948); *Engel* v. *Vitale*, 370 U.S. 421 (1962); *Abington School District* v. *Schempp*, 374 U.S. 203 (1963); *Epperson* v. *Arkansas*, 393 U.S. 97 (1968); *Swann* v. *Charlotte-Mecklenburg Board of Education*, 403 U.S. 912 (1971); *Roe* v. *Wade*, 410 U.S. 113 (1973).

16. Interview with Roy Jones, July 17, 1984.

17. Interview with Gary Jarmin, July 27, 1984.

18. Interview with Phil Crane, May 31, 1984; Henry Hyde, June 26, 1984; Forest Montgomery, June 13, 1984.

19. Anson Shupe and William Stacey, "The Moral Majority Constituency," in *The New Christian Right*, ed. Robert C. Liebman and Robert Wuthnow (New York: Aldine, 1983), 108. The authors found that 46 percent of Moral Majority supporters agreed that evolution should be taught in the schools.

20. Ibid.

21. Based on the mass-mailings of the Moral Majority that I received throughout 1984.

22. Interview with Stan Hastey, June 22, 1984.

23. The argument is that the Congress may strip, or restrict, the jurisdiction of the Supreme Court in accordance with Article III, Section 2, of the Constitution. As will be discussed later, the Christian Right backed such an approach in the 99th Congress (1985–86).

24. George Gallup, *The Gallup Poll: Public Opinion, 1972–1977* (Wilmington, Del.: Scholarly Resources, 1978), 1007–1008.

25. See Alvin M. Josephy, Jr., *On the Hill* (New York: Touchstone, 1979), 378–380.

26. For example, see U.S. Congress, House Committee on Standards of Official Conduct, *Ethics Manual for Members and Employees of the House of Representatives*, 98th Congress, 2nd sess., 1984.

27. Kevin P. Phillips, *Post-Conservative America* (New York: Random House, 1982), 190.

28. James Woods, "Religious Fundamentalism and the New Right," *Journal of Church and State* 22 (Autumn 1980): 419. Woods also cites other practical matters for the rise of the movement, such as the Supreme Court's abortion and school-prayer decisions.

29. Robert Wuthnow, "The Political Rebirth of American Evangelicals," in *The New Christian Right*, ed. Robert C. Liebman and Robert Wuthnow (New York: Aldine, 1983), 176–177.

30. Ibid., 176.

31. The trends are presented as gospel in American government texts. For example, see David Edwards, *The American Political Experience*, 3rd ed. (Englewood Cliffs, N.J.: Prentice-Hall, 1985), 588–589.

32. Interview with Phil Crane, May 31, 1984.

33. Winthrop S. Hudson, *Religion in America*, 3rd ed. (New York: Charles Scribner's Sons, 1981), 450.

34. Ibid. See also A. James Reichley, *Religion in American Public Life* (Washington, D.C.: Brookings Institution, 1985), 312.

35. John L. Kater, Jr., *Christians on the Right* (New York: Seabury Press, 1982), 13.

36. Tim LaHaye, *The Battle for the Mind* (Old Tappan, N.J.: Fleming H. Revell Co., 1980), 121.

37. Hal Lindsey, *The Late Great Planet Earth* (Grand Rapids, Mich.: Zondervan Publishing House, 1970), 60.

38. "Arab Lobby: Opening Doors That Were Previously Closed," *Current American Government* (Washington, D.C.: Congressional Quarterly, 1978), 93–99.

39. Ibid., 96.

40. Lindsey, *The Late Great Planet Earth*, 156.

41. Ibid., 145–155.

42. Ibid., 160–168.

43. Ibid., 43. Lindsey implies that Armageddon will occur around 1988 because the founding of Israel was 1948, a biblical generation is approximately forty years, and Armageddon is supposed to happen a generation after the founding of Israel.

44. Kater, *Christians on the Right*, 79.

45. Interview with Stan Hastey, August 17, 1984.

46. Reichley, *Religion in American Public Life*, 309.

47. Erling Jorstad, *The Politics of Moralism* (Minneapolis: Augsburg, 1981), 94–95.

48. Alan Crawford, *Thunder on the Right* (New York: Pantheon Books, 1980), 160.

49. Reichley, *Religion in American Public Life*, 308–309.

50. Ogintz, "Evangelists Seek Political Clout," 5.

51. Moral Majority fund-raising letter, April 30, 1984.

52. See LaHaye, *The Battle for the Mind*; James Robison, *Attack on the Family* (Wheaton, Ill.: Tyndale, 1982).

53. Shupe and Stacey, "The Moral Majority Constituency," 110.

54. Ibid.

55. Louise Lorentzen, "Evangelical Life Style Concerns Expressed in Political Action," *Sociological Analysis* 41 (Summer 1980): 153.

56. Shupe and Stacey, "The Moral Majority Constituency," 114.

57. Reichley, *Religion in American Public Life*, 243–244.

58. Moral Majority fund-raising letter, September 28, 1984.

59. Interview with Henry Hyde, June 26, 1984.

60. Richard A. Viguerie, *The New Right* (Falls Church, Va.: The Viguerie Co., 1981), 132.

61. Interview with Charles Bergstrom, August 6, 1984.

62. Reichley, *Religion in American Public Life*, 256–257.

63. See Constant H. Jacquet, Jr., ed., *Yearbook of American Churches* (New York: Council Press, 1970). See also Constant H. Jacquet, Jr., ed., *Yearbook of American and Canadian Churches* (Nashville: Abingdon Press, 1980). The numbers from these two sources were compared and the percentage increases calculated.

64. Ibid.

65. Dean M. Kelley, *Why Conservative Churches Are Growing* (Macon, Ga.: Mercer University Press, 1986), 175.

66. Ibid.

67. Wade Clark Roof and William McKinney, "Denominational America and the New Religious Pluralism," in *The Annals of the American Academy of Political and Social Science*, ed. Wade Clark Roof, 480 (July 1985): 31–32.

68. Benton Johnson, "Liberal Protestantism: End of the Road?" in *The Annals of the American Academy of Political and Social Science*, ed. Wade Clark Roof, 480 (July 1985): 42.

69. Ralph Clark Chandler, "Worshipping a Past That Never Was," *Christianity and Crisis*, February 15, 1982, 24. See also Viguerie, *The New Right*, 126.

70. Crawford, *Thunder on the Right*, 161.

71. Chandler, "Worshipping a Past That Never Was," 24.

72. Federal Communications Commission, Opinion 75-946, August 13, 1975, 1, available upon request from the FCC, 1919 M St., N.W., Washington, D.C., 20554.

73. Ibid.

74. Ibid., 10.

75. Ibid., 10.

76. Ibid., 1–2.

77. Federal Communications Commission, Report 8310-RM-

2493, 1, available upon request from the FCC, 1919 M St., N.W., Washington, D.C., 20554.

78. Phone conversation with FCC official, May 22, 1984. The official requested anonymity and therefore does not appear on the interview list in the Bibliography.

79. Elder Witt, "Court Upholds Power of the IRS to Deny Tax-Exempt Status to Schools That Discriminate," *Congressional Quarterly Weekly Report*, May 28, 1983, 1077.

80. Only thirteen states require state accreditation of private Christian schools. States that do not require it usually do not compile information on the number of such schools. Many private schools voluntarily seek accreditation, but because they are not required to do so, it is impossible to estimate their numbers. Many of those schools may be literally "household operations." For a general discussion of the issue, see George Hansen, *To Harass Our People* (Washington, D.C.: Positive Publications, 1984), ss12–ss20.

81. During the first Reagan term, the National Education Association lobbied against a number of measures involving religious expression in the public schools, including school prayer.

82. Interview with Bob Billings, July 26, 1984.

83. Civil rights groups argued that consistent application of the policy for white and black students was inherently discriminatory because of disparities in the numbers of students of each race. For a discussion of such matters, see House Committee on Ways and Means, *Administration's Change in Federal Policy Regarding the Tax Status of Racially Discriminatory Private Schools*, 97th Cong., 2nd sess., February 4, 1982.

84. Stan Hastey and Warner Ragsdale, "Right Religion Right Politics?" *Home Missions* 51 (September/October 1980): 68–69.

85. George Church, "Politics From the Pulpit," *Time*, October 13, 1980, 35.

86. Joan Sweeney, "Evangelicals Seeking to Establish Political Force," *Los Angeles Times*, May 19, 1980, 21.

87. 456 U.S. 922 (1983). The companion case was *Goldsboro Christian Schools* v. *U.S.* (1983).

88. Witt, "Court Upholds Power of IRS to Deny Tax-Exempt Status to Schools That Discriminate," 1077.

89. Among other things, the administraton initially sought to let the Voting Rights Act lapse, restrict affirmative action quotas, and limit regulations affecting the operations of private Christian schools. For the administration's view, see *Administration's Change in Federal Policy Re-*

garding the Tax Status of Racially Discriminatory Private Schools, 140–171.

90. Witt, "Court Upholds Power of IRS to Deny Tax-Exempt Status to Schools That Discriminate," 1077.

91. 456 U.S. 922 (1983).

92. Albert J. Menendez, *Religion at the Polls* (Philadelphia: Westminster Press, 1977), 102.

93. Ibid.

94. "Jimmy Carter: A Candid Conversation with the Democratic Candidate for the Presidency," *Playboy*, November 1976, 86.

95. Ibid.

96. Curtis Wilkie, "Righteousness from the Right," *Boston Globe*, October 12, 1980, 29.

97. Ibid.

98. Ibid.

99. Ibid.

100. Menendez, *Religion at the Polls*, 103.

101. Ibid., 103–104.

102. Gallup, *The Gallup Poll: Public Opinion, 1972–1977*, 875; Jeffrey Brudney and Gary Copeland, "Evangelicals as a Political Force," *Social Science Quarterly* 65 (December 1984): 1078.

103. Stan Hastey, "Carter: Religious Right Influence to Decline," *Baptist Press*, May 28, 1981, 1.

104. Jorstad, *The Politics of Moralism*, 21.

105. See Jeffrey K. Hadden and Charles E. Swann, *Prime Time Preachers* (Reading, Mass.: Addison-Wesley, 1981), 47–67. The authors emphasize the influence of television evangelism, not the conflicts with the secular state, as the central force behind the rise of the Christian Right.

Chapter 2. Rallies and Tallies

1. Interview with Charles Bergstrom, June 18, 1984.

2. Flo Conway and Jim Siegelman, *The Holy Terror* (Garden City, N.Y.: Doubleday & Co., 1982), 189.

3. Murray Edelman, *The Symbolic Uses of Politics* (Urbana: University of Illinois Press, 1964), 114–129.

4. Seymour Martin Lipset and Earl Rabb, *The Politics of Unreason* (New York: Harper & Row, 1970), 39–47, 209–245, 338–377.

5. For the definition, see Tim LaHaye, *The Battle for the Mind*

(Old Tappan, N.J.: Fleming H. Revell Co., 1980), 26. See also John W. Whitehead, *The Second American Revolution* (Elgin, Ill.: David C. Cook Publishing, 1982); Gary North, *Conspiracy: A Biblical View* (Fort Worth: Dominion Press, 1986).

6. LaHaye, *The Battle for the Mind*, 26.

7. Moral Majority fund-raising letters, February 9, 1984, and May 1, 1984.

8. LaHaye, *The Battle for the Mind*, 10.

9. Interview with Stan Hastey, June 22, 1984.

10. David Nyhan, "Attacks on Religious Right Put Its Influence in Doubt," *Boston Globe*, October 28, 1980, 2.

11. Interview with Forest Montgomery, June 13, 1984.

12. Donahue Transcript #02275, available from Multimedia Entertainment, Box 2011, Cincinnati, Ohio 45201.

13. Interview with Bob Edgar, May 31, 1984.

14. Interview with Robert Drinan, June 1, 1984.

15. Joseph L. Conn, "The New Christian Politics," *Church & State* 33 (July/August 1980): 16.

16. Jeffrey K. Hadden and Charles E. Swann, *Prime Time Preachers* (Reading, Mass.: Addison-Wesley, 1981), 127–129.

17. Ibid., 129. The rallies were part of a "Clean Up America" campaign.

18. Ibid., 129.

19. Conn, "The New Christian Politics," 16.

20. Wes McCune, *Group Research Report*, March 26, 1980, 9.

21. Conn, "The New Christian Politics," 16–17.

22. Ibid., 17. The author of the quote was Phil Shank, a contributor to *Sojourners* magazine.

23. Interview with Tom Bovard, July 11, 1984.

24. 2 Chronicles 7: 14. All Bible verses are taken from Herbert G. May and Bruce M. Metzger, eds., *The New Oxford Annotated Bible* (New York: Oxford University Press, 1973).

25. Conn, "The New Christian Politics," 16.

26. Interview with Stan Hastey, June 22, 1984.

27. Ibid.

28. Interview with Tom Bovard, July 11, 1984.

29. Hadden and Swann, *Prime Time Preachers*, 129.

30. Ibid.

31. Ibid., 129–130.

32. Interview with Tom Bovard, July 11, 1984.

33. Hadden and Swann, *Prime Time Preachers*, 130–131.

34. Ibid., 131.

35. "Religious Right Talks Politics," *Guardian*, September 3, 1980, 4.

36. Hadden and Swann, *Prime Time Preachers*, 130–131. The rally organizers deliberately staged a spectacle because the previous mass rally had attracted so little attention.

37. Bill Stall, "Evangelicals Pin Their Faith on Political Action," *Los Angeles Times*, August 24, 1980, 8; Kathy Sawyer, "Christian Soldiers March to Different Drummer," *Washington Post*, December 27, 1984, 1.

38. "Religious Right Talks Politics," 4.

39. Erling Jorstad, *The Politics of Moralism* (Minneapolis: Augsburg, 1981), 94.

40. Ibid., 95.

41. Ibid., 95–96.

42. Ibid., 95.

43. For an early analysis of the Robertson campaign, see Phil Gailey, "A Bitter Struggle Splits South Carolina G.O.P.," *New York Times*, April 6, 1987, B9.

44. Jorstad, *The Politics of Moralism*, 95.

45. Ibid., 96.

46. Interview with Forest Montgomery, June 13, 1984.

47. Frye Gaillard, "Right Wing Religion," *The Progressive* 44 (April 1980): 13.

48. George Vecsey, "Some Evangelicals Lean to Carter After Meetings," *New York Times*, January 28, 1980, 5.

49. See Eileen Ogintz, "Evangelists Seek Political Clout," *Chicago Tribune*, January 13, 1980, 5; George Vecsey, "Militant Television Preachers Try to Weld Fundamentalist Christians' Political Power," *New York Times*, January 21, 1980, A21; Joan Sweeney, "Evangelicals Seeking to Establish Political Force, " *Los Angeles Times*, May 19, 1980, 1 +; David Nyhan, "The Growing Political Clout of America's Christian Right," *Boston Globe*, June 15, 1980, 9, 11.

50. See James Mann, "Old Time Religion on the Offensive," *U.S. News and World Report*, April 7, 1980, 40–42; "Born Again at the Ballot Box," *Time*, April 14, 1980, 94; Allan Mayer, "A Tide of Born Again," *Newsweek*, September 15, 1980, 28 +.

51. Bill Keller, "Evangelical Conservatives Move from Pews to Polls, But Can They Sway Congress?" *Congressional Quarterly Weekly Report*, September 6, 1980, 2627.

52. See Jean M. Marra, ed., *Reader's Guide to Periodical Literature* 39–40 (New York: H. W. Wilson Co., 1980–81).

53. Joseph Bloomfield, ed., *Social Sciences Index* 6–9 (New York: H. W. Wilson Co., 1980–83).

54. Harvey L. Holmes, ed., *The New York Times Index, 1979* 67 (New York: New York Times Co., 1980).

55. See Richard A. Viguerie, *The New Right* (Falls Church, Va.: The Viguerie Co., 1981), 123–136.

56. Edelman, *The Symbolic Uses of Politics*, 14–16.

57. The establishment of such groups fits the "pluralist" paradigm in American politics. For example, see David B. Truman, *The Governmental Process*, 2nd ed. (New York: Alfred A. Knopf, 1971).

58. For a discussion of the organization's activities, see Arthur Unger, "TV Ads Try to Offset Religious Right," *Christian Science Monitor*, October 21, 1980, 6.

59. Keller, "Evangelical Conservatives Move from Pews to Polls, But Can They Sway Congress?" 2627.

60. "1986 Already Exceeds Most Election Years in Instances of Religious Intolerance, Study Finds," August 3, 1986, 2. This document was published by and available from People for the American Way, 2000 M Street N.W., Washington, D.C., 20036.

61. The McGovern campaign staff prepared a thirty-page document detailing the right-wing negative campaigning against him and distributed it to Democratic county committee chairpersons in July 1980.

62. Marjorie Hyer, "Outflanking the Right: Mainline Clerics Oppose the Evangelicals," *Washington Post*, October 21, 1980, 8.

63. Based on a visit I made to the center in June 1984, during which I examined its files.

64. Nyhan, "Attacks on Religious Right Put Its Influence in Doubt," 2.

65. Robert Linder, "Militarism in Nazi Thought and in the American Religious Right," *Journal of Church and State* 24 (Spring 1982): 263–279.

66. Nyhan, "Attacks on Religious Right Put Its Influence in Doubt," 2.

67. Hyer, "Outflanking the Right," 8.

68. Kenneth Briggs, "Evangelical Leaders Hail Election and Ask Continuation of Efforts," *New York Times*, January 28, 1981, 8.

69. Jim Castelli, "Senator Offers Plan to Battle Religious Right," *Washington Star*, June 20, 1981, 6.

70. "Christian Right Equated with Iran's Mullahs," *Washington Star*, September 24, 1980, 4.
71. Ibid.

Chapter 3. The Visible Actors

1. See Edwin Warner, "New Resolve by the New Right," *Time*, December 8, 1980, 24–25; Arthur Miller and Martin Wattenberg, "Politics from the Pulpit," *Public Opinion Quarterly* 48 (Spring 1984): 301–317; Jeffrey Brudney and Gary Copeland, "Evangelicals as a Political Force," *Social Science Quarterly* 65 (December 1984): 1072–1079.
2. John W. Kingdon, *Agendas, Alternatives, and Public Politics* (Boston: Little, Brown & Co., 1984), 4.
3. Ibid., 20.
4. Ibid.
5. Ibid., 54.
6. Ibid. Kingdon suggests that the interest groups probably perform the alternative specification role more than the agenda-setting role.
7. For the distinction between the two types of agendas, see Roger W. Cobb and Charles E. Elder, *Participation in American Politics: The Dynamics of Agenda-Building*, 2nd ed. (Baltimore: Johns Hopkins University Press, 1983), 14.
8. David Hoffman, "President Skips Church for Parishioners' Sakes," *Washington Post*, March 8, 1984, A3. Following a series of religious references by Reagan during the 1984 campaign, Democratic Speaker O'Neill pointed out that Reagan rarely attended church; this statement engendered a controversy.
9. John H. Simpson, "Moral Issues and Status Politics," in *The New Christian Right*, ed. Robert C. Liebman and Robert Wuthnow (New York: Aldine, 1983), 198.
10. Interview with Doug Shaddix, July 27, 1984.
11. Ibid.
12. Interview with Charles Bergstrom, June 18, 1984.
13. Kenneth Briggs, "Evangelical Preachers Gather to Polish Their Politics," *New York Times*, August 21, 1980, B9.
14. Lou Cannon, "Reagan Disagrees with Fundamentalist Teachings on Prayer," *Washington Post*, October 4, 1980, A6.
15. Adam Clymer, "Fire and Brimstone," *New York Times*, March 9, 1983, A18; William Schneider, "Old Politics Yield to New U.S. Ideologies," *Los Angeles Times*, March 13, 1983, 3; Arthur Schlesinger,

Jr., "Pretension in the Presidential Pulpit," *Wall Street Journal*, March 17, 1983, 26; "Preaching to the Choir," *Church & State* 36 (March 1983): 6–8.

16. Juan Williams, "Reagan Calls for Prayer Bill, Renewal of Moral Attitudes," *Washington Post*, March 7, 1984, A1+; Marjorie Hyer, "Evangelicals Back Reagan, But Reject Political Label," *Washington Post*, March 10, 1984, B6.

17. The interviewee also said that Reagan was not religious.

18. "1986 Already Exceeds Most Election Years in Instances of Religious Intolerance, Study Finds," August 3, 1986, 18. This document was published by and available from People for the American Way, 2000 M Street N.W., Washington, D.C., 20036.

19. Reprinted in the *Congressional Quarterly Almanac* XXXIX (Washington, D.C.: Congressional Quarterly, 1983), 3E–6E.

20. Reprinted in the *Congressional Quarterly Weekly Report*, January 28, 1984, 146–150. For a content analysis of Reagan's State of the Union messages that partially addresses his support for the moral agenda, see Matthew C. Moen, "The Political Agenda of Ronald Reagan," *Presidential Studies Quarterly*, XVIII (Fall 1988): 775–85.

21. Kingdon, *Agendas, Alternatives, and Public Policies*, 197.

22. The quote is reprinted in Dom Bonafede, "New Right Preaches a New Religion, and Ronald Reagan Is Its Prophet," *National Journal*, May 2, 1981, 779.

23. Nadine Cohodas, "Emphasis on Economy Kept Divisive Social Issues on Back Burner in 1981," *Congressional Quarterly Weekly Report*, January 2, 1982, 3.

24. Reprinted in the *Congressional Quarterly Weekly Report*, January 28, 1984, 148.

25. Bonafede, "New Right Preaches a New Religion, and Ronald Reagan Is Its Prophet," 780.

26. "Preaching to the Choir," 6. Reagan also drew criticism from the fundamentalist community when he replied in response to a reporter's question that he would "consult his horoscope." See Bill Keller, "Evangelical Conservatives Move from Pews to Polls, But Can They Sway Congress?" *Congressional Quarterly Weekly Report*, September 6, 1980, 2634. That remark later achieved new significance when former White House Chief of Staff Donald Regan revealed that astrology was a major factor in dictating the president's schedule. See Donald Regan, *For the Record* (New York: Harcourt Brace Jovanovich, 1988), 3–5.

27. Interview with John Buchanan, August 1, 1984.

28. Interview with Stan Hastey, August 17, 1984; "Preaching to the Choir," 8.

29. Dick Kirschten, "Reagan Looks to Religious Leaders for Continuing Support in 1984," *National Journal*, August 20, 1983, 1731.

30. Interview with Bill Billings, May 24, 1984.

31. Interview with Stan Hastey, August 17, 1984.

32. Interview with Gary Jarmin, July 27, 1984.

33. "Church and Politics," *Congressional Quarterly Weekly Report*, September 15, 1984, 2263.

34. Interview with Bob Edgar, July 23, 1984.

35. See Murray Edelman, *Politics as Symbolic Action* (New York: Academic Press, 1971).

36. Norman J. Ornstein, Robert L. Peabody, and David W. Rhode, "The Senate Through the 1980s," in *Congress Reconsidered*, 3rd ed., ed. Lawrence C. Dodd and Bruce I. Oppenheimer (Washington, D.C.: CQ Press, 1985), 19.

37. Senate Subcommittee on Separation of Powers, *Hearings on the Human Life Bill*, 97th Cong., 1st sess., S. 158; Senate Subcommittee on the Constitution, *Hearings on the Human Life Federalism Amendment*, 97th Cong., 1st sess., S.J. Res. 110; Senate Committee on the Judiciary, *Hearings on a Proposed Constitutional Amendment to Permit Voluntary Prayer*, 97th Cong., 2nd sess., S.J. Res. 199; Senate Committee on Finance, *Hearings on Tuition Tax Credits*, 97th Cong., 1st sess., S. 550; Senate Committee on Finance, *Hearings on Tuition Tax Credit Proposals*, 97th Cong., 2nd sess., S. 2673.

38. House Subcommittee on Elementary, Secondary, and Vocational Education, *Hearings on the Equal Access Act*, 98th Cong., 1st sess., H.R. 2723; Senate Committee on Finance, *Hearings on Tuition Tax Credits*, 98th Cong., 1st sess., S. 528; Senate Subcommittee on the Constitution, *Hearings on the Voluntary School Prayer Amendment*, 98th Cong., 1st sess., S.J. Res. 73; Senate Subcommittee on the Constitution, *Hearings on the Human Life Federalism Amendment*, 98th Cong., 1st sess., S.J. Res. 3.

39. Kingdon, *Agendas, Alternatives, and Public Policies*, 135.

40. Richard Cohen, "Frustrated House Republicans Seek More Aggressive Strategy for 1984 and Beyond," *National Journal*, March 3, 1984, 414.

41. Ibid.

42. Nadine Cohodas, "House Judiciary Committee Approves ERA," *Congressional Quarterly Weekly Report*, November 12, 1983, 2395.

43. Phil Crane related this story during an interview on May 31, 1984.

44. T. R. Reid, "O'Neill Pans Republicans," *Washington Post*, May 12, 1984, A1+.

45. The COS activities created a partisan atmosphere in the 98th Congress. See Diane Granat, "Legislative Business Proceeds Amidst Hill's Political Battles," *Congressional Quarterly Weekly Report*, July 7, 1984, 1599–1614.

46. Nadine Cohodas, "Prayer Issue Engulfs Congress as Senate Embarks on Debate," *Congressional Quarterly Weekly Report*, March 10, 1984, 538.

47. Interview with Gary Jarmin, July 27, 1984.

48. Interview with Morton Blackwell, August 29, 1984.

49. Interview with Phil Crane, May 31, 1984.

50. Kingdon, *Agendas, Alternatives, and Public Policies*, 16–17.

51. Edwin Diamond, "Should the Government Crack Down on TV's Evangelists?" *TV Guide*, November 14, 1981, 6. Diamond headed the "News Study Group" at the Massachusetts Institute of Technology.

52. Jeffrey K. Hadden and Charles E. Swann, *Prime Time Preachers* (Reading, Mass.: Addison-Wesley, 1981), 51.

53. Ibid., 57.

54. Brenda Jenkins, "What the Pastor and Church Can/Cannot Do in an Election," *Liberty* 77 (September/October 1982): 9–10.

55. Ibid., 10.

56. Diamond, "Should the Government Crack Down on TV's Evangelists?" 6.

57. Interview with Frances Zwenig, May 23, 1984.

58. Interview with Stan Hastey, June 22, 1984.

59. Interview with Phil Crane, May 31, 1984.

60. Interview with Roy Jones, July 17, 1984.

61. Interview with Tom Bovard, June 8, 1984.

62. For examples, see Kathy Sawyer, "Christian Soldiers March to Different Drummer," *Washington Post*, December 27, 1984, 1.

Chapter 4. The Hidden Contingent

1. The one exception was Morton Blackwell, who mentioned the role of an academic in drafting a school-prayer proposal. That role will be discussed in a later chapter.

2. Hundreds of sources were examined in connection with this

book; even "insider" publications like the *National Journal* and *Congressional Quarterly* that cover the Congress did not mention academics and bureaucrats in the context of alternative specification.

3. John W. Kingdon, *Agendas, Alternatives, and Public Policies* (Boston: Little, Brown & Co., 1984), 45.

4. Interview with Tom Bovard, June 8, 1984.

5. Interview with Tom Bovard, July 11, 1984.

6. Interview with Gary Jarmin, July 27, 1984.

7. See Alan Crawford, *Thunder on the Right* (New York: Pantheon Books, 1980), 159–164; James L. Guth, "The Politics of the Christian Right," in *Interest Group Politics*, ed. Allan J. Cigler and Burdett A. Loomis (Washington, D.C.: CQ Press, 1983), 68–69.

8. Interview with Stan Hastey, June 22, 1984.

9. For a description of the Library Court, see Richard A. Viguerie, *The New Right* (Falls Church, Va.: The Viguerie Co., 1981), 153–154.

10. L. J. Davis, "Onward Christian Soldiers," *Penthouse*, February 1981, 54.

11. Rob Gurwitt, "The New Right and the GOP: Can This Marriage Be Saved?" *Congressional Quarterly Weekly Report*, August 25, 1984, 2085.

12. Interview with Stan Hastey, June 22, 1984.

13. Interview with Bob Edgar, May 31, 1984.

14. Interview with James McKenna, May 18, 1984.

15. Interview with Phil Crane, May 31, 1984.

16. For the four points, see the following four sources, respectively, Robert Jordan, "Evangelical Victories and Defeats," *Boston Globe*, July 19, 1980, 27; Bruce Buursma, "Reagan's Dismayed Fans Plan Holy War," *Chicago Tribune*, February 1, 1981, 12; Dom Bonafede, "New Right Preaches a New Religion, and Ronald Reagan Is Its Prophet," *National Journal*, May 2, 1981, 779; Richard A. Viguerie, "America's Ruling Class Has Got to Go!" *Washington Post*, November 27, 1983, B1.

17. Gurwitt, "The New Right and the GOP: Can This Marriage Be Saved?" 2086.

18. Interview with Stan Hastey, August 17, 1984.

19. Gurwitt, "The New Right and the GOP: Can This Marriage Be Saved?" 2085.

20. Interview with Gary Jarmin, July 27, 1984.

21. Scheduled interviews with both Richard Viguerie and Howard

Phillips were canceled because of unanticipated events related to the 1984 election.

22. For example, see Viguerie, "America's Ruling Class Has Got to Go!" B1; Viguerie, *The New Right*, 1981.

23. Kingdon, *Agendas, Alternatives, and Public Policies*, 4.

24. For a statement to that effect, see Gurwitt, "The New Right and the GOP: Can This Marriage Be Saved?" 2085.

25. The relevant bills, respectively, were S.J. Res. 73, H.R. 2723, S.J. Res. 3.

26. Interview with Bill Billings, May 24, 1984.

27. Ibid.

28. Bill Keller, "Evangelical Conservatives Move from Pews to Polls, But Can They Sway Congress?" *Congressional Quarterly Weekly Report*, September 6, 1980, 2631.

29. Bill Billings even wrote a "how to become involved" book for fundamentalists entitled *The Christian's Political Action Manual* (Washington, D.C.: NCAC, 1980).

30. Interview with Bill Billings, May 24, 1984.

31. For a discussion of both the activities of Bob Billings and the NCAC, see Keller, "Evangelical Conservatives Move from Pews to Polls, But Can They Sway Congress?" 2628–2630.

32. Rowland Evans and Robert Novak, *The Reagan Revolution* (New York: E. P. Dutton, 1981), 220–221.

33. Billings, *The Christian's Political Action Manual*, 134.

34. Keller, "Evangelical Conservatives Move from Pews to Polls, But Can They Sway Congress?" 2628.

35. Viguerie, *The New Right*, 130. See also Maxwell Glen, "The Electronic Ministers Listen to the Gospel According to the Candidates," *National Journal*, December 22, 1979, 2144.

36. Davis, "Onward Christian Soldiers," 59.

37. Interview with Bob Billings, July 26, 1984.

38. Viguerie, *The New Right*, 9. See also Allan Stang, "Why Secular Humanists Are Making War on the Religious Right," *American Opinion* 25 (November 1982): 10; Joseph L. Conn, "The New Christian Politics," *Church & State* 33 (July/August 1980): 17.

39. Bill Stall, "Evangelicals Pin Their Faith on Political Action," *Los Angeles Times*, August 24, 1980, 9.

40. Interview with Stan Hastey, August 17, 1984.

41. McAteer failed to win the Republican primary and then lost the general election in a third-party bid.

42. Interview with Stan Hastey, August 17, 1984.

43. Jim Castelli, "Religious Groups Hope to Influence Elections," *Washington Star*, April 13, 1980, A3.

44. Jeffrey K. Hadden and Charles E. Swann, *Prime Time Preachers* (Reading, Mass.: Addison-Wesley, 1981), 139.

45. Keller, "Evangelical Conservatives Move from Pews to Polls, But Can They Sway Congress?" 2631.

46. Interview with Gary Jarmin, July 27, 1984.

47. Hadden and Swann, *Prime Time Preachers*, 139.

48. Viguerie, *The New Right*, 129.

49. James Endersby, "The Cross and the Flag," 3–5, paper delivered at the Annual Meeting of the Southwestern Political Science Association, Fort Worth, Texas, March 21–24, 1984.

50. Steven Weisman, "Appeals Backing GOP Said to Portray Views as Contrary to Bible," *New York Times*, November 1, 1980, 9; Jim Castelli, "Pro-Reagan Group Targets Sunday Worshippers," *Washington Star*, November 1, 1980, A4.

51. Interview with Gary Jarmin, July 27, 1984.

52. Steven Pressman and Lenore Webb, "Lobbies Issue Congressional Report Cards," *Congressional Quarterly Weekly Report*, July 14, 1984, 1690.

53. Erling Jorstad, *The Politics of Moralism* (Minneapolis: Augsburg, 1981), 74.

54. Keller, "Evangelical Conservatives Move from Pews to Polls, But Can They Sway Congress?" 2628.

55. Interview with Bob Billings, July 26, 1984.

56. Ibid.

57. Interview with Roy Jones, July 17, 1984.

58. George Church, "Politics from the Pulpit," *Time*, October 13, 1980, 28.

59. Interview with Roy Jones, July 17, 1984.

60. Robert C. Liebman, "Mobilizing the Moral Majority," in *The New Christian Right*, ed. Robert C. Liebman and Robert Wuthnow (New York: Aldine, 1983), 54–55.

61. Ibid., 55.

62. Jeffrey K. Hadden et al., "Why Jerry Falwell Killed the Moral Majority," in *The God Pumpers*, ed. Marshall Fishwick and Ray B. Browne (Bowling Green, Ohio: Bowling Green State University Popular Press, 1987), 106.

63. Ibid.

64. Ibid.

65. Ibid., 110.

66. Ibid.

67. Liebman, "Mobilizing the Moral Majority," 61.

68. Interview with Bob Billings, July 26, 1984.

69. Orrin Hatch, "Christian Conservatives Are a Major Force on U.S. Political Scene," *Human Events*, July 9, 1983, 11.

70. Interview with Bill Billings, May 24, 1984.

Chapter 5. The Agenda

1. Kenneth Briggs, "Evangelical Preachers Gather to Polish Their Politics," *New York Times*, August 21, 1980, B9.

2. Ibid.

3. Leroy Rieselbach, *Congressional Reform* (Washington, D.C.: CQ Press, 1986), 110.

4. Kay Lehman Schlozman and John T. Tierney, *Organized Interests and American Democracy* (New York: Harper & Row, 1986), 153.

5. Interview with Barry Lynn, June 1, 1984.

6. "Religious Right Goes for Bigger Game," *U.S. News and World Report*, November 17, 1980, 42.

7. Ibid.

8. Interview with Roy Jones, July 17, 1984.

9. Interview with Bill Billings, May 24, 1984.

10. James L. Guth, "The New Christian Right," in *The New Christian Right*, ed. Robert C. Liebman and Robert Wuthnow (New York: Aldine, 1983), 33.

11. Interview with Gary Jarmin, July 27, 1984.

12. Interview with Stan Hastey, August 17, 1984; Charles Bergstrom, August 6, 1984.

13. Tim Miller, "Two Competing Pro-Life Measures Split the Anti-Abortion Lobby," *National Journal*, March 20, 1982, 512.

14. See Louise Lorentzen, "Evangelical Life Style Concerns Expressed in Political Action," *Sociological Analysis* 41 (Summer 1980): 144–154; Anson Shupe and William Stacey, "The Moral Majority Constituency," in *The New Christian Right*, ed. Robert C. Liebman and Robert Wuthnow (New York: Aldine, 1983), 114. For a critique of the status-politics paradigm as applied to the Christian Right, see Matthew C. Moen, "Status Politics and the Political Agenda of the Christian Right," *Sociological Quarterly* 29 (September 1988): 429–437.

15. Seymour Martin Lipset and Earl Rabb, *The Politics of Unreason* (New York: Harper & Row, 1970), 485–487.

16. See Joseph Gusfield, *Symbolic Crusade* (Urbana: University of Illinois Press, 1963); Louis Zurcher and R. George Kirkpatrick, *Citizens for Decency* (Austin: University of Texas Press, 1976).

17. See Wilbur J. Scott, "The Equal Rights Amendment as Status Politics," *Social Forces* 64 (December 1985): 499–506; Ann Page and Donald Clelland, "The Kanawha County Textbook Controversy: A Study of the Politics of Life Style Concern," *Social Forces* 57 (September 1978): 265–281; Matthew C. Moen, "School Prayer and the Politics of Life Style Concern," *Social Science Quarterly* 65 (December 1984): 1065–1071.

18. Pamela Fessler, "Bill Permits Church Exit from Social Security," *Congressional Quarterly Weekly Report*, April 28, 1984, 952.

19. Alexis De Tocqueville, *Democracy in America* (New York: Doubleday, 1969), 9, 11.

20. Action in Congress is usually documented to the *Congressional Quarterly* rather than to the *Congressional Record*, which has a reputation for inaccuracy, partly because members can "revise and extend" their remarks. For insight into such matters, see "Congressional Record Not Always the Record," *Congressional Quarterly Weekly Report*, August 31, 1974, 2382.

Chapter 6. Starting Out

1. James Roberts, "The Christian Right: New Force in American Politics," *Human Events*, November 8, 1980, 10.

2. "Religious Right Goes for Bigger Game," *U.S. News and World Report*, November 17, 1980, 42.

3. Tom Minnery, "The Religious Right: How Much Credit Can It Take for the Electoral Landslide?" *Christianity Today* 24 (December 12, 1980): 52.

4. Interview with Philip Kiko, June 11, 1984.

5. Nadine Cohodas, "Peter Rodino Turns Judiciary into a Legislative Graveyard," *Congressional Quarterly Weekly Report*, May 12, 1984, 1099.

6. Interview with Henry Hyde, June 26, 1984.

7. Interview with Mike Synar, May 17, 1984.

8. Interview with Henry Hyde, June 26, 1984.

9. Nadine Cohodas, "Members Move to Rein in Supreme Court," *Congressional Quarterly Weekly Report*, May 30, 1981, 947.

10. Ibid.

11. Roger W. Cobb and Charles E. Elder, *Participation in American Politics: The Dynamics of Agenda-Building*, 2nd ed. (Baltimore: Johns Hopkins University Press, 1983), 127–128.

12. "House Roll Call Votes," *Congressional Quarterly Almanac* XXXVII (Washington, D.C.: Congressional Quarterly, 1981), 64-H.

13. Nadine Cohodas, "Emphasis on Economy Kept Divisive Social Issues on Back Burner in 1981," *Congressional Quarterly Weekly Report*, January 2, 1982, 5.

14. *Harris* v. *McRae*, 448 U.S. 917 (1980). See "Congress and the Hyde Amendment . . . How the House Moved to Stop Abortions," *Congressional Quarterly Weekly Report*, April 19, 1980, 1038–1039.

15. "Aid Bill Gives President Broader Authority," *Congressional Quarterly Almanac* XXXVII (Washington, D.C.: Congressional Quarterly, 1981), 163. See also in the same source, "Reagan Backing Helps Foreign Aid Bill," 342; "Treasury/Post Office Funds," 356–357.

16. Interview with Mike Synar, May 17, 1984.

17. Interview with Philip Kiko, June 11, 1984.

18. "Key Vote 14," *Congressional Quarterly Almanac* XXXIV (Washington, D.C.: Congressional Quarterly, 1978), 14-C.

19. Robert Lyke, "Legislative Activity on Tuition Tax Credits Prior to the 97th Congress," *Congressional Research Service Brief*, August 12, 1982, 1–3.

20. "Tuition Credit Friends, Foes Ready, Just in Case," *National Journal*, April 24, 1982, 736.

21. Rochelle Stanfield, "The Public School Lobby Fends Off Tuition Tax Credits—At Least for Now," *National Journal*, June 13, 1981, 1063.

22. "Congress Enacts President Reagan's Tax Plan," *Congressional Quarterly Almanac* XXXVII (Washington, D.C.: Congressional Quarterly, 1981), 98–100.

23. Dick Kirschten, "The Deferred Agenda," *National Journal*, July 25, 1981, 1346.

24. Dick Kirschten, "Putting the Social Issues on Hold: Can Reagan Get Away with It?" *National Journal*, October 10, 1981, 1810; Cohodas, "Emphasis on Economy Kept Divisive Social Issues on Back Burner in 1981," 3.

25. See Kirschten, "The Deferred Agenda," 1346; Kirschten,

"Putting the Social Issues on Hold: Can Reagan Get Away with It?" 1810.

26. Kirschten, "Putting the Social Issues on Hold: Can Reagan Get Away with It?" 1812.

27. "GOP Seeks Fruits of Victory as 97th Congress Convenes," *Congressional Quarterly Almanac* XXXVII (Washington, D.C.: Congressional Quarterly, 1981), 3.

28. "Capitol Boxscore," *Congressional Quarterly Weekly Report*, May 8, 1982, 1083.

29. Senate Committee on the Judiciary, *Hearings on a Proposed Constitutional Amendment to Permit Voluntary Prayer*, 97th Cong., 2nd sess., S.J. Res. 199, 1.

30. Walter Oleszek, *Congressional Procedures and the Policy Process* (Washington, D.C.: CQ Press, 1978), 66–68.

31. *Hearings on a Proposed Constitutional Amendment to Permit Voluntary Prayer*, 141–156.

32. Ibid., 273–279.

33. Ibid., 341–504.

34. Morrow Cater, "Helms' Back Door Approach to School Prayer May Fare Better Than Reagan's," *National Journal*, August 14, 1982, 1426.

35. "State, Justice, Commerce Appropriation," *Congressional Quarterly Almanac* XXXVII (Washington, D.C.: Congressional Quarterly, 1981), 367.

36. Ibid.

37. Nadine Cohodas, "State, Justice, Commerce Appropriations Bill Snarled by School Prayer Wrangle, *Congressional Quarterly Weekly Report*, November 21, 1981, 2281.

38. "State, Justice, Commerce Appropriation," 368.

39. "Senate Roll Call Votes," *Congressional Quarterly Almanac* XXVII (Washington, D.C.: Congressional Quarterly, 1981), 63-S.

40. Ibid., 64-S.

41. Nadine Cohodas, "Anti-Abortion Bill Advances in Senate Panel," *Congressional Quarterly Weekly Report*, July 11, 1981, 1253.

42. Senate Subcommittee on Separation of Powers, *The Human Life Appendix*, 97th Cong., 1st sess., S. 158.

43. Cohodas, "Anti-Abortion Bill Advances in Senate Panel," 1253.

44. Ibid.

45. Tim Miller, "Two Competing Pro-Life Measures Split the Anti-Abortion Lobby," *National Journal*, March 20, 1982, 512.

46. Nadine Cohodas, "Constitutional Amendment to Permit Ban on Abortion Approved by Senate Panel," *Congressional Quarterly Weekly Report*, December 19, 1981, 2526.

47. Ibid.

48. Miller, "Two Competing Pro-Life Measures Split the Anti-Abortion Lobby," 511.

49. Ibid.

50. Ibid.

51. Nadine Cohodas, "Panel Approves Anti-Abortion Amendment," *Congressional Quarterly Weekly Report*, March 13, 1982, 572.

52. Nadine Cohodas, "Senate Tables Anti-Abortion Amendment," *Congressional Quarterly Weekly Report*, September 18, 1982, 2299.

53. Nadine Cohodas, "Senate Caught in Filibuster on Abortion, School Prayer," *Congressional Quarterly Weekly Report*, August 21, 1982, 2102.

54. Cohodas, "Senate Tables Anti-Abortion Amendment," 2299.

55. Nadine Cohodas, "Senate Ends Long Debate on Social Issues," *Congressional Quarterly Weekly Report*, September 25, 1982, 2359.

56. Ibid.

57. Interview with Gary Curran, July 25, 1984.

58. Interview with Laura Clay, May 21, 1984.

59. Interview with Gary Curran, July 25, 1984.

60. Alan Murray, "House Tells Conferees to Lift Surgeon General Age Limit," *Congressional Quarterly Weekly Report*, May 23, 1981, 909.

61. Ann Pelham, "Conferees Vote on Medicaid Cuts, Block Grants," *Congressional Quarterly Weekly Report*, August 1, 1981, 1388.

62. "Reagan Backing Helps Foreign Aid Bill," 342.

63. Stanfield, "The Public School Lobby Fends Off Tuition Tax Credits—At Least for Now," 1063.

64. Jim Castelli, "Christian Right Sees Influence Widened," *Washington Star*, November 8, 1980, 4.

65. Senate Committee on Finance, *Hearings on Tuition Tax Credits*, 97th Cong., 1st sess., S. 550.

66. Ibid., 63–67.

67. Ibid., 188.

68. "Capitol Boxscore," *Congressional Quarterly Weekly Report*, April 17, 1982, 888.

69. Dick Kirschten, "Reagan Looks to Religious Leaders For Con-

tinuing Support in 1984," *National Journal*, August 20, 1983, 1727–1731.

70. Senate Committee on Finance, *Hearings on Tuition Tax Credit Proposals*, 97th Cong., 2nd sess., S. 2673, 72–74.

71. Ibid., 258–260.

72. Harrison Donnelly, "Senate Committee Approves Tuition Tax Credit Proposal," *Congressional Quarterly Weekly Report*, September 18, 1982, 2297.

73. Ibid.

74. For a summary of Goldwater's criticisms of the Christian Right, see Judith Miller, "Goldwater Vows to Fight Tactics of New Right," *New York Times*, September 16, 1981, A1.

75. Ann Pelham, "Family Protection Act: Dear to New Right, But Unlikely to Get Out of Committees," *Congressional Quarterly Weekly Report*, October 3, 1981, 1916.

76. "House Roll Call Votes," 72-H.

77. "Criminal Code Revision Dies," *Congressional Quarterly Almanac*, XXXVIII (Washington, D.C.: Congressional Quarterly, 1982), 416.

78. Ibid.

79. "Legal Services Corp. Kept Alive Temporarily," *Congressional Quarterly Almanac* XXXVII (Washington, D.C.: Congressional Quarterly, 1981), 413.

80. "House Roll Call Votes," 36-H.

81. U.S. House of Representatives, Office of Legislative Information.

82. Ibid.

83. Senate Subcommittee on Separation of Powers, *Hearings on the Human Life Bill*, 97th Cong., 1st sess., S. 158; Senate Subcommittee on the Constitution, *Hearings on the Human Life Federalism Amendment*, 97th Cong., 1st sess., S.J. Res.110; Senate Committee on the Judiciary, *Hearings on a Proposed Constitutional Amendment to Permit Voluntary Prayer*, 97th Cong., 2nd sess., S.J. Res. 199; Senate Committee on Finance, *Hearings on Tuition Tax Credits*, 97th Cong., 1st sess., S. 550; Senate Committee on Finance, *Hearings on Tuition Tax Credit Proposals*, 97th Cong., 2nd sess., S. 2673.

84. Compiled by the author from hearings on S. 158, S.J. Res. 110, S.J. Res. 199, S. 550, S. 2673.

85. Interview with Roy Jones, July 17, 1984. He estimated that the Moral Majority had working relationships with about 150 congressional offices in the 98th (1983–84) Congress.

Chapter 7. The Struggle Intensifies

1. Interview with Lilli Hausenfluck, May 29, 1984.

2. Nadine Cohodas, "Replay of 1982 Controversies Facing Judiciary Committees," *Congressional Quarterly Weekly Report*, January 22, 1983, 167.

3. See "Court, Senate Rebuff Anti-Abortion Efforts," *Congressional Quarterly Almanac* XXXIX (Washington, D.C.: Congressional Quarterly, 1983), 306; Pamela Fessler, "Conference OK's $12.8 Billion for Treasury, Postal Service," *Congressional Quarterly Weekly Report*, August 11, 1984, 1955; "Labor/HHS/Education Money Bill Cleared," *Congressional Quarterly Almanac* XXXIX (Washington, D.C.: Congressional Quarterly, 1983), 507.

4. Nadine Cohodas, "Campaign to Overturn Ban on Abortion Funding Began," *Congressional Quarterly Weekly Report*, August 20, 1983, 1689–1693.

5. Ibid., 1692.

6. Nadine Cohodas, "House Campaign Launched to Restore Abortion Funding," *Congressional Quarterly Weekly Report*, June 2, 1984, 1323.

7. Ibid.

8. Allen D. Hertzke, *Representing God in Washington* (Knoxville: University of Tennessee Press, 1988), 121.

9. 454 U.S. 263 (1981).

10. Ibid.

11. Interview with Charles Bergstrom, August 6, 1984.

12. Hertzke, *Representing God in Washington*, 180–181.

13. Ibid., 176. Hertzke's view is that the Christian Right favored equal access all along, placing pressure on the Congress to enact a vocal-prayer amendment with the hope of then obtaining an equal access bill. I suggest that was a "face-saving" interpretation given retrospectively by Christian Right elites after they had lost on the school-prayer amendment. My conclusion is based on the interviews I conducted, which took place just before the equal access and vocal-prayer debates.

14. Interview with Forest Montgomery, June 13, 1984.

15. Nadine Cohodas, "Two House Veterans Scrap on Issue of Equal Access," *Congressional Quarterly Weekly Report*, May 12, 1984, 1104.

16. Donahue Transcript #02275, available from Multimedia Entertainment, Box 2011, Cincinnati, Ohio 45201. The specific language was used by Senator Orrin Hatch and New Right activist Phyllis Schlafly.

17. Hertzke, *Representing God in Washington*, 167.

18. Cohodas, "Two House Veterans Scrap on Issue of Equal Access," 1103.

19. Janet Hook, "Schools Opened to Student Religious Groups," *Congressional Quarterly Weekly Report*, April 7, 1984, 814.

20. Ibid. I attended the hearings and witnessed the geniality.

21. Ibid.

22. Cohodas, "Two House Veterans Scrap on Issue of Equal Access," 1104.

23. Ibid.

24. Ibid.

25. Ibid. The signatures would have forced equal access into the Judiciary Committee via pressure from Democratic members, not via House rules.

26. I was in the House gallery on that day watching the equal access vote. The description of events is based on my observations. It is worth noting that, when Gingrich's attack began, the House gallery was largely empty; within thirty minutes, there was not an available seat.

27. "House Votes," *Congressional Quarterly Weekly Report*, May 19, 1984, 1208.

28. Interview with Forest Montgomery, June 13, 1984.

29. "Senate Votes," *Congressional Quarterly Weekly Report*, June 30, 1984, 1580.

30. Janet Hook, "House Clears Bill Allowing Prayer Meetings in Schools, "*Congressional Quarterly Weekly Report*, July 28, 1984, 1807.

31. Interview with Stan Hastey, August 17, 1984.

32. Cohodas, "Two House Veterans Scrap on Issue of Equal Access," 1104.

33. Hertzke, *Representing God in Washington*, 178–179.

34. Janet Hook, "Bill Requires Schools to Permit Silent Prayer," *Congressional Quarterly Weekly Report*, July 28, 1984, 1809.

35. Senate Committee on the Judiciary, *Human Life Federalism Amendment*, 98th Cong., 1st sess., S.J. Res. 3, Report 98–149, 1.

36. Ibid., 4.

37. Ibid.

38. Interview with Gary Curran, July 25, 1984.

39. Nadine Cohodas, "Senate Rejects Amendment Designed to Ban Abortion," *Congressional Quarterly Weekly Report*, July 2, 1983, 1362.

40. Ibid., 1361.

41. Ibid.

42. 456 U.S. 922 (1983).

43. 463 U.S. 388 (1983).

44. Brian Nutting, "Senate Rejects Tuition Tax Credit Plan," *Congressional Quarterly Weekly Report*, November 19, 1983, 2424.

45. Interview with David Boren, June 14, 1984.

46. Nutting, "Senate Rejects Tuition Tax Credit Plan," 2424.

47. Interview with David Boren, June 14, 1984.

48. Interview with Bob Edgar, May 31, 1984.

49. Steven Pressman, "Religious Organizations Urge Administration Not to Name Ambassador to the Vatican," *Congressional Quarterly Weekly Report*, December 17, 1983, 2677.

50. "Senate Votes," *Congressional Quarterly Weekly Report*, March 10, 1984, 585.

Chapter 8. The High-Water Mark

1. Interview with Gary Jarmin, July 27, 1984. Because the interviews for this book were conducted during the fight over the school-prayer amendment, they are the basis for much of the discussion in this chapter. The interview with Gary Jarmin is drawn from heavily because he was closely involved in the prayer fight and graciously donated two hours of his time for an interview, the bulk of which was devoted to the prayer amendment.

2. Senate Committee on the Judiciary, *Hearings on a Proposed Constitutional Amendment to Permit Voluntary Prayer*, 97th Cong., 2nd sess., S.J. Res. 199, 153.

3. Interview with Gary Jarmin, July 27, 1984.

4. Ibid.

5. Nadine Cohodas, "Senate Panel Bows to Pressure: Postpones School Prayer Vote," *Congressional Quarterly Weekly Report*, May 28, 1983, 1052.

6. Interview with Gary Jarmin, July 27, 1984.

7. Ibid.

8. Nadine Cohodas, "Two School Prayer Measures Approved by Senate Panel," *Congressional Quarterly Weekly Report*, June 11, 1983, 1144.

9. Interview with Morton Blackwell, August 29, 1984.

10. Senate Committee on the Judiciary, *Voluntary School Prayer Amendment*, 98th Cong., 2nd sess., Report 98–348, 7–9.

11. Interview with Frances Zwenig, May 23, 1984.

12. Interview with Gary Jarmin, July 27, 1984.

13. For an analysis of the language, see *Voluntary School Prayer Amendment*, 7–9.

14. Interview with Gary Jarmin, July 27, 1984.

15. Ibid.

16. Interview with Morton Blackwell, August 29, 1984.

17. Interview with Gary Jarmin, July 27, 1984.

18. Interview with Morton Blackwell, August 29, 1984.

19. March 24, 1983, *Congressional Record*, 98th Cong., 1st sess., 3918.

20. Cohodas, "Two School Prayer Measures Approved by Senate Panel," 1144.

21. Ibid.

22. Ibid.

23. Ibid.

24. Interview with Gary Jarmin, July 27, 1984.

25. Ibid.

26. *Voluntary School Prayer Amendment*, 3.

27. Interview with Gary Jarmin, July 27, 1984.

28. *Voluntary School Prayer Amendment*, 3.

29. See S.J. Res. 218, 98th Cong., 2nd sess., 2.

30. Nadine Cohodas, "Senate Vote Set on Vocal Prayer Amendment," *Congressional Quarterly Weekly Report*, March 17, 1984, 633.

31. Interview with Frances Zwenig, May 23, 1984.

32. Steven Pressman, "Famous Faces Fighting Hard for School Prayer," *Congressional Quarterly Weekly Report*, March 3, 1984, 491; Nadine Cohodas, "Prayer Issue Engulfs Congress as Senate Embarks on Debate," *Congressional Quarterly Weekly Report*, March 10, 1984, 538.

33. Interview with David Boren, June 14, 1984.

34. Based on my viewing D.C. area television programs on Reverend Falwell's activity, covered as a local-interest story for Virginia residents.

35. Interview with Frances Zwenig, May 23, 1984.

36. Pressman, "Famous Faces Fighting Hard for School Prayer," 490.

37. Interview with David Boren, June 14, 1984. Senator Boren graciously had a staff member compile the information, which was given to me after the interview.

38. Pressman, "Famous Faces Fighting Hard for School Prayer," 490.

39. Ibid.

40. Interview with Frances Zwenig, May 23, 1984.

41. Interview with Stan Hastey, June 22, 1984.

42. Based on my examination of letters from both sides while on Capitol Hill as a congressional aide.

43. Pressman, "Famous Faces Fighting Hard for School Prayer," 490.

44. Ibid., 491.

45. Anne Saker, "House Republicans Conduct an All-Night Prayer Vigil," *Roll Call*, March 18, 1984, 3. This source is the "insider's" newspaper covering events on Capitol Hill and the people who work there.

46. Based on my attendance at the rally.

47. Cohodas, "Prayer Issue Engulfs Congress as Senate Embarks on Debate," 538.

48. Interview with Barry Lynn, June 1, 1984.

49. For a discussion of these matters, see T. R. Reid, "Say Amen, Senator," *Washington Post*, March 21, 1984, B1; T. R. Reid, "Sens. Weicker, Hatch Do Battle over Prayer Issue," *Washington Post*, March 8, 1984, A2; Jim Buie, "An Answer to Prayer," *Church & State* 4 (April 1984): 4–6.

50. Interview with Barry Lynn, June 1, 1984.

51. Interview with Frances Zwenig, May 23, 1984.

52. Cohodas, "Prayer Issue Engulfs Congress as Senate Embarks on Debate," 538.

53. Ibid.

54. Ibid., 540.

55. Ibid., 538.

56. Interview with Gary Jarmin, July 27, 1984.

57. Cohodas, "Senate Vote Set on Vocal Prayer Amendment," 633.

58. I was in the Senate gallery on the day of the vote, sitting just behind the artists who were sketching the proceedings.

59. Steven Pressman, "Senate Rejects School Prayer Amendment," *Congressional Quarterly Weekly Report*, March 24, 1984, 643. When Hart entered the Senate chamber, he was surrounded by his Democratic colleagues. After visiting with them, he approached Vice-President Bush, who was presiding over the debate while at the same time autographing pictures of himself. The two exchanged laughs as Hart reached for a signed picture. I observed the episode from my seat in the Senate gallery.

Chapter 9. A Term of Accomplishment

1. Steven Pressman, "Religious Right: Trying to Link Poll Power and Lobby Muscle," *Congressional Quarterly Weekly Report*, September 22, 1984, 2315.

2. Based on the discussions of those issues in the previous chapter. For an analysis of the problem of assessing interest-group influence, see Kay Lehman Schlozman and John T. Tierney, *Organized Interests and American Democracy* (New York: Harper & Row, 1986), 7–9.

3. The information on the numbers of bills was obtained from the U.S. House of Representatives, Office of Legislative Information. For the hearings, see Senate Subcommittee on the Constitution, *Hearings on the Human Life Federalism Amendment*, 98th Cong., 1st sess., S.J. Res. 3; Senate Subcommittee on the Constitution, *Hearings on the Voluntary School Prayer Amendment*, 98th Cong., 1st sess., S.J. Res. 73; House Subcommittee on Elementary, Secondary, and Vocational Education, *Hearings on the Equal Access Act*, 98th Cong., 1st sess., H.R. 2723; Senate Committee on Finance, *Hearings on Tuition Tax Credits*, 98th Cong., 1st sess., S. 528. The information on the individuals who testified was compiled from the hearings; the testimony was given by Adrian Rogers (S.J. Res. 3), Gary Jarmin and Dick Dingman (S.J. Res. 73), and Dick Dingman (S. 528).

4. Roger W. Cobb and Charles E. Elder, *Participation in American Politics: The Dynamics of Agenda-Building*, 2nd ed. (Baltimore: Johns Hopkins University Press, 1983), 28.

5. Ibid., 152.

6. John W. Kingdon, *Agendas, Alternatives, and Public Policies* (Boston: Little, Brown & Co., 1984), 134–135.

7. Ibid., 135.

8. Interview with David Boren, June 14, 1984.

9. Interview with Forest Montgomery, June 13, 1984.

10. Interview with Gary Jarmin, July 27, 1984.

11. Interview with Lilli Hausenfluck, May 29, 1984.

12. Interview with Tom Ashcraft, August 3, 1984.

13. For example, see Norman J. Ornstein, Robert L. Peabody, and David W. Rhode, "The Senate Through the 1980s," in *Congress Reconsidered*, 3rd ed., ed. Lawrence C. Dodd and Bruce I. Oppenheimer (Washington, D.C.: CQ Press, 1985), 13–33.

14. Interview with Roy Jones, July 17, 1984.

15. Ibid.

16. Jean M. Marra, ed., *Reader's Guide to Periodical Literature* 39–43 (New York: H. W. Wilson Co., 1980–84).

17. Joseph Bloomfield, ed., *Social Sciences Index* 4–9 (New York: H. W. Wilson Co., 1978–83).

18. Interview with Tom Bovard, June 8, 1984.

Chapter 10. Reputation Problems

1. Bill Keller, "Evangelical Conservatives Move from Pews to Polls, But Can They Sway Congress?" *Congressional Quarterly Weekly Report*, September 6, 1980, 2629.

2. Ibid.

3. T. R. Reid, "Sens. Weicker, Hatch Do Battle over Prayer Issue," *Washington Post*, March 8, 1984, A2; Steven Roberts, "Fervent Debate on School Prayer," *New York Times*, March 9, 1984, A16.

4. Interview with Barry Lynn, June 1, 1984.

5. James L. Guth, "The Politics of the Christian Right," in *Interest Group Politics*, ed. Allan J. Cigler and Burdett A. Loomis (Washington, D.C.: CQ Press, 1983), 72.

6. Interview with Gary Curran, July 25, 1984.

7. Interview with Roy Jones, July 17, 1984.

8. Based on my examination of letters being sent from various offices on Capitol Hill.

9. Interview with Gary Curran, July 25, 1984.

10. Interview with Gary Jarmin, July 27, 1984.

11. Letter to me from Gary Jarmin, April 16, 1985, in response to a convention paper I had sent him outlining the general views expressed here. See Matthew C. Moen, "The Christian Right and the Legislative Agenda, 1981–1984," paper delivered at the Annual Meeting of the Southwestern Political Science Association, Houston, Texas, March 20–23, 1985.

12. Jeffrey K. Hadden et al., "Why Jerry Falwell Killed the Moral Majority," in *The God Pumpers*, ed. Marshall Fishwick and Ray B. Browne (Bowling Green, Ohio: Bowling Green State University Popular Press, 1987), 112.

Chapter 11. The Transition Period

1. Janet Hook, "Reagan Continues to Push Tuition Tax Breaks," *Congressional Quarterly Weekly Report*, June 15, 1985, 1164.

2. Julie Rovner, "Senate Passes Labor-HHS Appropriations

Bill," *Congressional Quarterly Weekly Report*, September 13, 1986, 2167.

3. Ibid.

4. Nadine Cohodas, "School Prayer Advocates Split over Best Approach to Issue," *Congressional Quarterly Weekly Report*, June 29, 1985, 1275.

5. 105 S. Ct. 2479 (1985).

6. Cohodas, "School Prayer Advocates Split over Best Approach to Issue," 1275.

7. Nadine Cohodas, "Senate Rejects Bill to Permit School Prayer," *Congressional Quarterly Weekly Report*, September 14, 1985, 1842.

8. Ibid.

9. Nadine Cohodas, "Panel Approves School Prayer Amendment," *Congressional Quarterly Weekly Report*, October 5, 1985, 2008.

10. Cohodas, "School Prayer Advocates Split over Best Approach to Issue," 1275.

11. Cohodas, "Panel Approves School Prayer Amendment," 2008.

12. "NSF Authorization Cleared," *Congressional Quarterly Almanac* XLI (Washington, D.C.: Congressional Quarterly, 1985), 288–289.

13. Jacqueline Calmes, "Reagan Seeks More Power over Annual Budget Process," *Congressional Quarterly Weekly Report*, February 8, 1986, 263.

14. Barbara Hinckley, *Congressional Elections* (Washington, D.C.: CQ Press, 1981), 113–132.

15. Interview with Roy Jones, July 17, 1984.

16. Nebraska Democratic Senator Edward Zorinsky died and was replaced in March 1987 by Republican David Karnes, who was appointed by Republican Governor Kay Orr.

17. "Conservative Groups Retreat from Politics," *Washington Post*, January 17, 1987, D14.

18. Based on my examination of the 1987 indexes of the *Congressional Quarterly Weekly Report*.

19. For a discussion of this affair, see Larry Martz et al., "God and Money," *Newsweek*, April 6, 1987, 19–20.

20. For the following description of the events surrounding the Bakkers, see Martz et al., "God and Money," 16–22; Richard N. Ostling, "TV's Unholy Row," *Time*, April 6, 1987, 60–67; Larry Martz et al., "Gospelgate II: Target Falwell," *Newsweek*, June 1, 1987, 56–59.

21. Mark Miller, "Goodbye to All That," *Newsweek*, November 16, 1987, 10.

22. Jean McNair, "Robertson Lays Off 470, Blames TV Ministry Scandals," *Boston Globe*, June 6, 1987, 1 +.

23. "TV Preachers to Testify," *Newsweek*, August 31, 1987, 64.

24. With respect to the American Coalition for Traditional Values, Swaggart was on the Executive Committee and Bakker on the Board of Directors. Roberts was not involved with that organization.

Chapter 12. Off the Hill

1. Samuel Freedman, "Falwell Disseminates Views Through Liberty U.," *New York Times*, June 4, 1987, I1.

2. Ibid.

3. "Prospectus: The Leadership Institute," 5. The publication was given to me during an interview with Blackwell. It was obtainable from: The Leadership Institute, 8001 Braddock Road, Suite 402, Springfield, Virginia 22151.

4. Ibid. See also the "Leadership Training Service Directory," 16. This publication was also given to me during an interview with Blackwell; it was obtainable from the same address as the Leadership Institute Prospectus.

5. Martin Tolchin, "Reagan's Power to Name Judiciary Going Lame," *New York Times*. Reprinted in the *Maine Sunday Telegram*, December 6, 1987, 20.

6. The parochial schools case was *Aguilar* v. *Felton*, 105 S. Ct. 3232 (1985); the "moment of silence" case was *Wallace* v. *Jaffree*, 105 S. Ct. 2479 (1985); the Connecticut Sabbath case was *Estate of Thornton* v. *Calder Inc.*, 105 S. Ct. 2914 (1985).

7. The Louisiana case was *Edwards* v. *Aguillard*, 107 S. Ct. 2573 (1987); the textbook case was *Smith* v. *Board of School Commissioners of Mobile County*, 655 F. Supp. 939 (1987).

8. 106 S. Ct. 1326 (1986). See also Elder Witt, "Court Dodges Ruling on Equal Access Issue," *Congressional Quarterly Weekly Report*, March 29, 1986, 717.

9. "Major Rulings of 1985–1986 Court Term," *Congressional Quarterly Weekly Report*, July 12, 1986, 1576.

10. The Reagan administration assisted the Christian Right in attempts to influence the courts in part by filing more "friend of the court" briefs than any other administration in American history. See Elder

Witt, "Reagan Crusade before Court Unprecedented in Intensity," *Congressional Quarterly Weekly Report*, March 15, 1986, 616.

11. On the "abortion pill," see James Franklin, "New Pill May Alter Abortion Debate," *Boston Globe*, December 22, 1986, 1.

12. *Smith* v. *Board of School Commissioners of Mobile County*, 655 F. Supp. 939 (1987).

13. Ezra Bowen, "A Courtroom Clash over Textbooks," *Time*, October 27, 1986, 94.

14. The two chains are LaVerdiere's and Wellby, both of which initially removed the magazines but have since reinstated them.

15. This picketing of the office building of Cox Cable in Oklahoma City gained considerable publicity for the fundamentalists, based on my observations while living in the area at the time.

16. See "Unexpected Landslide," *Maine Times*, June 13, 1986, 11.

17. Interview with John Buchanan, August 1, 1984.

18. The case was *Edwards* v. *Aguillard*, 107 S. Ct. 2573 (1987). For a discussion of it, see Ethan Bronner, "Justices Say States Can't Order Teaching of Creationism," *Boston Globe*, June 20, 1987, 1+.

19. Congressional Research Service, 98th Cong., 2nd sess. The furor in Nebraska attracted the attention of a number of fundamentalist ministers from Indiana, who then contacted the office of Phil Sharp (where I was working as a congressional fellow) to complain about the treatment accorded Reverend Sileven. At that time, I requested the information from the Congressional Research Service about the number of states that had laws similar to those of Nebraska.

20. Rob Gurwitt, "1986 Elections Generate GOP Power Struggles," *Congressional Quarterly Weekly Report*, April 12, 1986, 803.

21. Ibid., 802.

22. Larry Martz, "Day of the Preachers," *Newsweek*, March 7, 1988, 44.

23. Interview with Gary Jarmin, July 27, 1984.

24. Joan Sweeney, "Evangelicals Seeking to Establish Political Force," *Los Angeles Times*, May 19, 1980, 21.

Bibliography

"Aid Bill Gives President Broader Authority." *Congressional Quarterly Almanac* XXXVII (Washington, D.C.: Congressional Quarterly, 1981): 161–184.

"Arab Lobby: Opening Doors That Were Previously Closed." *Current American Government* (Washington, D.C.: Congressional Quarterly, 1978): 93–99.

Billings, Bill. *The Christian's Political Action Manual*. Washington, D.C.: NCAC, 1980.

Bloomfield, Joseph, ed. *Social Sciences Index*. 10 vols. New York: H. W. Wilson Co., 1975–1984.

Bonafede, Dom. "New Right Preaches a New Religion, and Ronald Reagan Is Its Prophet." *National Journal* 18 (May 2, 1981): 779–782.

"Born Again at the Ballot Box." *Time* 115 (April 14, 1980): 94.

Bowen, Ezra. "A Courtroom Clash over Textbooks." *Time* 128 (October 27, 1986): 94.

Briggs, Kenneth. "Evangelical Leaders Hail Election and Ask Continuation of Efforts." *New York Times* (January 28, 1981): 8.

———. "Evangelical Preachers Gather to Polish Their Politics." *New York Times* (August 21, 1980): B9.

———. "Evangelicals Hear a Plea: Politics Now." *New York Times* (August 24, 1980): 33.

Bronner, Ethan. "Justices Say States Can't Order Teaching of Creationism." *Boston Globe* (June 20, 1987): 1 + .

Brudney, Jeffrey, and Gary Copeland. "Evangelicals as a Political Force." *Social Science Quarterly* 65 (December 1984): 1072–1079.

Buie, Jim. "An Answer to Prayer." *Church & State* 4 (April 1984): 4–6.

Buursma, Bruce. "Reagan's Dismayed Fans Plan Holy War." *Chicago Tribune* (February 1, 1981): 12.

Calmes, Jacqueline. "Reagan Seeks More Power over Annual Budget Process." *Congressional Quarterly Weekly Report* 6 (February 8, 1986): 263.

Campbell, Bruce. *The American Electorate*. New York: Holt, Rinehart & Winston, 1979.

Cannon, Lou. "Reagan Disagrees with Fundamentalist Teachings on Prayer." *Washington Post* (October 4, 1980): A6.

"Capitol Boxscore." *Congressional Quarterly Weekly Report* 16 (April 17, 1982): 888–889.

"Capitol Boxscore." *Congressional Quarterly Weekly Report* 19 (May 8, 1982): 1083.

Castelli, Jim. "Christian Right Sees Influence Widened." *Washington Star* (November 8, 1980): 3–4.

———. "Pro-Reagan Group Targets Sunday Worshippers." *Washington Star* (November 1, 1980): A4.

———. "Religious Groups Hope to Influence Elections." *Washington Star* (April 13, 1980): A3.

———. "Senator Offers Plan to Battle Religious Right." *Washington Star* (June 20, 1981): 6.

Cater, Morrow. "Helms' Back Door Approach to School Prayer May Fare Better Than Reagan's." *National Journal* 33 (August 14, 1982): 1426–1428.

Chandler, Ralph Clark. "Worshipping a Past That Never Was." *Christianity and Crisis* 42 (February 15, 1982): 20–29.

"Christian Right Equated with Iran's Mullahs." *Washington Star* (September 24, 1980): 4.

Church, George. "Politics from the Pulpit." *Time* 116 (October 13, 1980): 28 + .

"Church and Politics." *Congressional Quarterly Weekly Report* 37 (September 15, 1984): 2263–2264.

Clymer, Adam. "Fire and Brimstone." *New York Times* (March 9, 1983): A18.

Cobb, Roger W., and Charles E. Elder. *Participation in American Politics: The Dynamics of Agenda-Building*. 2nd ed. Baltimore: Johns Hopkins University Press, 1983.

Cohen, Richard. "Frustrated House Republicans Seek More Aggressive Strategy for 1984 and Beyond." *National Journal* 9 (March 3, 1984): 413–417.

Cohodas, Nadine. "Anti-Abortion Bill Advances in Senate Panel." *Congressional Quarterly Weekly Report* 28 (July 11, 1981): 1253.

———. "Campaign to Overturn Ban on Abortion Funding Began." *Congressional Quarterly Weekly Report* 33 (August 20, 1983): 1689–1693.

———. "Constitutional Amendment to Permit Ban on Abortion Approved by Senate Panel." *Congressional Quarterly Weekly Report* 51 (December 19, 1981): 2526.

———. "Emphasis on Economy Kept Divisive Social Issues on Back Burner in 1981." *Congressional Quarterly Weekly Report* 1 (January 2, 1982): 3–5.

———. "House Campaign Launched to Restore Abortion Funding." *Congressional Quarterly Weekly Report* 22 (June 2, 1984): 1323.

———. "House Judiciary Committee Approves ERA." *Congressional Quarterly Weekly Report* 45 (November 12, 1983): 2395.

———. "Members Move to Rein in Supreme Court." *Congressional Quarterly Weekly Report* 22 (May 30, 1981): 947–951.

———. "Panel Approves Anti-Abortion Amendment." *Congressional Quarterly Weekly Report* 11 (March 13, 1982): 572.

———. "Panel Approves School Prayer Amendment." *Congressional Quarterly Weekly Report* 40 (October 5, 1985): 2008.

———. "Peter Rodino Turns Judiciary into a Legislative Graveyard." *Congressional Quarterly Weekly Report* 19 (May 12, 1984): 1097–1102.

———. "Prayer Issue Engulfs Congress as Senate Embarks on Debate." *Congressional Quarterly Weekly Report* 10 (March 10, 1984): 538–540.

———. "Replay of 1982 Controversies Facing Judiciary Committees." *Congressional Quarterly Weekly Report* 3 (January 22, 1983): 167.

———. "School Prayer Advocates Split over Best Approach to Issue." *Congressional Quarterly Weekly Report* 26 (June 29, 1985): 1275.

———. "Senate Caught in Filibuster on Abortion, School Prayer." *Congressional Quarterly Weekly Report* 34 (August 21, 1982): 2102.

———. "Senate Ends Long Debate on Social Issues." *Congressional Quarterly Weekly Report* 39 (September 25, 1982): 2359.

———. "Senate Panel Bows to Pressure: Postpones School Prayer Vote." *Congressional Quarterly Weekly Report* 21 (May 28, 1983): 1051–1052.

———. "Senate Rejects Amendment Designed to Ban Abortion."

Congressional Quarterly Weekly Report 26 (July 2, 1983): 1361–1362.

———. "Senate Rejects Bill to Permit School Prayer." *Congressional Quarterly Weekly Report* 37 (September 14, 1985): 1842.

———. "Senate Tables Anti-Abortion Amendment." *Congressional Quarterly Weekly Report* 38 (September 18, 1982): 2299.

———. "Senate Vote Set on Vocal Prayer Amendment." *Congressional Quarterly Weekly Report* 11 (March 17, 1984): 633.

———. "State, Justice, Commerce Appropriations Bill Snarled by School Prayer Wrangle." *Congressional Quarterly Weekly Report* 47 (November 21, 1981): 2281.

———. "Two House Veterans Scrap on Issue of Equal Access." *Congressional Quarterly Weekly Report* 19 (May 12, 1984): 1103–1105.

———. "Two School Prayer Measures Approved by Senate Panel." *Congressional Quarterly Weekly Report* 23 (June 11, 1983): 1144.

"Congress and the Hyde Amendment . . . How the House Moved to Stop Abortions." *Congressional Quarterly Weekly Report* 16 (April 19, 1980): 1038–1039.

"Congress Enacts President Reagan's Tax Plan." *Congressional Quarterly Almanac* XXXVII (Washington, D.C.: Congressional Quarterly, 1981): 98–100.

Congressional Record. 98th Cong., 1st sess., March 24, 1983, 3918.

"Congressional Record Not Always the Record." *Congressional Quarterly Weekly Report* 31 (August 31, 1974): 2382–2383.

Conn, Joseph L. "The New Christian Politics." *Church & State* 33 (July/August 1980): 14–22.

"Conservative Groups Retreat from Politics." *Washington Post* (January 17, 1987): D14.

Conway, Flo, and Jim Siegelman. *The Holy Terror.* Garden City, N.Y.: Doubleday & Co., 1982.

"Court, Senate Rebuff Anti-Abortion Efforts." *Congressional Quarterly Almanac* XXXIX (Washington, D.C.: Congressional Quarterly, 1983): 306.

Crawford, Alan. *Thunder on the Right.* New York: Pantheon Books, 1980.

"Criminal Code Revision Dies." *Congressional Quarterly Almanac* XXXVIII (Washington, D.C.: Congressional Quarterly, 1982): 416.

Davis, L. J. "Onward Christian Soldiers." *Penthouse* 12 (February 1981): 52+.

Diamond, Edwin. "Should the Government Crack Down on TV's Evangelists?" *TV Guide* (November 14, 1981): 2 + .

Donnelly, Harrison. "Senate Committee Approves Tuition Tax Credit Proposal." *Congressional Quarterly Weekly Report* 38 (September 18, 1982): 2297.

Edelman, Murray. *Politics as Symbolic Action.* New York: Academic Press, 1971.

———. *The Symbolic Uses of Politics.* Urbana: University of Illinois Press, 1964.

Edwards, David. *The American Political Experience.* 3rd ed. Englewood Cliffs, N.J.: Prentice-Hall, 1985.

Endersby, James. "The Cross and the Flag." Paper delivered at the Annual Meeting of the Southwestern Political Science Association, Fort Worth, Texas, March 21–24, 1984.

Evans, Rowland, and Robert Novak. *The Reagan Revolution.* New York: E. P. Dutton, 1981.

Federal Communications Commission Opinion. No. 75–946, August 13, 1975.

Fessler, Pamela. "Bill Permits Church Exit from Social Security." *Congressional Quarterly Weekly Report* 17 (April 28, 1984): 952.

———. "Conference OK's $12.8 Billion for Treasury, Postal Service." *Congressional Quarterly Weekly Report* 32 (August 11, 1984): 1955.

Franklin, James. "New Pill May Alter Abortion Debate." *Boston Globe* (December 22, 1986): 1.

Freedman, Samuel. "Falwell Disseminates Views Through Liberty U." *New York Times* (June 4, 1987): I1.

Gailey, Phil. "A Bitter Struggle Splits South Carolina G.O.P." *New York Times* (April 6, 1987): B9.

Gaillard, Frye. "Right Wing Religion." *The Progressive* 44 (April 1980): 12–13.

Gallup, George. *The Gallup Poll: Public Opinion, 1972–1977.* Wilmington, Del.: Scholarly Resources, 1978.

Glen, Maxwell. "The Electronic Ministers Listen to the Gospel According to the Candidates." *National Journal* 50–51 (December 22, 1979): 2142–2145.

"GOP Seeks Fruits of Victory as 97th Congress Convenes." *Congressional Quarterly Almanac* XXXVII (Washington, D.C.: Congressional Quarterly, 1981): 3.

Granat, Diane. "Legislative Business Proceeds Amidst Hill's Political Battles." *Congressional Quarterly Weekly Report* 27 (July 7, 1984): 1599–1614.

Gurwitt, Rob. "The New Right and the GOP: Can This Marriage Be Saved?" *Congressional Quarterly Weekly Report* 34 (August 25, 1984): 2084–2086.

———. "1986 Elections Generate GOP Power Struggles." *Congressional Quarterly Weekly Report* 15 (April 12, 1986): 802–807.

Gusfield, Joseph. *Symbolic Crusade*. Urbana: University of Illinois Press, 1963.

Guth, James L. "The New Christian Right." In *The New Christian Right*, edited by Robert C. Liebman and Robert Wuthnow, 31–45. New York: Aldine, 1983.

———. "The Politics of the Christian Right." In *Interest Group Politics*, edited by Allan J. Cigler and Burdett A. Loomis, 60–83. Washington, D.C.: CQ Press, 1983.

Hadden, Jeffrey K., Anson Shupe, James Hawdon, and Kenneth Martin. "Why Jerry Falwell Killed the Moral Majority." In *The God Pumpers*, edited by Marshall Fishwick and Ray B. Browne, 101–115. Bowling Green, Ohio: Bowling Green State University Popular Press, 1987.

Hadden, Jeffrey K., and Charles E. Swann. *Prime Time Preachers*. Reading, Mass.: Addison-Wesley, 1981.

Hansen, George. *To Harass Our People*. Washington, D.C.: Positive Publications, 1984.

Hastey, Stan. "Carter: Religious Right Influence to Decline." *Baptist Press* (May 28, 1981): 1.

Hastey, Stan, and Warner Ragsdale. "Right Religion Right Politics? *Home Missions* 51 (September/October 1980): 67–72.

Hatch, Senator Orrin. "Christian Conservatives Are a Major Force on U.S. Political Scene." *Human Events* (July 9, 1983): 10–12.

Hertzke, Allen D. *Representing God in Washington*. Knoxville: University of Tennessee Press, 1988.

Hinckley, Barbara. *Congressional Elections*. Washington, D.C.: CQ Press, 1981.

Hoffman, David. "President Skips Church for Parishioners' Sakes." *Washington Post* (March 8, 1984): A3.

Holmes, Harvey L., ed. *The New York Times Index 1979 67*. New York: New York Times Co., 1980.

Hook, Janet. "Bill Requires Schools to Permit Silent Prayer." *Congressional Quarterly Weekly Report* 30 (July 28, 1984): 1809–1810.

———. "House Clears Bill Allowing Prayer Meetings in Schools."

Congressional Quarterly Weekly Report 30 (July 28, 1984): 1807–1808.

———. "Reagan Continues to Push Tuition Tax Breaks." *Congressional Quarterly Weekly Report* 24 (June 15, 1985): 1164.

———. "Schools Opened to Student Religious Groups." *Congressional Quarterly Weekly Report* 14 (April 7, 1984): 814.

"House Roll Call Votes." *Congressional Quarterly Almanac* XXXVII (Washington, D.C.: Congressional Quarterly, 1981): 36-H, 64-H, 72-H.

"House Votes." *Congressional Quarterly Weekly Report* 20 (May 19, 1984): 1208.

Hudson, Winthrop S. *Religion in America.* 3rd ed. New York: Charles Scribner's Sons, 1981.

Hyer, Marjorie. "Evangelicals Back Reagan, But Reject Political Label." *Washington Post* (March 10, 1984): B6.

———. "Outflanking the Right: Mainline Clerics Oppose the Evangelicals." *Washington Post* (October 21, 1980): 8.

Interviews, special, conducted for this book. See Special Interviews section at the end of this Bibliography.

Jacquet, Constant H., Jr., ed. *Yearbook of American and Canadian Churches.* Nashville: Abingdon Press, 1980.

———, ed. *Yearbook of American Churches.* New York: Council Press, 1970.

Jenkins, Brenda. "What the Pastor and Church Can/Cannot Do in an Election." *Liberty* 77 (September/October 1982): 9–10.

"Jimmy Carter: A Candid Conversation with the Democratic Candidate for the Presidency." *Playboy* (November 1976): 86.

Johnson, Benton. "Liberal Protestantism: End of the Road?" In *The Annals of the American Academy of Political and Social Science,* edited by Wade Clark Roof, 480 (July 1985): 39–52.

Jordan, Robert. "Evangelical Victories and Defeats." *Boston Globe* (July 19, 1980): 27.

Jorstad, Erling. *The Politics of Moralism.* Minneapolis: Augsburg, 1981.

Josephy, Alvin M., Jr. *On the Hill.* New York: Touchstone, 1979.

Kater, John L., Jr. *Christians on the Right.* New York: Seabury Press, 1982.

Keller, Bill. "Evangelical Conservatives Move from Pews to Polls, But Can They Sway Congress?" *Congressional Quarterly Weekly Report* 36 (September 6, 1980): 2627–2634.

Kelley, Dean M. *Why Conservative Churches Are Growing.* Macon, Ga.: Mercer University Press, 1986.

"Key Vote 14." *Congressional Quarterly Almanac* XXXIV (Washington, D.C.: Congressional Quarterly, 1978): 14-C.

Kingdon, John W. *Agendas, Alternatives, and Public Policies.* Boston: Little, Brown & Co., 1984.

Kirschten, Dick. "The Deferred Agenda." *National Journal* 30 (July 25, 1981): 1346.

————. "Putting the Social Issues on Hold: Can Reagan Get Away with It?" *National Journal* 41 (October 10, 1981): 1810–1815.

————. "Reagan Looks to Religious Leaders for Continuing Support in 1984." *National Journal* 34–35 (August 20, 1983): 1727–1731.

"Labor/HHS/Education Money Bill Cleared." *Congressional Quarterly Almanac* XXXIX (Washington, D.C.: Congressional Quarterly, 1983): 507.

LaHaye, Tim. *The Battle for the Mind.* Old Tappan, N.J.: Fleming H. Revell Co., 1980.

"Legal Services Corp. Kept Alive Temporarily." *Congressional Quarterly Almanac* XXXVII (Washington, D.C.: Congressional Quarterly, 1981): 413.

Liebman, Robert C. "Mobilizing the Moral Majority." In *The New Christian Right*, edited by Robert C. Liebman and Robert Wuthnow, 49–73. New York: Aldine, 1983.

Linder, Robert. "Militarism in Nazi Thought and in the American Religious Right." *Journal of Church and State* 24 (Spring 1982): 263–279.

Lindsey, Hal. *The Late Great Planet Earth.* Grand Rapids, Mich.: Zondervan Publishing House, 1970.

Lipset, Seymour Martin, and Earl Rabb. *The Politics of Unreason.* New York: Harper & Row, 1970.

Lorentzen, Louise. "Evangelical Life Style Concerns Expressed in Political Action." *Sociological Analysis* 41 (Summer 1980): 144–154.

Lyke, Robert. "Legislative Activity on Tuition Tax Credits Prior to the 97th Congress." *Congressional Research Service Brief*, August 12, 1982.

McCune, Wes. *Group Research Report* 3 (March 26, 1980): 1–12.

McNair, Jean. "Robertson Lays Off 470, Blames TV Ministry Scandals." *Boston Globe* (June 6, 1987): 1+.

"Major Rulings of 1985–1986 Court Term." *Congressional Quarterly Weekly Report* 28 (July 12, 1986): 1576.

Mann, James. "Old Time Religion on the Offensive." *U.S. News and World Report* 13 (April 7, 1980): 40–42.

Marra, Jean M., ed. *Reader's Guide to Periodical Literature*. Vols. 39–43. New York: H. W. Wilson Co., 1980–84.

Martz, Larry. "Day of the Preachers." *Newsweek* 106 (March 7, 1988): 44.

Martz, Larry, Vern E. Smith, Daniel Pedersen, Daniel Shapiro, Mark Miller, and Ginny Carroll. "God and Money." *Newsweek* 105 (April 6, 1987): 16–22.

Martz, Larry, Kenneth L. Woodward, Ginny Carroll, Daniel Pedersen, and Rich Thomas. "Gospelgate II: Target Falwell." *Newsweek* 105 (June 1, 1987): 56–59.

May, Herbert G., and Bruce M. Metzger, eds. *The New Oxford Annotated Bible*. New York: Oxford University Press, 1973.

Mayer, Allan. "A Tide of Born Again." *Newsweek* 96 (September 15, 1980): 28 +.

Menendez, Albert J. *Religion at the Polls*. Philadelphia: Westminster Press, 1977.

———. "Religious Lobbies." *Liberty* 77 (March/April 1982): 2 +.

Mikva, Abner J., and Patti B. Saris. *The American Congress*. New York: Franklin Watts, 1983.

Miller, Arthur. "Political Issues and Trust in Government, 1964–1970." *American Political Science Review* 68 (September 1974): 951–972.

Miller, Arthur, and Martin Wattenberg. "Politics from the Pulpit." *Public Opinion Quarterly* 48 (Spring 1984): 301–317.

Miller, Judith. "Goldwater Vows to Fight Tactics of New Right." *New York Times* (September 16, 1981): A1 +.

Miller, Mark. "Goodbye to All That." *Newsweek* 110 (November 16, 1987): 10.

Miller, Tim. "Two Competing Pro-Life Measures Split the Anti-Abortion Lobby." *National Journal* 12 (March 20, 1982): 511–513.

Minnery, Tom. "The Religious Right: How Much Credit Can It Take for the Electoral Landslide?" *Christianity Today* 24 (December 12, 1980): 52.

Moen, Matthew C. "The Christian Right and the Legislative Agenda, 1981–1984." Paper delivered at the Annual Meeting of the Southwestern Political Science Association, Houston, Texas, March 20–23, 1985.

———. "The Political Agenda of Ronald Reagan." *Presidential Studies Quarterly*. XVIII (Fall 1988): 775–85.

———. "School Prayer and the Politics of Life Style Concern." *Social Science Quarterly* 65 (December 1984): 1065–1071.

————. "Status Politics and the Political Agenda of the Christian Right." *Sociological Quarterly* 29 (September 1988): 429–437.

Murray, Alan. "House Tells Conferees to Lift Surgeon General Age Limit." *Congressional Quarterly Weekly Report* 21 (May 23, 1981): 909.

North, Gary. *Conspiracy: A Biblical View*. Fort Worth: Dominion Press, 1986.

"NSF Authorization Cleared." *Congressional Quarterly Almanac* XLI (Washington, D.C.: Congressional Quarterly, 1985): 288–289.

Nutting, Brian. "Senate Rejects Tuition Tax Credit Plan." *Congressional Quarterly Weekly Report* 23 (November 19, 1983): 2424.

Nyhan, David. "Attacks on Religious Right Put Its Influence in Doubt." *Boston Globe* (October 28, 1980): 1–2.

————. "The Growing Political Clout of America's Christian Right." *Boston Globe* (June 15, 1980): 9, 11.

Ogintz, Eileen. "Evangelists Seek Political Clout." *Chicago Tribune* (January 13, 1980): 5.

Oleszek, Walter. *Congressional Procedures and the Policy Process*. Washington, D.C.: CQ Press, 1978.

Ornstein, Norman J., Robert L. Peabody, and David W. Rhode. "The Senate Through the 1980s." In *Congress Reconsidered*, 3rd ed., edited by Lawrence C. Dodd and Bruce I. Oppenheimer, 13–33. Washington, D.C.: CQ Press, 1985.

Ostling, Richard N. "TV's Unholy Row." *Time* 129 (April 6, 1987): 60–67.

Page, Ann, and Donald Clelland. "The Kanawha County Textbook Controversy: A Study of the Politics of Life Style Concern." *Social Forces* 57 (September 1978): 265–281.

Pelham, Ann. "Conferees Vote on Medicaid Cuts, Block Grants." *Congressional Quarterly Weekly Report* 31 (August 1, 1981): 1387–1389.

————. "Family Protection Act: Dear to New Right, But Unlikely to Get Out of Committees." *Congressional Quarterly Weekly Report* 40 (October 3, 1981): 1916.

Phillips, Kevin P. *Post-Conservative America*. New York: Random House, 1982.

"Preaching to the Choir." *Church & State* 36 (March 1983): 6–8.

Pressman, Steven. "Famous Faces Fighting Hard for School Prayer." *Congressional Quarterly Weekly Report* 9 (March 3, 1984): 490–491.

————. "Religious Organizations Urge Administration Not to Name Ambassador to the Vatican." *Congressional Quarterly Weekly Report* 50 (December 17, 1983): 2677.

———. "Religious Right: Trying to Link Poll Power and Lobby Muscle." *Congressional Quarterly Weekly Report* 38 (September 22, 1984): 2315–2319.

———. "Senate Rejects School Prayer Amendment." *Congressional Quarterly Weekly Report* 12 (March 24, 1984): 643.

Pressman, Steven, and Lenore Webb. "Lobbies Issue Congressional Report Cards." *Congressional Quarterly Weekly Report* 28 (July 14, 1984): 1689–1691.

"Reagan Backing Helps Foreign Aid Bill." *Congressional Quarterly Almanac* XXXVII (Washington, D.C.: Congressional Quarterly, 1981): 342.

Regan, Donald. *For The Record*. New York: Harcourt Brace Jovanovich, 1988.

Reichley, A. James. *Religion in American Public Life*. Washington, D.C.: Brookings Institution, 1985.

Reid, T. R. "O'Neill Pans Republicans." *Washington Post* (May 12, 1984): A1+.

———. "Say Amen, Senator." *Washington Post* (March 21, 1984): B1.

———. "Sens. Weicker, Hatch Do Battle over Prayer Issue." *Washington Post* (March 8, 1984): A2.

"Religious Right Goes for Bigger Game." *U.S. News and World Report* 89 (November 17, 1980): 42.

"Religious Right Talks Politics." *Guardian* 33 (September 3, 1980): 4.

Rieselbach, Leroy. *Congressional Reform*. Washington, D.C.: CQ Press, 1986.

Roberts, James. "The Christian Right: New Force in American Politics." *Human Events* 40 (November 8, 1980): 10+.

Roberts, Steven. "Fervent Debate on School Prayer." *New York Times* (March 9, 1984): A16.

Robison, James. *Attack on the Family*. Wheaton, Ill.: Tyndale, 1982.

Roof, Wade Clark. "The New Fundamentalism: Rebirth of Political Religion in America." In *Prophetic Religions and Politics: Religion and the Political Order*, edited by Jeffrey K. Hadden and Anson Shupe, 18–34. New York: Paragon House, 1986.

Roof, Wade Clark, and William McKinney. "Denominational America and the New Religious Pluralism." In *The Annals of the American Academy of Political and Social Science*, edited by Wade Clark Roof, 480 (July 1985): 24–38.

Rovner, Julie. "Senate Passes Labor-HHS Appropriations Bill." *Congressional Quarterly Weekly Report* 37 (September 13, 1986): 2167.

Saker, Anne. "House Republicans Conduct an All-Night Prayer Vigil." *Roll Call* (March 18, 1984): 3.

Sawyer, Kathy. "Christian Soldiers March to Different Drummer." *Washington Post* (December 27, 1984): 1.

———. "Linking Religion and Politics." *Washington Post* (August 24, 1980): A12.

Schlesinger, Arthur, Jr. "Pretension in the Presidential Pulpit." *Wall Street Journal* (March 17, 1983): 26.

Schlozman, Kay Lehman, and John T. Tierney. *Organized Interests and American Democracy.* New York: Harper & Row, 1986.

Schneider, William. "Old Politics Yield to New U.S. Ideologies." *Los Angeles Times* (March 13, 1983): 3.

Scott, Wilbur J. "The Equal Rights Amendment as Status Politics." *Social Forces* 64 (December 1985): 499–506.

"Senate Roll Call Votes." *Congressional Quarterly Almanac* XXVII (Washington, D.C.: Congressional Quarterly, 1981): 63S–64S.

"Senate Votes." *Congressional Quarterly Weekly Report* 10 (March 10, 1984): 585.

"Senate Votes." *Congressional Quarterly Weekly Report* 26 (June 30, 1984): 1580.

Shupe, Anson, and William Stacey. "The Moral Majority Constituency." In *The New Christian Right*, edited by Robert C. Liebman and Robert Wuthnow, 103–116. New York: Aldine, 1983.

Simpson, John H. "Moral Issues and Status Politics." In *The New Christian Right*, edited by Robert C. Liebman and Robert Wuthnow, 187–205. New York: Aldine, 1983.

Stall, Bill. "Evangelicals Pin Their Faith on Political Action." *Los Angeles Times* (August 24, 1980): 1+.

Stanfield, Rochelle. "The Public School Lobby Fends Off Tuition Tax Credits—At Least for Now." *National Journal* 24 (June 13, 1981): 1063–1066.

Stang, Allan. "Why Secular Humanists Are Making War on the Religious Right." *American Opinion* (November 1982): 7+.

"State, Justice, Commerce Appropriation." *Congressional Quarterly Almanac* XXXVII (Washington, D.C.: Congressional Quarterly, 1981): 367.

Sweeney, Joan. "Evangelicals Seeking to Establish Political Force." *Los Angeles Times* (May 19, 1980): 1+.

Tocqueville, Alexis De. *Democracy in America.* Translated from the

French by George Lawrence and edited by J. P. Mayer. New York: Doubleday, 1969.

Tolchin, Martin. "Reagan's Power to Name Judiciary Going Lame." *New York Times*. Reprinted in the *Maine Sunday Telegram* (December 6, 1987): 20.

"Treasury/Post Office Funds." *Congressional Quarterly Almanac* XXXVII (Washington, D.C.: Congressional Quarterly, 1981): 356–357.

Truman, David B. *The Governmental Process*. 2nd cd. New York: Alfred A. Knopf, 1971.

"Tuition Credit Friends, Foes Ready, Just in Case." *National Journal* 17 (April 24, 1982): 736–737.

"TV Preachers to Testify." *Newsweek* 105 (August 31, 1987): 64.

"Unexpected Landslide." *Maine Times* (June 13, 1986): 11.

Unger, Arthur. "TV Ads Try to Offset Religious Right." *Christian Science Monitor* (October 21, 1980): 6.

U.S. Congress. House. Committee on Education and Labor. Subcommittee on Elementary, Secondary, and Vocational Education. *Hearings on the Equal Access Act*. 98th Cong., 1st sess., 1983. H.R. 2723.

———. Committee on Standards of Official Conduct. *Ethics Manual for Members and Employees of the House of Representatives*. 98th Cong., 2nd sess., 1984.

———. Committee on Ways and Means. *Administration's Change in Federal Policy Regarding the Tax Status of Racially Discriminatory Private Schools*. 97th Cong., 2nd sess., February 4, 1982.

U.S. Congress. Senate. Committee on Finance. *Hearings on Tuition Tax Credit Proposals*. 97th Cong., 2nd sess., 1982. S. 2673.

———. Committee on Finance. *Hearings on Tuition Tax Credits*. 98th Cong., 1st sess., 1983. S. 528.

———. Committee on Finance. *Hearings on Tuition Tax Credits*. 97th Cong., 1st sess., 1981. S. 550.

———. Committee on the Judiciary. *Hearings on a Proposed Constitutional Amendment to Permit Voluntary Prayer*. 97th Cong., 2nd sess., 1982. S.J. Res. 199.

———. Committee on the Judiciary. *Hearings on the Human Life Federalism Amendment*. 98th Cong., 1st sess., 1983. S.J. Res. 3.

———. Committee on the Judiciary. *Human Life Federalism Amendment*. 98th Cong., 1st sess., 1983. S. Report 98–149.

———. Committee on the Judiciary. *Voluntary School Prayer Amendment*. 98th Cong., 2nd sess., 1984. S. Report 98–348.

————. Committee on the Judiciary. Subcommittee on Separation of Powers. *Hearings on the Human Life Bill.* 97th Cong., 1st sess., 1981. S. 158.

————. Committee on the Judiciary. Subcommittee on Separation of Powers. *The Human Life Appendix.* 97th Cong., 1st sess., 1981. S. 158.

————. Committee on the Judiciary. Subcommittee on the Constitution. *Hearings on the Human Life Federalism Amendment.* 97th Cong., 1st sess., 1981. S.J. Res. 110.

————. Committee on the Judiciary. Subcommittee on the Constitution. *Hearings on the Human Life Federalism Amendment.* 98th Cong., 1st sess., 1983. S.J. Res. 3.

————. Committee on the Judiciary. Subcommittee on the Constitution. *Hearings on the Voluntary School Prayer Amendment.* 98th Cong., 1st sess., 1983. S.J. Res. 73.

Vecsey, George. "Militant Television Preachers Try to Weld Fundamentalist Christians' Political Power." *New York Times* (January 21, 1980): A21.

————. "Some Evangelicals Lean to Carter After Meetings." *New York Times* (January 28, 1980): B9.

Viguerie, Richard A. "America's Ruling Class Has Got to Go!" *Washington Post* (November 27, 1983): B1.

————. *The New Right.* Falls Church, Va.: The Viguerie Co., 1981.

Warner, Edwin. "New Resolve by the New Right." *Time* 23 (December 8, 1980): 24–25.

Weisman, Steven. "Appeals Backing GOP Said to Portray Views as Contrary to Bible." *New York Times* (November 1, 1980): 1–9.

Whitehead, John W. *The Second American Revolution.* Elgin, Ill.: David C. Cook Publishing, 1982.

Wilcox, Clyde. "Evangelicals and Fundamentalists in the New Christian Right." *Journal for the Scientific Study of Religion* 25 (September 1986): 355–363.

Wilkie, Curtis. "Righteousness from the Right." *Boston Globe* (October 12, 1980): 29.

Williams, Juan. "Reagan Calls for Prayer Bill, Renewal of Moral Attitudes." *Washington Post* (March 7, 1984): A1 +.

Witt, Elder. "Court Dodges Ruling on Equal Access Issue." *Congressional Quarterly Weekly Report* 13 (March 29, 1986): 717.

————. "Court Upholds Power of IRS to Deny Tax-Exempt Status to Schools that Discriminate." *Congressional Quarterly Weekly Report* 21 (May 28, 1983): 1077–1078.

———. "Reagan Crusade before Court Unprecedented in Intensity." *Congressional Quarterly Weekly Report* 11 (March 15, 1986): 616.

Woods, James. "Religious Fundamentalism and the New Right." *Journal of Church and State* 22 (Autumn 1980): 419.

Wuthnow, Robert. "The Political Rebirth of American Evangelicals." In *The New Christian Right*, edited by Robert C. Liebman and Robert Wuthnow, 167–185. New York: Aldine, 1983.

Zurcher, Louis, and R. George Kirkpatrick. *Citizens for Decency*. Austin: University of Texas Press, 1976.

Special Interviews

As part of the research for this volume, the author conducted a series of interviews in Washington, D.C., from May 17 through August 29, 1984. The procedure he followed was to take a list of basic questions to the interview, jot down key phrases or words during the responses to these and other questions, and then reconstruct the interview on a typewriter immediately after it was completed. The only exception was the interview with William Billings, the reconstruction of which was not begun until about thirty minutes after it ended.

After completing the reconstruction, a copy was given to the respondent, who was allowed to edit it. That was done to encourage the participants to speak freely during the interviews. The result is that some of their original comments are reported anonymously in this study.

The veracity of the reconstruction, of course, is an issue in such an interview method. In that regard, it can only be said that one respondent asked the author of this book upon receiving the reconstructed interview whether he had secretly taped it. Moreover, only one interviewee took serious issue with the author's reconstruction; the disputed comments are not used anywhere in this book.

All the interviews were face-to-face with one exception. Father Robert Drinan preferred to respond to written questions; his answers to them were received by the author on June 1, 1984, which is the date listed for the interview. The Reverend Pat Robertson declined an interview, but sent a copy of one of his books along with a personal letter broadly outlining his thoughts on the Christian Right and his place in it. Those materials were received on July 18, 1984.

The interviews varied widely in length. Some were as short as twenty minutes (for example, Marlow, Synar, and McCurdy); others were as long as an hour (for example, Bergstrom, Blackwell, and William Billings). The longest single one was approximately two and one-half hours, with Gary Jarmin, of Christian Voice. Some individuals participated in two separate interviews.

Together, the reconstructed interviews totaled more than two hundred, single-spaced typewritten pages.

The interviewees, their primary position at the time of the interview, and its date are listed below in alphabetical order:

Ashcraft, Tom
Legislative Assistant, Senator Jesse Helms, August 3, 1984.
Bergstrom, Reverend Charles
Executive Director, Office of Governmental Affairs, Lutheran Council in the USA, June 18, August 6, 1984.
Billings, Robert
Director, Regional Liaison, Department of Education, July 26, 1984.
Billings, William
Executive Director, National Christian Action Coalition, May 24, 1984.
Blackwell, Morton
White House Liaison, August 29, 1984.
Boren, Hon. David
Senator, Oklahoma, June 14, 1984.
Bovard, Tom
Counsel, Separation of Powers Subcommittee, Senate Judiciary, June 8, July 11, 1984.
Buchanan, Reverend John
Director, People for the American Way, August 1, 1984.
Clay, Laura
Legislative Assistant, Senator Don Nickles, May 21, 1984.
Crane, Hon. Phil
Congressman, Illinois, May 31, 1984.
Curran, Gary
Director, American Life Lobby, July 25, 1984.
Daschle, Hon. Tom
Congressman, South Dakota, May 31, 1984.
Drinan, Father Robert
Faculty Member, Georgetown Law School, June 1, 1984.
Edgar, Hon. Bob
Congressman, Pennsylvania, May 31, July 23, 1984.
Hastey, Reverend Stan

Director, Information Services, Baptist Joint Committee on Public Affairs; Bureau Chief, Baptist Press, June 22, August 17, 1984.

Hausenfluck, Lilli
Legislative Assistant, Senator Roger Jepsen, May 29, 1984.

Hyde, Hon. Henry
Congressman, Illinois, June 26, 1984.

Jarmin, Gary
Legislative Director, Christian Voice, July 27, 1984.

Jones, Roy
Legislative Director, Moral Majority, July 17, 1984.

Kiko, Philip
Minority Counsel, Civil and Constitutional Rights Subcommittee, House Judiciary Committee, June 11, 1984.

Lee, Susan
Staff, National Christian Action Coalition, May 24, 1984.

Lynn, Reverend Barry
Legislative Counsel, American Civil Liberties Union, June 1, 1984.

McCune, Wes
Director, Group Research, Inc., May 25, 1984.

McCurdy, Hon. Dave
Congressman, Oklahoma, June 6, 1984.

McKenna, James
Legislative Assistant, Congressman George Hansen, May 18, 1984.

Marlow, Deanna
Legislative Assistant, Senator Mark Andrews, June 14, 1984.

Montgomery, Forest
Counsel, National Association of Evangelicals, June 13, 1984.

Shaddix, Doug
Deputy Field Director, American Coalition for Traditional Values, July 27, 1984.

Synar, Hon. Mike
Congressman, Oklahoma, May 17, 1984.

Zwenig, Frances
Lobbyist, People for the American Way, May 23, 1984.

Index